Your Everyday Answer Book

Publisher's Note

This book is intended for general information only. It does not constitute medical, legal, or financial advice or practice. The editors of FC&A have taken careful measures to ensure the accuracy and usefulness of the information in this book. While every attempt has been made to ensure accuracy, errors may occur and information may change. Addresses, telephone numbers, and Internet website addresses were accurate at the time this book was printed. We cannot guarantee the safety or effectiveness of any advice or treatments mentioned. Readers are urged to consult with their professional financial advisors, lawyers, and health care professionals before making any changes.

Any health information in this book is for information only and is not intended to be a medical guide for self-treatment. It does not constitute medical advice and should not be construed as such or used in place of your doctor's medical advice. Readers are urged to consult with their health care professionals before undertaking therapies suggested by the information in this book, keeping in mind that errors in the text may occur as in all publications and that new findings may supersede older information.

The publisher and editors disclaim all liability (including any injuries, damages, or losses) resulting from the use of the information in this book.

But the fruit of the Spirit is love, joy, peace, longsuffering, gentleness, goodness, faith, meekness, temperance: against such there is no law.

— Galatians 5:22-24

FC&A Publishing®
103 Clover Green
Peachtree City, GA 30269
www.fca.com

Produced by the staff of FC&A

ISBN 978-1-935574-31-6

Table of Contents

Appliances

Amp up performance & productivity

Score big bargains on small appliances. Get the best price for new appliances like coffee makers and food processors at these surprising places – Amazon.com, QVC, and your local Kohl's store. A recent *Consumer Reports* survey found that only the wholesale clubs Costco and Sam's Club could compete with the low prices offered by these three sellers. To find deals on larger appliances, like refrigerators and washing machines, remember these tips.

- Research prices on the Web and in stores before you buy. Knowing more about the product and its price helps you haggle for a better deal, and you could save $75 or more. Don't forget to ask about free delivery when you're haggling.

- Sign up for email alerts, or register with appliance retailers and manufacturers. This can lead to rebates, discount coupons, and members-only sales.

- Buy last year's model around the time new models come out after August. If you must buy at a different time, consider the floor model displayed in the store or a new appliance that was recently returned. Ask about the warranty on returns and floor models before you buy.

- Pick your favorite models and wait for them to go on sale if you're not pressed for time. Sales often happen in January, May, September, and October.

- Keep an eye out for package deals if you need more than one appliance.

- Ask about scratch and dent models at regular appliance stores, or look for them at outlets, scratch-and-dent warehouse stores, or clearance centers. Just remember to check the appliance very thoroughly, and ask a salesperson how you can verify that the appliance is in working condition and isn't missing any parts. Scratch-and-dent models are usually sold as-is, and you may need to make your own delivery arrangements.

- Find out the price match policy of every retailer you might buy from. Some stores may not only match another store's price, but offer to beat it.

- Look into new mover's discounts if you are moving.

GREAT IDEA

Fix it yourself with free help from experts

That rattle in your vacuum or the problem with your clothes dryer may be easier to fix than you think. Use these sources to help.

- User manuals. These invaluable guides often include pages specifically for addressing problems, so find the manual for your machine. If it's long gone, download an electronic version from the support section of the manufacturer's website or from *www.manualsonline.com*. Look for pages in the manual labeled "troubleshooting" or "problems." You may be able to fix the appliance yourself.

- Customer help lines. If the manual's troubleshooting section does not solve your problem, check for a customer help phone number. Some companies will help you diagnose and repair a problem over the phone.

- Websites. Visit the support section of the manufacturer's website to check for additional repair advice. Try websites like *www.repairclinic.com* or *www.fixya.com* or even search *www.youtube.com* for advice on how to fix your problem.

The shopping mistake you don't want to make. Don't be fooled by brand names when buying major appliances. Even brand name manufacturers famous for making quality products don't always make every appliance well. For example, a brand manufacturer that makes fantastic clothes dryers may produce lousy dishwashers.

What's more, a brand that makes quality washing machines can still come out with the occasional clunker — and here's the proof. A recent *Consumer Reports* rating of refrigerators, based on their product testing, found that four different manufacturers offered both top-scoring and low-scoring models.

Instead of depending on a particular brand name, check out reviews and ratings of individual models. Also, ask around to see if friends or relatives have any experience with models you are considering. And, if you have Web access, check out user reviews to see how a particular model behaves in homes like yours. You may pick up valuable information and tips you can't find anywhere else.

GREAT IDEA

Make your kitchen gentle on your joints

Think about your arthritis when shopping for — or using — kitchen appliances. For example, your refrigerator can be kinder to hand arthritis if you plan ahead. Just loop some attractive fabric around the handle, and slip your wrist or forearm through the loop to open the refrigerator door hands-free.

If you are lucky enough to be shopping for a new refrigerator, and arthritis makes bending a problem for you, consider choosing a side-by-side refrigerator or other model that keeps the most frequently used items at eye level. If you're buying a stove, hunt for models with controls on the front to avoid having to do a lot of reaching and bending.

Let your microwave clean itself. Why use elbow grease to clean the inside of your microwave oven? Try this clever trick instead. Wet a sturdy paper towel thoroughly. If your paper towels aren't sturdy, tear off several, pile them together, and then wet them. Toss your paper towel in the microwave, and heat for four minutes. After it's done, don't open your microwave right away. Let the steam work its magic while you put on rubber gloves. After a couple of minutes, open the microwave door, and use the paper towel to wipe down the inside of your microwave. You'll be amazed at how easily the grime just wipes away.

If you'd like to deodorize your microwave as well as clean it, switch to this method. Combine one-third cup of lemon juice with two-thirds cup of water in a microwave-safe bowl. Bring the liquid to a boil in your microwave, and let boil for about three minutes. Carefully remove the bowl and immediately wipe down the interior with a wet cloth.

GREAT IDEA

Fight allergies while you clean your floors

Here's a dirty little secret about vacuuming. Standard vacuums can raise an invisible cloud of dust, pet allergens, and other tiny particles that takes several hours to settle. Choosing a vacuum with a high efficiency particulate air (HEPA) filter keeps more than 99 percent of these particles out of the air.

But if you have serious allergies, you may need a vacuum with extra design features that are even more effective against allergens. To find these vacuums, visit *www.asthma andallergyfriendly.com*. This is where the Asthma and Allergy Foundation of America lists products that earn their "asthma & allergy friendly" certification. These vacuums aren't required to have HEPA filters, but they have passed rigorous tests of their ability to clean well, to avoid adding allergens to the air during vacuuming, and to limit your exposure to allergens during bag changes or canister-emptying.

Vacuum your carpet like a pro. Vacuuming back-and-forth isn't the best way to clean your carpet. Instead, treat your vacuum cleaner as if it were a lawn mower for your carpet. Before you vacuum a room, quickly examine the carpet for any clutter or small items that could jam up your vacuum. After all, you would remove your hose and other items from the grass if you were mowing, so take a similar approach for inside.

When you're ready, turn on your vacuum and start cleaning in one direction in long strips. Let your strips overlap just slightly to be sure you never miss a spot. Also, remember to go slowly to give the vacuum more time to suction up the dirt. When you need to save time, you can vacuum a little faster in low traffic areas that may be less dirty. Change your vacuuming direction every few weeks or months to help suction up dirt that may have escaped the vacuum on previous passes.

GREAT IDEA

Clean your lint trap for faster drying

Months of using fabric softener or dryer sheets can cause buildup that coats your lint trap and dryer sensors. This can make your clothes take longer to dry — especially the ones made from thick or heavy fabrics.

To solve this problem, check your dryer's manual to find out where the sensors are. Once you know, remove the lint trap and wash both the sensors and the lint filter with warm soapy water. Scrub the trap, if needed, and rinse it well before sliding it back into its slot in the dryer. Don't be surprised if you notice heavy clothes drying more quickly right away. You may even notice a difference in your electricity bill.

As long as you continue using dryer sheets or fabric softener, be sure to clean the lint filter and dryer sensors periodically to keep residue from building up.

Dry clothes in half the time. People who switch from fabric softener to wool dryer balls say their clothes dry up to 50 percent faster – and that means a lower electric bill. These balls separate clothes, increase the air flow between them, and absorb moisture. Wool dryer balls also get rid of wrinkles, soften your clothes, and reduce static in every load. Best of all, they last for years, so you can stop spending money on fabric softener sheets and liquids. Depending on how much fabric softener you use, you could save $15 to $100 every year.

Here's another reason to switch to wool – fabric softeners can coat your dryer's lint trap with waxy buildup so your clothes take even longer to dry. For best results, clean your lint trap to remove this buildup before using dryer balls for the first time. Shop around to discover the best deal on wool dryer balls. You'll find them at fabric stores, Target, and Etsy.com, as well as other Internet sources.

MONEYSAVER

What to check first to avoid a dryer repair bill

Steve called the repair service because his dryer wouldn't heat. But when the repairer arrived, he noticed the dryer was set to the no-heat or air-fluff setting. Once he changed the setting, it worked just fine. Steve later found out his wife had used the air-fluff setting earlier in the day. Repairers say things like this happen more often than you might expect. So play it safe, and check your dryer setting before you call for repairs.

Clean a glass cook top with baking soda. Combine the scratch-free scrubbing power of baking soda with lemon slices or hot water, and you may be surprised at how easy cleaning your glass cook top can be. Just try one of these clever techniques:

- Lemon method. Scatter baking soda across your cook top, and use a slice of lemon to rub it across the entire surface. With a damp cloth, wipe down the cook top to remove any leftover baking soda and lemon juice. Buff with a dry cloth.

- Hot water method. Fill a bowl with hot water and a squeeze of dish soap. Drop a large cleaning rag into the water, and let it get thoroughly wet. Wring it out slightly so it stops dripping, but it's still very wet. Open up the rag, and rest it flat on the cook top for about 20 minutes. For really stubborn messes, leave the rag on a few minutes longer. When time is up, use the rag to scrub the entire surface of your cook top with baking soda. Wipe off the baking soda with a clean, damp cloth. Dry the surface and enjoy the scratch-free shine.

3 garbage disposal fixes you can do yourself. Don't panic when your garbage disposal stops working. It might be easier to fix than you think.

- Check the power. Make sure the garbage disposal really is the problem. If your unit plugs into the wall, check that the plug hasn't been dislodged. If it doesn't plug into the wall, make a quick trip to your fuse box to see if the circuit breaker for the disposal has tripped and turned off the power.

- Try the reset button. If electricity is not the problem, check the user's manual for your garbage disposal to see if it has a reset button. Most have a red or black button on the part of the unit underneath your kitchen sink. Push the button, and your garbage disposal may work just fine.

- Dislodge a jam. If something is caught in your disposal, don't put your hand down there to fish it out. Not only is that incredibly dangerous, but better tools are available. First, turn off the garbage disposal or cut power to it. Grab long-handled tongs, chopsticks, extra-long needle-nose pliers, or even a bent coat hanger. With help from a flashlight, find the caught object, and use your tool to coax it out. If you don't need to fish out the item, some experts recommend inserting a broom handle carefully into the disposal and using it to gently turn the disposal blade. That may be enough to release the item.

GREAT IDEA

Clean your dishwasher with lemonade

Eliminate mineral deposits and clogs from your dishwasher, and leave it smelling lemon-fresh. When your dishwasher is empty, pour a packet of any sugar-free lemonade mix in the soap dispenser — or substitute a couple of ounces of lemon juice. Run a cleaning cycle if your dishwasher has one, or just run a normal cycle. The citric acid from the lemon helps dissolve clogs and mineral deposits, and the lemon scent is a fabulous way to deodorize a foul-smelling dishwasher.

Try this for cleaner dishes. Small changes in how you load your dishwasher can sometimes make a big difference in cleaning. Try these tips, and find out how much cleaner your dishes can be.

- Put cups and glasses between the tines of the top rack instead of over each tine. This keeps them from rattling around during washing.

- Instead of turning plates in one direction on that lower rack, point them all toward the center of the dishwasher. They get cleaner that way. Stagger smaller and larger plates so the water and soap can get between them more easily.

- Place large items like baking sheets and big pans around the outer edge of the lower rack, so they're less likely to block the sprayers.

- Position smaller bowls on the top rack. Tilt them slightly so their undersides point toward the sprayers.

- Instead of tucking long-handled or tall utensils in with the silver-ware, rest them on their sides in the upper rack.

- Keep bowls and any large spoons in the upper rack facing downward so they won't fill with water.

- Turn knives blade down, but alternate the rest of the utensils so some handles point up while others point down. If you don't do this, some items may press together or nest, prevent-ing them from getting clean.

- Keep dishes from touching one another, so the spray and soap reach all parts of each dish. This also prevents chipping.

Oven features you really need — and some you don't.
Today's range ovens come with a confusing array of new features. Experts recommend you include these first:

- At least one high-heat or high-powered burner for quick-heating methods like searing.

- Controls that can't be bumped or reset easily. That's a good reason to choose controls on top of the range instead of the front. Or be sure front controls have a lockout feature that prevents accidental changes.

- At least five rack positions to allow cooking on more than one rack or simply to leave enough room for large items like that Thanksgiving turkey.

You'll also want to know about options like these – even if you decide to turn some of them down:

- A warming drawer keeps food warm until you are ready to serve it.

- Smooth-topped models offer an easy-to-clean flat surface, but models with coils are often less expensive.

- Convection ovens use air circulation to reduce cooking time.

- Dual ovens mean you can roast a chicken in one oven, while you bake a cake in another.

- Induction cook tops cook faster than other cook tops, but raise the oven's price and require special magnetic cookware.

- Self-cleaning options are a high-heat feature that burns off oven spills so you won't have to clean your oven with elbow grease.

- Decide whether your range should be powered by natural gas or electricity, or choose the professional dual-fuel models that feature a gas-powered cook top paired with an electric oven.

Also, keep this in mind — the more people you cook for, the bigger your oven should be. And, if you often cook for a crowd, you may get more value from warming drawers and high heat burners than someone who only cooks for one or two people.

Declare war on stubborn disposal odors. When throwing lemon or orange peels in your garbage disposal isn't enough to get rid of an awful smell, call in more powerful reinforcements. Pour some baking soda down the drain, but don't rinse. Instead, let it sit there and hammer away at the odor for several hours before you turn on the water and disposal. To get rid of odors even faster, measure 4 tablespoons of Borax into the drain, and let it sit for an hour or longer. Then turn on the water, run the disposal, and declare victory.

Clean refrigerator spills in seconds. Don't wait until the next time something spills in your fridge. Lay the groundwork for an easy-to-clean refrigerator today. Clear off a shelf, clean and disinfect it, and dry it with an absorbent cloth. When fully dry, wrap it in plastic wrap, or line it with plastic place mats. Follow the same process with each of the shelves in your refrigerator. The next time something spills or your refrigerator shelves seem grimy, just replace the plastic wrap, or clean the place mat.

If the place mats won't cover the entire shelf, or if you have to change the plastic wrap so often it becomes too expensive, try this instead. Cover each shelf with plastic wrap, and top it with a plastic place mat. If a spill hits the place mat, but fails to reach the plastic wrap, remove the place mat for cleaning, and the shelf will still be protected. What's more, you won't have to change the plastic wrap unless a spill happens before you can put the place mat back.

MONEYSAVER

Score smarter savings on vacuum filters and bags

Don't just hunt for cheaper replacement dust bags and filters for your vacuum. Compare the cost of cheap filters and bags to reusable filters and bags, and see which ones come out ahead. Also, when shopping for bags, pay close attention to whether the bag you're considering has the same filtering capabilities as the bag you have. If it doesn't, you might be unhappy with the results.

---

5 essential buying questions. Ask these questions when you shop for appliances, so you won't end up with the wrong one.

- What are its measurements? You need to know how wide, tall, and deep the appliance is to be sure it will fit into your space, and through the doorway when it's delivered. Before you shop, measure the place where the appliance will go, as well as the doorways and hallways it must pass through to get there. Don't forget to allow extra inches for ventilation or clearance if the appliance requires it.

- How noisy is it? Most conversations occur between 40 and 60 decibels, and a whisper is 30 decibels. If you want to carry on a conversation while standing near your dishwasher or refrigerator, choose a model famed for its quiet operation or one that scores lower than 40 decibels.

- Does it have high maintenance costs? Some appliances have filters or other parts that regularly need changing. But humidifiers and air purifiers are particularly notorious for requiring pricey filters that must frequently be replaced. Before you buy an appliance, check whether it comes with extra costs like these that could make it more expensive to own.

- How much does it cost to run? When comparing the prices of two appliances, also look at the yellow EnergyGuide label. This label displays how much each appliance costs to run in both dollars and kilowatt-hours per year. If the appliance with the higher price has much cheaper operating costs, its total cost may actually be less expensive in the long run.

- Does it have any special electrical requirements? Some extra-large window air conditioners require so much power you might need special circuits or wiring.

MONEYSAVER

Money-saving laundry room secret

You can save a significant amount of money if you don't buy your washer and dryer as a matched set. Instead, buy a higher performing washing machine to do a better job of getting clothes clean, and pair it with a less-expensive dryer.

Straight talk about dishwashers. Your old dishwasher finally conked out, but you feel guilty spending money on a new one when you could wash your dishes by hand. Take comfort knowing today's dishwashers are so efficient that washing by hand costs more than running a full load in a new dishwasher.

You can find both budget and premium models that do a great job of cleaning your dishes. Individual features will probably determine your final price. You just have to decide which features are worth the extra costs and where you can save.

- Steam. Some pricey dishwashers generate steam to loosen dirt before washing. However, tests suggest dishes will probably come out just as clean without steam.

- Power scrub. If you usually pre-rinse, don't pay extra for power-scrubbing features.

- Custom wash cycles. You may not need additional custom wash cycles. Experts say most dishwasher buyers only need three cycles – normal, heavy-duty, and a quick or delicate cycle. An extra sanitizing cycle doesn't necessarily provide better cleaning.

- Two-drawers. If a dishwasher features two separate drawers, you can run both drawers at once or just one. These dishwashers are often less efficient and more expensive.

- Location of controls. Controls mounted along the dishwasher door's top rim vanish neatly when you close the door, but you can't see the time left until the dishes are finished. Consider partially hidden or front-mounted controls instead.

- Stainless steel. A stainless steel interior contributes to a quieter wash, helps dishes dry faster, and is more resistant to stains than a plastic interior.

- Noise. Cheaper dishwashers are often louder.

- Easier loading. Features that make loading your dishwasher easier include adjustable racks, fold-down tines, a third rack, extra flatware slots, tines set closer together to allow more dishes, or tines positioned farther apart to accommodate larger dishes.

- Drying options. Some dishwashers offer both heated drying and an air-dry function for utility savings.

- Soil sensors. These sensors detect how dirty your dishes are, so your dishwasher can use just enough water and water pressure to get them squeaky clean.

- Energy efficiency. For an energy efficient dishwasher, look for a Consortium for Energy Efficiency (CEE) rating of Tier One or higher, or check the yellow EnergyGuide label.

Secrets to keeping stainless steel looking new. You don't need to use expensive cleaners every day on your stainless steel appliances. Try these thrifty super heroes instead.

- Glass cleaner. To remove fingerprints, whip out your glass cleaner spray and a clean cloth.

- White vinegar. If your stainless steel develops water stains, wipe them away with white vinegar.

- Baking soda. For bits of food that have stubbornly glued them-selves to the stainless steel, apply a mixture of warm water and baking soda, and rub gently with a sponge.

- Baby oil. You may even be able to make scratches fade almost instantly by buffing them with baby oil or mineral oil and dry-ing with a clean cloth.

Unbeatable way to pick the best dehumidifier. Choose the wrong dehumidifier, and it won't dry out your space. Even worse, the dehumidifier may be a hassle to use and waste energy. Fortunately, the following tips can help you get the most bang for your buck.

- Figure the size of your room. Dehumidifiers are sized by how many pints of water they can remove from the air in 24 hours. To figure what size dehumidifier you need, measure the room you want to dry and figure the square footage. For example, if your basement is 25 feet long and 20 feet wide, the square footage is 25 x 20 or 500 square feet. Some experts recommend no more than a 30-pint humidifier for rooms this size. They also recommend sizes ranging from 40 to 70 pints if your space is between 800 and 1,400 square feet, but the correct size may vary depending on the conditions in the space. Regardless of the size of the room, be sure to increase your square footage by at least 20 percent for ceilings higher than 8 feet, but reduce the original number by at least 25 percent if the space is air conditioned.

- Consider the temperature. If the temperature in your space could drop below 65 degrees, consider a "low temperature" model. These dehumidifiers come with an automatic defrost function that prevents the dehumidifier's coils from freezing.

- Choose hose or bucket. To remove the water that collects, you'll need a hose that can empty to a drain, or be prepared to empty the bucket regularly. Some models have a built-in pump that drains the unit. Check which options each model provides. If you prefer to empty the bucket, remember that smaller buckets are easier to lift, but they must be emptied more often. Models with auto shutoff turn off when the bucket is full.

- Determine optimal humidity level. Some models include an adjustable humidistat you can set to the recommended 50 percent level. These units only run when the humidity is not at your chosen level. Without this programmable humidistat, you'll need a hygrometer to measure the humidity so you can set the unit to get the results you want.

- Take noise into consideration. Check the noise levels on the label, or test them in the store. Models over 60 decibels will probably drown out conversation in the same room. Choose a dehumidifier with casters if you need to move it easily.

- Look for an easy-to-clean filter. Since you must clean the unit's filter regularly, find one that's easy to clean.

- Plan ahead. You can save money if you buy your dehumidifier during summer sales, but don't rush. Closeout sales usually happen in late fall or early winter.

Boost your dehumidifier's efficiency

Make your dehumidifier work more efficiently with two changes. If the dehumidifier is in a cold room, turn on a space heater. This helps dry the air faster because dehumidifiers work better in warmer air. Placing your dehumidifier in the center of the room may dry the room faster, too.

Keep in mind that your dehumidifier works fastest when it only has to dehumidify one room or one closed-off space. If you have two rooms separated by an open door, putting a smaller dehumidifier in each room will dry the rooms faster than one large dehumidifier in one of the rooms.

Silence a vibrating washer. Your brand new washer is so loud it could wake the dead, and it vibrates so hard it actually moves a few inches by the time each load finishes. You could try putting carpet scraps under the feet to dull the noise, but check this first. When the washer is empty and not running, check the tags and stickers until you find one with instructions for removing the bolts that hold the washer drum in place during shipping. These bolts should be removed during installation, but installers often forget. If you don't find any information on the back of the washer, check your washer's manual or the manufacturer's website for information on removing shipping bolts.

If the shipping bolts have already been removed, you may need to balance the washer legs. To check the balance, place a carpenter's level on the surface of the washer, and make sure the machine is not tilted in any direction. If the washer is tilted, play it safe, and ask someone to help you level it.

Before you begin, get your adjustable wrench and a block of wood or 2x4. Ask your assistant to tilt the washer so the front legs come off the floor. While the washer is tilted, shove the wood under the washer. Now your assistant can lower the washer, but the wood will keep the washer legs from touching the floor. Each washer leg has a locking nut that holds it in place. Loosen each one with the wrench so you can adjust the legs. When the legs are adjusted, tighten the locking nuts. Ask your helper to tilt the washer up again so you can remove the wood.

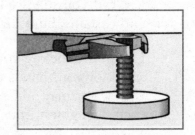

To level the rear legs, tilt the washer forward so you raise them about 4 inches off the floor. Unlike the front legs, the rear legs are self-leveling, so they should adjust to the proper height when you set them back on the floor. Use your carpenter's level to make sure the legs are balanced from left to right and from front to back.

Stop wasting energy in the laundry room. Your dryer must work harder and longer to dry your clothes when the lint trap is clogged. That means wasted utility dollars. Even if you clean the filter after every load, do you give any thought to the dryer's exhaust tube? It can get clogged, too, which is especially dangerous since a blocked exhaust has been known to cause household fires. Professionals could charge you $100 or more to clean this tube, but why not take care of the problem yourself? Take your outdoor leaf blower and insert the nozzle into the exhaust opening in your dryer. A couple of short blasts of air should blow out any lint caught in the tube.

7 things to consider when buying an iron. A cordless steam iron or an iron with a nonstick surface may seem like a great idea, but *Consumer Reports* was disappointed with the models they tested in both categories. So ignore all the flashy features and marketing hype, and use tips like these to find the right iron for your clothes.

- Decide whether you want a steam iron or a garment steamer. If you don't need that just-ironed look and only want to remove wrinkles from your clothes, a steamer may work faster. If you still need an iron, but also want to steam clothes and curtains, hunt for an iron with a vertical steaming option.

- Lift an iron before you buy it to make sure it isn't too large or small for your hands or too heavy. Remember, filling the iron with water may add enough weight to make a difference. If even the lightest irons are too hefty, consider a travel iron.

- Hold the iron the way you would while using it. Check that you can easily read its controls and markings and adjust the settings.

- Be sure your iron includes an auto-shutoff that turns off the iron if it sits idle too long.

- Check out models with a spill-resistant, removable water reservoir if you're fed up with spills that happen while refilling an iron.

- Look for irons that let you control the amount of steam.

- Choose an iron with spray and burst of steam functions if you often deal with stubborn wrinkles or heavy fabrics.

Say goodbye to washing machine odors. You might be surprised to learn that washing machines can develop mold, mildew, gunky buildup, and even smelly germs, in spite of regular washing with hot water. But that doesn't mean you have to break out nasty-smelling cleaners. Just use vinegar and baking soda.

For a front-loading washer, pour one cup of vinegar and one-fourth cup of baking soda into your machine. If you have a top loader, pour in four cups of vinegar and three-fourths cup of baking soda. Choose a hot water wash, allow the washer to agitate for a minute or two, and then let sit for 45 minutes. When you restart your washer, let it run through the rest of the wash and rinse cycles. After it empties, wipe down the tub with vinegar to remove any left-over residue.

This washing process works well with conventional washers, but cleaning a high efficiency (HE) washer works differently. Some HE washers have a maintenance cycle you should run on a regular basis, but you can also run your own version of the cycle using a hot water or stain setting, along with an extra rinse cycle. Check your HE washer manual to find out the right way to run a maintenance cycle for your machine. Plan to run this cycle without any laundry in the washer. In general, you should run the maintenance cycle every month with one-fourth cup of bleach, a cup of white vinegar, or the cleaner specified by your user's manual.

After the HE cleaning cycle finishes, wipe down the inside of the washer with white vinegar to remove any lingering residue. In addition, scrub the rubber seal around the washer door with bleach or vinegar before wiping it dry with a fresh cloth.

Banish mold and mildew from your washer

Whether you own a conventional washing machine or HE washer, experts say you can help prevent mold, mildew, and bad odors by simply leaving the door open between washes. It gives everything a chance to dry out.

Secret to a problem-free garbage disposal. Clogged garbage disposals are one reason why the day after Thanksgiving is Roto-Rooter's busiest day of the year. Garbage disposals can handle many foods, but some items are a clog waiting to happen. Unfortunately, those foods may be more likely to find their way into disposals at Thanksgiving and Christmas. To keep your disposal problem-free every day, make sure these notorious cloggers never go into your disposal.

- Stringy or tough foods. This includes food with clingy fibers and fruits or vegetables with tough parts or peels like potato skins, corn husks, asparagus ends, artichokes, celery, string beans, chard, carrot peels, banana peels, onion skins – and, strangely enough, eggshells.

- Expandable foods. Rice, pasta, and other starchy foods expand in your pipes and disposal just as they do on your stove.

- Oils, fats, or grease. These can create a clog by accumulating into a solid mass or by building up over time.

- Hot water. If grease is in your disposal, hot water helps it accumulate into a clog.

Beware of hidden danger lurking in your blender. Your freshly washed blender may be hiding a colony of germs and mold. A study by NSF International found that yeast, mold, and food-poisoning bacteria like *E. coli* and *Salmonella* lurked in the gaskets of household blenders. In fact, their study found that these appliances are the third-most contaminated item in the kitchen.

The reason a perfectly clean blender can be so germy is because most people wash their blenders without removing the gasket, that rubber seal at the base of the blender. This means any food in the gasket may stay there for weeks, months, or even longer.

Fortunately, this problem is easy to fix and prevent. Check the manufacturer's instructions for cleaning your blender. If your blender jar can be disassembled and removed from the blender base, remove the gasket and clean it separately after every use. Do the same for other nonelectric parts that can be detached from the blender jar. If the gasket is not dishwasher safe, NSF recommends cleaning it with hot, soapy water and rinsing well. Just make sure everything has dried thoroughly before you reassemble the blender.

But don't stop there. NSF also recommends taking a little time to regularly clean the germiest spots in their study – your refrigerator's meat and vegetable compartments. Your can opener may also collect germs in its nooks and crannies, so clean its blades carefully after each use.

Exterminate dangerous fungus lurking in your dishwasher

After checking nearly 200 dishwashers on six continents, scientists found that 62 percent of them contained fungus, especially in the rubber seal around the dishwasher's edge. The fungus survived in spite of the detergents and high water temperatures in the dishwashers, but they won't survive this.

Scrub down your dishwasher's rubber seal with a mixture of vinegar and baking soda, making sure to completely remove any black moldy deposits if you find them. When you are done, fill a bowl with two cups of vinegar, place it on the top rack, and run the dishwasher on its hot setting. For the final blow against the fungus, pour one cup of baking soda on the floor of your dishwasher, and run it again.

Hassle-free way to move your refrigerator. Nobody wants to scrape or rip the kitchen floor, but sometimes, moving the refrigerator out from the wall causes damage – especially on vinyl floors. Fortunately, preventing that damage is incredibly easy. First, even if you are only moving your refrigerator a foot from its original spot, play it safe. Tie the doors shut, and make sure the length of your refrigerator's power cord, ice maker water connection, and any other connections are long enough to reach where you want your refrigerator to go.

Ask someone to tilt the refrigerator slightly so you can slip a slider – thick cardboard, carpet scraps, or plastic sliding disks – under the refrigerator's legs. If you try carpet scraps, make sure the carpet side faces the floor so the refrigerator legs rest on the carpet's underside. And remember, the trick to making carpet and cardboard sliders work well is for two people to slowly move the refrigerator, while keeping it on the sliders. One person should push the refrigerator from the back, while the other pulls on the cardboard or carpet scraps from the front.

MONEYSAVER

The costly truth about refrigerator ice makers

Before you pay extra for a refrigerator ice maker or an in-the-door ice and water dispenser, be aware that refrigerators with these features are much more likely to need repairs than models that don't have them. The ice maker or dispenser may also add to your electricity costs. So you may pay more for the ice maker when you buy, more to run it, and more for repairs in a few years.

Super solutions for hard water problems. Hard water clogs appliances with mineral deposits and makes soaps and detergents less effective. Take these steps to protect your appliances.

- Pour vinegar instead of water into the reservoir when your coffee maker is empty, and run the coffee maker as usual. If this doesn't remove all the mineral deposits in your coffee maker's carafe, repeat the process until the deposits are gone.

- Turn your water heater down to 130 degrees to reduce the mineral deposits you see on your dishes. Also, pour vinegar into the rinse agent slot, or spoon some vinegar into a cup or bowl on the dishwasher rack before running each load of dishes.

- Add one-third cup of washing soda to your rinse cycle for cleaner clothes if you use powdered detergent. If you are not completely satisfied with the result and your water is very hard, try this with the next load. Add one-half cup of washing soda. That should give you a better result.

Smart way to stop losing small lids. Small plastic items –
like cup lids, corncob holders, and storage container lids – need to
go in your dishwasher's top rack, but the dishwasher isn't usually
set up so you can keep them in one place. Buy a mesh lingerie bag
for dishwasher use. Fill it with your small plastic items and hook it
onto the tines of the top rack. When your dishwasher's cycle is finished, your items will still be in the same place, but they'll be clean.

Meanwhile, make the lingerie bag in your laundry room do double
duty by using it to solve the orphan sock problem. By washing your
socks in the lingerie bag, you'll eliminate the chances of one sock
getting lost.

Find appliance manuals with ease. Round up all your
kitchen appliance manuals. If any are missing, download them for
free from the support section of the manufacturer's website or
www.manualsonline.com. To make sure you can easily find these
manuals in the future, drop them into a gallon-size resealable bag.

Mount a couple of small hooks inside the cabinet under your
kitchen sink or install a small expandable curtain rod. Hang large
office binder clips from the hooks or rod, and use the clips to hold
your resealable bag of manuals. The next time you need a manual,
you'll know right where to go.

Cars & Trucks

The road to smart buys & easy care

Learn the real cost of ownership. Often the cheapest car is not the smartest deal. When you factor in other expenses like insurance, gas, maintenance, repairs, and fees, suddenly that bargain isn't so wallet-friendly. But figuring out all these costs on your own can be daunting. For help, turn to IntelliChoice, a website that claims to help you choose your car wisely. Here you can plug in a make, model, year, and options, and you'll see details on the real cost to own that car over a five-year period. Visit the site at *www.intellichoice.com*.

Car-buying service saves time and money. Whether you're in the market for a new or used car, a buying service is one option you should consider, especially if you hate the idea of haggling with a dealer. Warehouse clubs, credit unions, and organizations like AAA and USAA offer a car-buying service to their members for free. You need to first have an idea of the car you want and a good feel for its average price. The service then locates vehicles in your area that match your criteria. They can usually negotiate lower prices with the dealer because of the volume of sales they send their way.

Atlanta car-buyer David Horner didn't have time to search for a new car, so he used the Credit Union of Georgia's free Car Buying Program to locate the exact Subaru model he was looking for. They locked in a price for him that was invoice plus transportation and docking fees, and ended up saving him $950 on the deal.

Avoid expensive dealer add-ons. You don't really win if you've haggled your new car price down by several thousand dollars only to spend that much – or more – on hidden add-ons. Check the fine print, question the salesperson, and make sure you're not paying for extras you don't want or need.

- Dealer fees. Some may be negotiable, some may be outright outrageous, and some you'll just have to pay. Regardless, question them all. Look for lines in the contract containing terms like Processing Fees, Dealer Preparation, Delivery Charge, Advertising Fee, or Documentation Fee. Be especially wary of Additional Dealer Mark-up (ADM), which is solely for extra profit.

- Vin etching. It's an excellent idea to permanently engrave your vehicle's identification number (VIN) on the car's windshield or windows. In fact, police and insurance agencies recommend you do so to make a stolen car harder to dispose of and easier to recover. Your insurance carrier may even give you a discount if your car has VIN etching. Doing this yourself is easy and cheap – a kit averages about $25 and takes under 15 minutes. A car dealer, on the other hand, may demand anywhere from $150 to $300.

- Environmental protection package. A fancy phrase for rust-proofing and paint sealant, it will cost you an extra $200 up to a whopping $1,200. But most experts say you can safeguard your chassis and paint job just as well with the protective coating that comes standard from the factory plus regular washing and waxing. Cost to you – zip.

- Fabric upholstery protection. Splatters and spills are part of a busy commute, but you can protect your car's upholstery with an inexpensive can of stain repellent spray. The dealer may ask $200 for this add-on, while a can of spray is less than $15.

Inspect before you buy. You would never purchase a home without having it appraised, so why would you buy a used car without having a professional give it the once-over first? It may seem like a beauty to you, but what do you really know about the frame, suspension, brakes, radiator, or battery? A qualified mechanic can conduct a pre-purchase inspection (PPI) for about one hour and

$100 – although this can vary depending on where you live, the specific vehicle, and how thorough the inspection is. That seems a small investment for peace of mind.

Skip extended warranties for auto protection

Buying that extra coverage is a lot like betting against your new car. You're wagering it will need more repairs than the warranty cost. These overpriced service contracts never cover all vehicle repairs and limit you to only certain approved repair facilities. That means you could end up paying for an "excluded" repair or be forced to use an inconvenient service location.

Worse, you might never use the protection plan at all. In fact, according to a *Consumer Reports* survey, 42 percent of their respondents didn't need the extra coverage because either the standard manufacturer's warranty was enough or their cars simply didn't need repairs. For many people, the smartest move is to buy a car with proven reliability, then set aside a repair fund.

Protect yourself from flood-damaged cars. Whenever superstorms, hurricanes, or flash floods recede, they leave behind a deluge of water-damaged vehicles – hundreds of thousands of cars corroded from salt water, ruined by silt, and overrun with mold. Unfortunately, many of these will be spiffed up on the outside by swindlers and sold to unsuspecting buyers. Don't let that be you.

The most incriminating evidence will be deep inside the car's engine, transmission, brakes, electrical system, and other innermost parts, and may not even impact the car's functionality for months or even years. But there are ways you can spot a storm-damaged car if you know how.

- Look inside the trunk and pop the hood. Hunt for silt, lines, or water stains, especially around the spare.

- Sniff. Mold and mildew have a distinctive odor which is a dead giveaway, but even the overpowering aroma of air freshener or disinfectants should raise a red flag.

- Check under the carpet, on the seats and seatbelts, around metal screws and hinges, and along the door panels. You're looking for silt, discolorations, rust, and warping. Make sure the headlights and taillights aren't fogged or have water lines.

- Take it for a test spin and note if the engine is rough or lurches.

Of course, the best precaution is to have the vehicle inspected by a qualified mechanic before you buy.

WARNING

Beware of title scams

Never purchase a used car without giving its title a thorough inspection — front and back. Those extra minutes could save you from an expensive, and potentially life-threatening, mistake. What you're looking for are danger words, part of a branding strategy to warn unsuspecting buyers that a vehicle has suffered severe damage from a collision, theft, or disaster. Branding terms include flood, salvage, rebuilt, fire, junk, and irreparable.

But be aware that a "clean" title is sometimes misleading. Criminals can take a branded title to a state that does not require branding, register the vehicle there, and get a new, clean title. This is called "title washing." If you suspect someone is trying to sell a damaged car with a washed title, contact your auto insurance company, local police, or the NICB at 800-835-6422.

Use VIN to check title. If you want to be sure a car's title is "clean," get the vehicle identification number (VIN) from the seller and dig a little deeper. Go online to the Department of Justice's National Motor Vehicle Title Information System (NMVTIS) at *www.vehiclehistory.gov*

or the National Insurance Crime Bureau (NICB) database at *www.nicb.org,* and request a report on the vehicle's damage history. The NICB report is free, but there's a small fee for reports via NMVTIS. You can also pay a few extra dollars for a more in-depth report from AutoCheck at *www.autocheck.com.* If the seller will not give you the VIN, walk away from the deal — they have something to hide.

Smart features help seniors drive safer and longer.
Arthritic knees, diminished hand strength, hip pain, and failing eyesight all make driving more of a challenge than it was years ago. But these common symptoms of aging don't necessarily mean you must throw in the car keys. The University of Florida National Older Driver Research and Training Center in conjunction with AAA have recommendations that address the challenges senior drivers face. Take advantage of existing features in your car or look for these specific elements if you're thinking of buying another vehicle.

- Safety features — front and rear warning systems, antilock brakes, adjustable head restraints with extra padding, dynamic stability control, backup cameras, parallel parking assistance, and dual-stage air bags.

- Ergonomics — adjustable seats, low door thresholds, adjustable accelerator and brake pedals, and tilting and telescoping steering wheels.

- Comfort — thick steering wheels, automatic door openers and closers, power mirrors and seats, heated mirrors and seats, large dashboard buttons, pushbutton ignition, and keyless entry.

In addition, you can add inexpensive assistive devices to your car — like pedal extenders, swivel seats, leg lift straps, lumbar supports, and hand controls — either through your car's manufacturer or a third party. Just make sure any add-ons don't compromise the existing safety features in your car. Find out by contacting an occupational therapy-driver rehabilitation specialist (OT-DRS) online at *www.aota.org/olderdriver* or by calling 301-652-6611. If you want help selecting a vehicle that fits your needs, visit the interactive website *SeniorDriving.AAA.com/SmartFeatures.*

Recall database keeps you safe. The National Highway Traffic Safety Administration (NHTSA) has the challenging task of recalling cars and other vehicles with safety issues, and ensuring all problems are fixed. Since 1966, they've risen to this challenge by recalling more than 390 million cars, trucks, buses, and motorcycles, perhaps saving countless lives. As a car owner, you are notified of these problems on your vehicle.

But what about a used car you're thinking of purchasing? You would certainly like to know if there's been a recall issued for it and if the owner followed up properly. Peace of mind is but a few mouse clicks away, thanks to the NHTSA recall database. Search by vehicle year, make, and model, and see all safety recalls, complaints, service bulletins, and NHTSA investigation documents. Find this online at *www.safercar.gov/Vehicle+Owners*.

When leasing makes sense. Leasing may have a bad reputation with many financial experts, but there are several situations where leasing a car could be a good fit for you.

- If you don't have a lot of cash on hand to buy a car outright, the low upfront cost of leasing could be a blessing. In fact, some dealers will waive a down payment altogether. Just remember, the lower your down payment, the higher your monthly payments will be.

- If you can't afford the high monthly payments that often come with a car loan, the amount you'll pay each month for a lease may be within your budget. Since you're only paying off the depreciation on the car, monthly payments could be half what you'd expect.

- If you like driving a new car every few years, or if you only need a car for a few years, leasing means easy turnover or turn in. Simply hand the keys to the dealer when your initial lease is up, and drive out with a brand new car or walk away — no haggling, no hassles.

- If you don't want to deal with maintenance and repairs common when a new car turns three or four years old, the short life span of a lease could be perfect. Most new cars are covered by a manufacturer's warranty during this time, and all you have to pay for is routine maintenance, like oil changes, tire rotations, and the like.

WARNING

Distracted driving is deadly

Hands-free technology makes it easier than ever to talk or text and drive. But just because you can do it doesn't mean you should. New research shows hands-free does not mean risk-free. You can experience dangerous mental distractions even when your hands are on the wheel and your eyes are on the road.

Comprehensive testing showed when talking on the phone, your reaction time slows, you scan the area less, and your brain even fails to recognize things right in front of you, like pedestrians and stop signs. In short, you enter the phone zone. This is different, researchers say, from having a conversation with a passenger in the car, because you both are likely to react to things like sirens, accidents, and traffic. A person on the phone just keeps talking.

The bottom line — turn your phone off while driving.

Cut the cost of your car lease. Many leasing companies offer a little-known program that can significantly reduce your monthly payment. It's called the Multiple Security Deposit (MSD) lease, and here's how it works.

Most leases require a security deposit – usually equal to one monthly payment rounded up to the nearest $50. This is returned to you at the end of your lease. Note, a security deposit is different from a down payment, which is rolled into the lease price of your car, and is never returned.

In addition, every lease has something called the money factor or lease factor. It is essentially the interest rate you are charged for the lease. You'll see it as a decimal – something like 0.0033. This money factor is used to calculate your monthly lease payments. The kicker is, your money factor automatically goes down by a certain percentage when you pay a security deposit.

If your leasing company offers an MSD program, you are allowed to pay more than one security deposit, reducing your money factor with each one. The bottom line is you pay less every month plus get all your security deposits back at the end of the lease. Just remember to do the math ahead of time to make sure your overall savings will be more than you could otherwise make by investing the total amount of your MSDs.

Bust a gas-saving myth. Changing your car's air filter will certainly improve acceleration, but it won't get you more miles to the gallon. Today's cars have fuel-injected, computer-controlled engines, and the air filter simply doesn't affect fuel economy. This myth is a holdover from the days when cars had carburetors – those built prior to the 1980s. So change your air filter when it's dirty because it's good for your car, but don't expect to save any money at the pump. What will make your car more fuel-efficient? Drive with an empty trunk, keep your tires inflated properly, use cruise control when possible, eliminate jackrabbit starts and sudden stops, don't drive with a loose or missing gas cap, and fix serious problems like a faulty oxygen sensor.

Do the math before buying a hybrid. It may seem that the time for hybrids and electric cars has come. After all, they tout some remarkable miles per gallon claims. And who doesn't support reducing pollution and minimizing greenhouse gasses? But when all is said and done, don't discount the value of a truly fuel-efficient gasoline-powered car. Because of improvements in engineering and design, you can get excellent gas mileage and a comfortable interior at a reasonable price.

And that's the bottom line – price. In order for a hybrid or electric car to make economic sense, you must factor in purchase price, fuel savings, tax credits, repair and maintenance costs, insurance, and depreciation. To do this more easily, visit the U.S. Department of Energy's website at *www.fueleconomy.gov* and navigate to its "Save Money & Fuel" tab. Here you'll find the cost calculator "Can a Hybrid Save Me Money?"

GREAT IDEA

Record your car's maintenance history

You can purchase an auto care notebook specifically designed for car maintenance, or download forms off the Internet and print them out. Simply Google terms like "car maintenance log," and browse through your options. Or create your own register, cheaply and easily.

The simplest solution is a spiral notebook that fits in your glove box. But you can also use graph paper and a three-ring binder, or print out a spreadsheet you've created on your computer. If you decide to record two types of information — gas mileage and maintenance — create different pages or areas in your notebook for them.

To record gas mileage, make columns for the date, odometer reading, number of miles, number of gallons purchased, and miles per gallon calculation. Keep a separate log for maintenance. You'll want columns for the date, odometer reading, type of maintenance, the cost, and any helpful notes for future reference. Record oil changes, tire replacements and rotations, filter replacements, various fluid changes, and other services.

A diary like this will be invaluable in helping you stay up-to-date on your car's service schedule, plus you'll feel more confident when speaking to your mechanic about maintenance issues. In addition, when you go to sell your car, proving it was well-maintained could give you a negotiating boost.

Buy used tires with care. Good tires mean better grip and handling on roads as well as better gas mileage. For that reason, experts urge you to replace your tires when the tread becomes worn down. As a quick test, hold a penny upside down in the tread. If you can see the top of Lincoln's head, your tires flunk. But should you buy used and save some money? It's a classic case of buyer beware. Sure, you can look for tread wear, plugs, and patches, but there could be less obvious defects or damage.

Take a few extra moments to get up close and personal with that used tire before you buy it. Look for exposed steel cords or wires in the tread, bumps or irregularities in the surface, and even missing chunks of rubber near the wheel. In addition, the Rubber Manufacturers Association says tire repairs should be limited to the tread area only. Don't buy a tire with a patch, plug, or repair on the sidewall.

Remember, tread is not the only indicator of an aging tire. The rubber deteriorates over time, and even a tire that has never spent one mile on the road can be dangerous. Look for a Tire Identification Number (TIN) on the sidewall. It should start with the letters DOT. The last four numbers represent the week and year the tire was manufactured. A code of 1110, for instance, means the tire was made in week 11 of 2010. Don't purchase tires that are more than six years old.

Car maintenance you should question. If you weren't born with a compression gauge in hand, you may feel like you're at the mercy of every mechanic with an agenda. Here are some maintenance tasks you may not be too familiar with, and guidance for scheduling them.

- Transmission flush. Fresh, clean transmission fluid is the lifeblood of your car. And for that reason, you don't want it to get so old it gums up the works. Unfortunately, experts disagree on exactly how often you should replace this important fluid. Many car manuals say you can wait until you've driven 100,000 miles, while some experts say you should change it every 60,000 or even every 30,000 miles. If you can physically check your transmission fluid, change it if it looks or smells burnt or contains particles.

- Engine flush. Many car manufacturers – including Honda and GM – recommend against this process, which claims to clean sludge out of your engine. They state some of the chemicals used could damage engine parts.

- Fuel-injector cleaning. Under normal circumstances, this is not part of required routine maintenance. That's because most brand-name gasolines contain detergents that prevent clogged fuel injectors. But if your check engine light comes on, and a specific problem is found, you could need them cleaned.

Sidestep the coolant controversy. You may choose to save money by changing the coolant in your car yourself. This is the liquid that protects your engine from temperature extremes. You may also know it as antifreeze. And while it may sound like a pretty straight-forward do-it-yourself job, using the wrong coolant can cause major damage to your engine.

The issue is especially confusing because there's no standard across the industry. Vehicle manufacturers recommend specific coolant types for their cars, while coolant manufacturers use different labels and colors as they choose. Two different coolants may even use the same color dye. Most standard antifreeze is green, but some are yellow. Long life coolants are typically orange or yellow, but could be red, pink, blue, purple, or even green. While all coolants perform the same basic function, certain chemicals are not compatible with others. That makes mixing types – and colors – dangerous to your engine.

You may think a "universal" coolant would be a safe solution. These are marketed as acceptable for all cars and mixable with whatever coolant is already in your system. But car manufacturers still dis-agree, to the point they've issued service bulletins warning against them. Your best bet – find the coolant your car manufacturer rec-ommends and use it exclusively.

Avoid a dead car battery this winter. Don't let winter morn-ings slow down your commute. Get your car battery tested before there's even a hint of Jack Frost in the air, and you won't be stranded in the driveway. When temperatures dip below freezing, your battery loses a third of its power. And when the mercury plunges to zero, your battery nosedives right along with it — to 50 percent power. That's why you want to start out winter with as much juice as possible.

According to AAA, most batteries have a life span of three to five years, so consider replacing it if you're near that mark. Check the date code on yours if you're not sure how old it is. Most manufacturers use a letter-number combination, which you'll find on a sticker or stamped on the top edge of the battery case.

If you think your battery still has some life left in it, take it to an auto parts store or a mechanic, and ask them to test it. Or buy a multimeter, starting at around $20, and test it yourself. Remember, when shopping for a replacement, you're more likely to get a "fresh" battery if you buy from a retailer with a high turnover — where batteries don't sit on the shelf for months.

4 hot tips for cold car care. You and your car can survive the fury of Old Man Winter with these clever tips that will make frosty outings less troublesome.

- Apply a coat of wax to your car's alloy wheels. This protects them from the corroding effects of road salt.

- Slip a pair of long socks over your wiper blades whenever your car sits outside during a freeze. Then when you're ready to go, pull off the socks without fighting any ice.

- Drain and refill your radiator with fresh antifreeze just before winter hits. Since antifreeze needs to be fairly pure to protect your engine properly from cold temperatures, experts recommend you do this every other year.

- Keep a stash of plastic grocery bags in your car, and tie one around each side-view mirror before a frost. Remove in the morning, and you're on your way with no scraping.

Secrets to a well-ordered trunk. You should always keep some essentials in your trunk, like a first aid kit, tire gauge, flashlight, jumper cables, flares, a blanket, sanitizing wipes, and bottled water. During winter, you may want to throw in a few more items like kitty litter, an ice scraper, snacks, and extra clothes. An old shower curtain is great to include for when you need to protect your trunk from the mud and wet, plus it's handy as a tarp in emergencies.

So now that you're prepared for almost anything, can you find what you need when you need it? It's simple to get – and stay – organized. First, lay a good foundation in your clean, empty trunk with a non-slip rug pad. This will keep everything from sliding around. Then grab whatever size container suits your needs and your space. Recycle something from the house or garage, like a milk crate, plastic tub, laundry basket, or even a wicker planter. Place the larger items in this. A small cooler can do double duty as a container, but remember you'll have to empty it out when you need to use it for cold food.

Then get creative with things like plastic shower caddies and shoe organizers with clear pouches. Even consider an old large handbag, tote, or briefcase with lots of pockets and compartments. Use these – plus hooks and suction cups – to keep small items contained and off the floor of your trunk. After all, you may need to actually use your trunk for groceries or luggage.

WARNING

Don't shorten the life of your headlights

When changing the bulb, if you touch it with your bare fingers, oil on your skin transfers to the glass and causes the bulb to burn out faster. Keep your headlights burning longer by changing the bulbs properly. Always handle a new bulb with a cloth, tissue, or when wearing latex gloves.

Replace a high-tech key for less. Along with a GPS and heated seats, your late-model car may have come with a fancy key fob. Simply push a button and you can remotely lock and unlock doors, set the car alarm, and even start the engine. Life is good — until the fob stops working. Don't panic. First, try replacing the battery. There's most likely a small screw or slot that gives you access to the inner workings. Pop the fob open and remove the old battery. Look for a replacement at your local hardware or battery store or at an electronics store like Radio Shack. It should run you less than $10. If you don't leave the battery out too long, your fob might not even lose its programming. Otherwise, check your car's manual for steps to reprogram it.

If you need to replace the key fob, you have a few choices. A dealer will get the job done quickly and easily, but you'll pay top dollar — anywhere from $150 to several hundred dollars, depending on the model. A cheaper option is to order a replacement online. One source is Keyless Ride at *www.keylessride.com*. They claim up to 75 percent off dealer prices. Or find a local locksmith who belongs to the Associated Locksmiths of America at *www.FindALocksmith.com*. He might have the blank fobs and can cut a new key for you at a reasonable price.

DIY scratch repair is fast and cheap. No need to report minor dings and scrapes to your insurance company, especially if they happen at home and won't cost enough to meet your deductible. You may be able to fix them yourself.

Buff out a small scuff or light scratch with a commercial product like Quixx Paint Scratch Remover, found at stores like Wal-Mart and Ace Hardware. It works like a mildly abrasive car polish to integrate the surrounding paint into the scratch. You might spend about $20, a half-hour, and some elbow grease.

If you can see metal in the chip or scrape, don't ignore the problem. This could lead to rust and more expensive damage. Get miniature bottles of touch-up paint from an auto parts store or car dealer. They probably won't blend perfectly, but if the scratch is small, you should be happy with the cost — about $15 — and the results.

For anything bigger than a breadbox, you'll want to step the repair process up a notch. Look for your car's color code. It's often found on the driver side door jamb. Then go to the Internet, where you'll find companies selling spray paint kits that could match your color exactly. Check out Automotive Touchup at *www.automotivetouchup.com*, where you can get a 12-ounce spray can for about $20 or a pint can for $45.

Get the best service from your mechanic

Simply avoid the busiest times in his day. For the most part, people drop off cars in the morning — between 7 and 9 a.m. — and pick them up late afternoon — from about 4 to 6 p.m. During these hours, your mechanic may have his mind on just moving business along. But bring your car in between 10 a.m. and 2 p.m., and you're more likely to get his undivided attention. Without a line of impatient people to hold you up or distract you both, you'll have time for questions and detailed answers. Even better — call ahead and ask if he takes appointments.

Cellphones

Straight talk & smart solutions

Tap into the best phone apps for seniors. Can an app a day keep the doctor away? Possibly, if it's a health app, a mind game app, or one of the thousands of other beneficial apps on the market. But what exactly is an app and why would a cellphone user want one? Here's the lowdown. The word "app" is short for application, and it's simply a piece of software that you can load on to your smartphone. Some apps provide entertainment like the popular Angry Birds game. Others provide services from digital coupons to heart rate monitoring. Many are free, and others cost a few dollars.

Whether you own a smartphone or are thinking about getting one, consider making apps part of your mobile experience. Here's a sampling of apps that will make your life easier and just plain better.

Health – WebMD provides information about diseases and symptoms. My Medical is a digital file cabinet for your medical records. Instant Heart Rate can take your pulse from your fingertip through the lens of your phone's camera.

News and weather – Read, watch, or listen to your favorite news programs with apps from NPR, CNN, or Fox News. Check current conditions and forecasts on The Weather Channel.

Social – Share family pictures with friends and relatives on Facebook. Twitter gives seniors a chance to follow up-to-date posts from their favorite resources be it a retail store or a beloved grandchild.

Music – Stream free music with Pandora or Spotify.

Games – Lumosity for iPhone or Mind Games for Android will keep your mind sharp.

GPS – Google Maps and StreetPilot by Garmin will get you where you need to go.

Inspirational – The Bible and popular devotional books like "Jesus Calling" and "Streams in the Desert" are available as apps.

Shopping – Retail Me Not delivers coupons directly to your phone. Or you can scan and save coupons to your phone, and then redeem them in stores with SnipSnap.

Everyday living – EyeReader and Magnifying Glass with Light will magnify your reading material and shine extra light on it. If you have trouble remembering where you park your car, try the Find My Car app.

Top places to shop for a new phone. The next time you're in the market for a new phone, there are plenty of walk-in stores to choose from. Check out Apple, Best Buy, Costco, Wal-Mart, or Radio Shack. You'll find good deals, friendly customer service, and a great selection. For online shopping, check out Apple and Amazon Wireless for lots of phone options, with or without contracts from major service providers.

Cut a deal when your contract is up. Most service providers will do whatever it takes to keep you as a customer. Take advantage and ask for the terms that work best for you the next time your contract expires. If they're not willing to work with you, take your business elsewhere.

Five ways to cancel your contract. You found "the one," signed on the dotted line, and thus began your two-year commitment to your new cellphone. But one day you realize you want out of your contract, and don't want to pay the hefty termination fees. Luckily, there are some steps you can take to drop your plan.

- Read the fine print. You may have a way out and not realize it.

- Stay up to date with changes made to your agreement. By law, if a carrier changes its terms, consumers must be notified and given 30 days to break their contract.

- Plead your case. If you're moving out of the carrier's service area for a noteworthy reason – job transfer, retirement, death of a loved one – you may find a sympathetic ear.

- Make a trade. Chances are you're not the only person who wants out of their contract. Look into swapping services like Celltrade, Cellswapper, and TradeMyCellular to find someone who needs what you've got. The site handles the paperwork, and you end up without a contract.

- Tweet or post. Airing a grievance on social media is like running a commercial during Super Bowl. It's fast, effective, and can reach thousands within seconds. No company wants to look like the bad guy in front of its customers. Use Twitter, Facebook, or any other social media outlet to broadcast your desire to bail, and see if you get a response.

Save money with phone alerts. Avoid overage charges by paying attention to your mobile's alerts. According to the Federal Communications Commission, cellphone companies must tell consumers when they get close to, reach, and surpass their plan's limits on voice, data, texting, and international roaming. You can set up alerts to arrive via text message or email. Once you receive a notice, limit or stop your usage until the start of a new billing cycle.

Slash what you pay for your plan. Major cellphone service providers offer discounts to employers and senior adults. If you or a family member work for a large company, nonprofit, corporation, university, or government entity, you could qualify for a price break on your personal cellphone service. Plus, plans for seniors like Verizon's Nationwide 65 Plus Plan and 65 Plus Two-Line Share Plans deliver great packages at affordable prices.

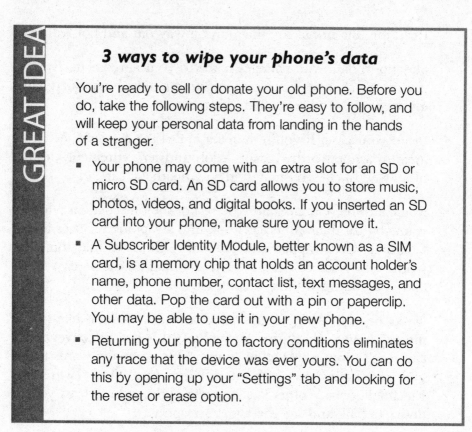

GREAT IDEA

3 ways to wipe your phone's data

You're ready to sell or donate your old phone. Before you do, take the following steps. They're easy to follow, and will keep your personal data from landing in the hands of a stranger.

- Your phone may come with an extra slot for an SD or micro SD card. An SD card allows you to store music, photos, videos, and digital books. If you inserted an SD card into your phone, make sure you remove it.

- A Subscriber Identity Module, better known as a SIM card, is a memory chip that holds an account holder's name, phone number, contact list, text messages, and other data. Pop the card out with a pin or paperclip. You may be able to use it in your new phone.

- Returning your phone to factory conditions eliminates any trace that the device was ever yours. You can do this by opening up your "Settings" tab and looking for the reset or erase option.

Score the best price for your old phone. When it comes to selling your old cellphone, you've got plenty of options – from online sites to brick-and-mortar stores, and the "go to" staples of eBay, Craigslist, and Amazon.

For good payouts and quick turnarounds, check out Gazelle (*www.gazelle.com*), You Renew (*www.yourenew.com*), and Exchange My Phone (*www.exchangemyphone.com*). All three sites offer quotes online, free shipping, and payment options such as a check, PayPal, or an Amazon gift card.

Best Buy and Radio Shack all run trade-in programs for phones. So does Target in partnership with NextWorth, an online service. The process generally starts online. You then drop off the old phone at the store or mail it in using a prepaid label. Payment is in gift cards.

Charities will also take your old phones off your hands, and put them to good use. Verizon's HopeLine program provides used cellphones to victims of domestic abuse. Cellphones for Soldiers supports troops stationed overseas. And the National Cristina Foundation uses them to help people with disabilities and at-risk students.

Easy ways to boost your battery. It's inevitable – every time you need to make a call, your phone's battery is in the red. If it's any consolation, you're not alone. But there are a few simple tricks you can perform to make your cellphone's battery charge last much longer. And there's no reason not to do them.

- Turn on airplane mode via your phone's settings menu. This will turn off Wi-Fi applications that drain your battery, and charge your phone in half the time.

- Change the brightness setting from auto to manual, and keep it as dim as you can without straining your vision.

- Set your device to lock or time out after a minute of not using it.

- Never place your phone in a desk drawer. Your phone will work harder to find a signal, zapping its power in the process.

- Keep your phone from getting too hot or too cold. A temperature between 32 and 95 degrees will best conserve your battery.

Best battery charger is in your garage. When your power goes out and you need to recharge your cellphone, turn to your car for help. Your vehicle's battery packs enough power to charge up your phone during an outage. It can juice up tablets, too.

High-tech solution for the hearing impaired. Have you heard? Bluetooth technology will help you hear your cellphone conversations crystal clear. A Bluetooth device can turn a pair of hearing aids into a wireless headset with no audio interference. The results are an enjoyable cellphone experience for hearing impaired individuals. The technology also allows people who wear hearing aids to listen to MP3 players, hear the television, conduct video chats with ease, and tune into GPS apps with driving instructions. Check with your audiologist for more information or search online for an accessory that will work with your hearing aids.

Surprising way to send text messages. When it comes to texting a message, you might feel like a klutz. Your fingers just can't seem to press the right keys on those tiny keyboards. But if you're willing to use a phone with voice recording capabilities, you can dictate your text messages with the press of a button. Many Android devices and iPhones come equipped with a microphone. By pressing the microphone icon on the keyboard, you can dictate a few sentences into a text message. You can also use the feature to dictate memos on to your phone's notepad or answer emails without typing a single word.

GREAT IDEA

How to wipe away phone grime

Never spray your device with a glass cleaner or disinfectant. In fact, it's best not to spray anything directly on to your phone or wipe it with a paper towel. Use a microfiber cloth or a dry Swiffer cloth to clean your phone's screen. If you need a little moisture to remove sticky gunk, mix 60 percent water with 40 percent alcohol. Isopropyl alcohol dries quickly, keeping moisture from seeping into your device.

To remove caked on grime from the unit's USB port, headphone jack, and other slots, use a cotton swab dipped in the water and alcohol solution. Or try a few bursts of compressed air.

Beware of eavesdroppers. You can walk away from a crowd, use hushed tones, or lock yourself in a restroom stall. No matter — if you're talking on your cellphone in public, anyone can overhear you. To protect yourself from wandering ears, keep the conversation short and never give out personal information such as a Social Security number or credit card number. If you must, cover your mouth and speak quickly. Always assume that someone is listening. And remember, public restrooms are just that — public, not private.

Dim your phone to catch some zzz's. If your body's natural sleep rhythm is disrupted night after night, your cellphone may be the culprit. According to a Mayo Clinic study, checking your phone in bed exposes you to bright light. That light can interfere with your production of melatonin, the hormone that regulates your sleep-wake cycle. Essentially, the light from your phone may trick your body into thinking it's daytime. Researchers suggest a simple way to get around this. Turn down the brightness setting on your device, and hold your phone at least 14 inches from your face. You may find your sleep problems put to rest.

GREAT IDEA

Pull the plug on robocalls

Charities. Politicians. Marketing companies. They all make them — those prerecorded phone calls that drive consumers crazy. Thankfully, there is something you can do to keep robocalls to a minimum or eliminate them completely. Register your mobile number with the National Do Not Call Registry created by the Federal Trade Commission and the Federal Communications Commission. Placing your cellphone number on the list should prevent telemarketers from calling or using autodial. Simply visit *www.donotcall.gov* to sign up. To file a complaint against a company or organization that is violating robocall rules, visit *www.fcc.gov* and search for Form 1088G: Wireless Communications Device.

Clothing & accessories

Fast fixes to fashion dilemmas

Secret to saving on clothing costs. Make a beeline for the back of a store to grab the best bargains. It's the single best way to save money on clothing. Retailers generally hang their clearance merchandise in the back, forcing customers to walk past their regularly priced items. Don't be tempted to look. Head straight back, then browse the racks along the walls for more deals. Leave full-priced clothes hanging.

You've heard the phrase, "three strikes and you're out." Apply this baseball rule when you shop for clothes. No matter how badly you want that top, if it doesn't go with three items in your wardrobe, it's out. Don't waste your money on something that goes with nothing – you'll never wear it.

Of course, nothing beats the value of simply taking care of what you already own. If you have a skirt in need of a new zipper, fix it. A repair may cost you a little money, but it will save you lots of money in the long run.

10 items every woman should have in her closet. Do you ever look in your closet and say, "I have nothing to wear?" Always keep these 10 wardrobe basics on hand and you'll never run out of options.

- black pants – for a polished, slimming look

- dark denim jeans – dress them up with pearls, dress them down with a T-shirt

- black dress – for dinner parties and elegant affairs

- dressy jacket – will complement even the most casual outfit

- cute flats – a comfortable pair for everyday wear with jeans, a skirt, or a dress

- dressy shoes in silver or gold – for special occasions

- figure-flattering skirt – pair with a variety of tops to achieve different looks

- khaki pants – to go with sweaters in the fall and tank tops in the spring

- cardigans – a collection of short- and long-sleeve will give you options year-round

- well-fitting undergarments – make sure they flatter your figure and your outfits

10 items every man should have in his closet. Men, take stock of your wardrobe. Keep the following fashion fundamentals in your closet, and look dapper at the drop of a hat.

- khaki pants – a tailored, relaxed pair delivers a trendy yet classic look

- white button down shirt – mix and match with anything from a pair of jeans to a suit

- navy blue blazer or sport coat – never goes out of style

- slim pair of black dress shoes – take good care of them and you'll wear them to every special occasion from now until forever

- cashmere or cotton-cashmere sweater in a neutral color – it's a splurge, but you'll find many opportunities to wear one

- polo shirt – the ultimate answer to casual wear

- dark blue jeans – every man should own a comfy pair of jeans

- attractive watch – don't leave home without one

- tie in classic colors like red and navy – for special occasions

- brown or black belt – because you don't want your pants to sag

3 ways to a perfect fit. Tired of trying on clothes in multiple sizes to figure out what fits you? Or guessing what would look good on you? Retail stores have come up with a variety of services to help you.

Online stores like Macys.com, Nordstrom.com, Belk.com, and many others offer a free service called True Fit. You create a profile by answering questions about your height, body type, and favorite brands, and they recommend sizes for clothing found in their stores. The more you use the True Fit system, the better it gets at helping you. See how it works at *www.truefit.com*.

Some online companies offer free trials of their clothing and accessories to make sure you have the perfect fit. Try out a pair of yoga pants from Athleta, and if they're not up to snuff, just send them back. You don't even have to wash them. Other companies that offer this perk include Norma Kamali for high-end fashion and Warby Parker for eyeglasses.

For a high-tech perfect fit, step inside a 3D sizing station found at malls in various parts of the country. The 10-second body scan will collect information from 200,000 points of reference to determine the styles and sizes that best suit you. It will then give you a printout of recommended sizes at your favorite stores. If you can't find one in a mall near you, go to *www.me-ality.com*, and submit your measurements to get your "me-ID" profile.

4 secrets of the well-dressed bargain hunter. Never pay retail again. That's the motto behind the books and blogs of savvy shoppers who know where to pay rock-bottom prices for high-end fashion — thrift stores. You, too, can join their ranks by learning a few tricks of the trade. Thrifty shoppers take note — here are four, no-fail tips for successful thrift store shopping.

- Get the skinny on special sale days. Some thrift stores slash prices by 10 percent once a week to 50 percent on holidays. Learn the schedule. Plus, ask about senior discount days.

- Know what day of the week your favorite thrift store sets out new merchandise. It could be daily or once a week. Shop early on those days to get the first shot at the newest offerings.

- Volunteer. Many thrift stores benefit the community. Not only will you get dibs on the latest selection, you will make new friends while helping out a worthwhile cause.

- Shop for name brands. Don't dish out cash for cheap duds. Pick up quality threads at affordable prices.

Get the best price on anything. Don't go running all over town trying to find the cheapest prices. Do some homework first to see if your favorite store will match competitors' prices and offer price adjustments. It pays to shop at stores that do. Wal-Mart, Target, and Kohl's, for example, will match a price if you find the item cheaper somewhere else. Just bring in the competitor's ad that shows the lower price. Home Depot, Lowe's, and Sears go even further and offer to beat competitors' prices by 10 percent. If the item you bought goes on sale, many stores will refund the difference, usually within a certain amount of time. Just make sure you read the fine print so you're aware of loopholes in store policies.

Perk up your wardrobe with rewards. All credit cards are not created equal. Many cards come with store perks that slash the cost of new clothes. Just make sure you know what you're signing up for — charge cards can only be used in-store and on the store's website, while credit cards with a store's logo and the Visa or MasterCard emblem, can be used anywhere. Take the Gap card, for instance, with its $10 rewards for every $200 spent plus 10 percent off every Tuesday. The store card is good only at Gap and Gap-related stores like Old Navy, Banana Republic, Piperlime, and Athleta. Gap also offers a Visa card, which can be used to make purchases anywhere.

Department stores like Kohl's deliver the goods, too, with two coupons for 15 percent off upon registering, plus cash rewards and 12 bonus discounts of 15 to 30 percent off annually. A Kohl's card is only valid in-store and on Kohls.com.

From Target's 5 percent off every purchase reward to JCPenney's monthly double point bonus, check your favorite fashion store's rewards card – it may be packed with perks.

Curb the urge to splurge online. Blowing your hard-earned bucks is easy on the Internet. Shoppers must break out their credit cards to buy online – and therein lies the problem. Studies show that consumers spend more when they shop with a credit card than when they shop with cash. Websites will also lure you with free shipping offers and time limits. These never-ending deals get you every time. But they don't have to. Follow these five easy tips to end overspending online.

- Prevent one-click shopping by never keeping a credit card on file with an online retailer. Taking a few extra minutes to enter your information gives you time to ask yourself, "Do I really want this?"

- Forward your finds to a few friends. Ask them if they think the item is worth buying.

- Limit your budget and time online. Know how much you can spend before you log on. Then set a time limit. You can browse hundreds of fashion items and accessories in a short amount of time online. Don't get sucked in.

- Walk away. If you see something you can't live without, log off and get busy doing something else. Give yourself a few minutes or longer to think about it. If you still can't live without it, log back on and buy it.

- Clean out your computer's cookies. Web browsers track your buying habits online, and then show you ads for items you may also like. Go to your browser's preferences to delete your history and change your tracking preferences.

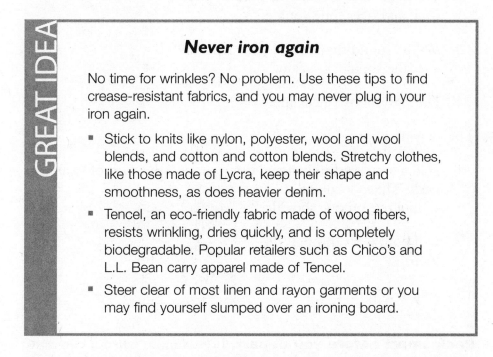

GREAT IDEA

Never iron again

No time for wrinkles? No problem. Use these tips to find crease-resistant fabrics, and you may never plug in your iron again.

- Stick to knits like nylon, polyester, wool and wool blends, and cotton and cotton blends. Stretchy clothes, like those made of Lycra, keep their shape and smoothness, as does heavier denim.

- Tencel, an eco-friendly fabric made of wood fibers, resists wrinkling, dries quickly, and is completely biodegradable. Popular retailers such as Chico's and L.L. Bean carry apparel made of Tencel.

- Steer clear of most linen and rayon garments or you may find yourself slumped over an ironing board.

Easy ways to tie a scarf. A scarf can transform a boring outfit into a fabulous fashion statement. For fresh ways to wear this versatile accessory, follow these easy steps.

The slip knot —

1. Drape a long scarf around the back of your neck and over your shoulders. One end should hang longer than the other.

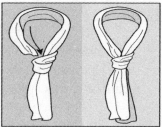

2. Tie a simple, loose knot about halfway up the longer end.

3. Slip the shorter end through the knot and tighten. Both ends should hang at about the same length. If they don't, try again.

The double wrap –

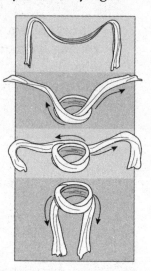

1. Drape a super long scarf around the back of your neck and over your shoulders.

2. Wrap the ends around the front of your neck and over the shoulders.

3. Wrap around the back of your neck and over the shoulders again.

4. Fluff around the neckline.

The hacking knot –

1. Fold a long scarf in half and drape around the back of your neck. The looped end should rest on one shoulder.

2. Pull both ends through the loop.

3. Adjust and fluff.

Pack smart before you depart. Less is more when it comes to packing for vacation. By picking a neutral color palette and selecting a handful of basics, you can travel in style and create plenty of outfits without stuffing your suitcase.

Packing list for ladies –

■ two bottoms, one dressy and one casual, or a pair of "convertible" pants – pants that unzip just below the knees to create a pair of capris

■ two to three tops including one tank top and one dressy blouse

- one pair of nice walking shoes and one pair of dressy shoes

- one dress, preferably in black

- accessories to change the look of each outfit, such as one to two scarves, a belt, a couple of necklaces, a few pairs of earrings, and a sweater

Packing list for men —

- one colored T-shirt

- two long-sleeve and two short-sleeve shirts

- one blazer

- one or two pairs of shorts and/or one or two pairs of jeans, depending on the season and destination

- one pair of pants, such as khakis, that can be dressed up with a blazer or dressed down with a T-shirt

- one pair of dress shoes and one pair of sneakers

- several ties

- dress suit optional, depending on the vacation

Both ladies and men should pack enough socks, sleepwear, and undergarments to last the duration of the trip.

Cut out trips to the cleaners. Just because the label says, "dry clean" doesn't mean you can't wash it. By law, clothing manufacturers only need to include one set of cleaning instructions per garment. If a piece of clothing is labeled "dry clean only," it should definitely go to the cleaners. But if it simply says "dry clean," you're in luck. Dry clean is a recommendation, and not your only laundering option.

Consider the fabric — if the label says cotton, cashmere, linen, nylon, or polyester, you can wash it. To play it safe, take a few precautions. Make sure accents like beads and sequins are sewn on, not glued on. Check for colorfastness by wetting a cotton swab with a little water and laundry detergent, and applying it to an inside seam or on an accent. If any dye comes off, dry clean the garment. If not, turn the garment inside out and place it in a mesh laundry bag. Run your washing machine on the delicate cycle. Or hand wash the item in your sink using lukewarm water and a few drops of detergent for delicate fabrics.

To dry, lay the garment on a clean, white towel and roll to absorb excess moisture. Unroll and lay flat on a fresh, dry towel or on a drying rack.

GREAT IDEA

Quick fixes for fashion emergencies

You never know when you're going to face a clothing crisis. Wardrobe woes strike suddenly, like in the middle of a wedding or when you're running out the door to an appointment. But with a little savvy, you can repair the mishap in no time. Here's a short guide on what to do if ...

- your hem falls out. Hold it in place with duct tape or masking tape.

- your zipper gets stuck. Rub a bar of soap or a wax candle along the teeth, and slide it free.

- you rip your blouse. Pull the threads through to the inside of your garment and tape the tear.

- your earring back falls out. Grab a pencil and snip off the eraser for a new back.

- your shiny shoes get scuffed up. Reach for a permanent marker of the same color and touch up the scuff marks.

- you break a heel. Super Glue to the rescue.

- you find a wad of chewing gum stuck to your clothes. Lift with duct tape or spritz with hairspray then scrap away.

- your button pops off your shirt, blouse, or pants. Reach for a twist tie. Remove the paper and "sew" the button back on with the wire.

Smart storage solutions. No one wants to take a favorite wool sweater out of storage — or any other article of clothing — only to find it's covered in mold or ruined by moths. Try these storage tips to keep varmints off your garments. Your favorite sweater will look fabulous from season to season

Fabric	How to store properly
Cashmere and wool	Best stored in a cedar chest, or in a drawer or closet with cedar chips or cedar balls.
Cotton	Layer garments in a storage container with acid-free tissue between items of different colors. Drill a few holes in the container's lid to allow the fabric to "breathe."
Leather	Stuff arms, shoes, boots, and bags with acid-free tissue paper. Cover with cloth and leave in a cool location.
Linen	Cover in cloth, not plastic. Don't store in cardboard boxes or cedar chests.
Polar fleece	Keep in a cotton sack with cedar balls.
Rayon	Best stored flat in a cool, dry place.
Silk	Use a padded hanger and store in a dark, cool closet with cedar balls, cedar blocks, or lavender.

Tackle stains without pricey spot removers. Look around your house and chances are you've got everything you need to fight stains within reach. But first, check the garment's label. If it says, "dry clean only," don't attempt to remove a stain. Take it to the cleaners and pay a professional to tackle it. Otherwise, squelch stains using the following guidelines, then follow the garment's laundry instructions.

- Butter or cooking grease — Dab on dishwashing liquid with a sponge. For stubborn spots, try rubbing alcohol.

- Coffee and tea – Pour hot water over the stain or reach for the dishwashing liquid.

- Ketchup and spaghetti sauce – Rub hydrogen peroxide on the stain or soak it in a mixture of 2 tablespoons white vinegar, 1 tablespoon dishwashing liquid, and cold water.

- Mustard – Blot to remove excess liquid, then try rubbing alcohol or glycerin.

- Red wine – Sprinkle with salt, then rinse with cold water. For a dried-in spot, rinse with club soda.

- Chocolate – Treat with a tablespoon of ammonia and 1/2 cup water – or try hydrogen peroxide. With chocolate, you want to blot the stain, not scrub it.

- Underarm – For whites, mix 1/4 cup each of baking soda, hydrogen peroxide, and water. Rub on the stain. For color garments that hide stains, but feel stiff from caked-on deodorant, fill your washing machine with cool water and add a cup of white vinegar. Soak for 30 minutes.

- Ink – Spray hairspray on the spot and blot. Place a rag or paper towel behind the stain to absorb the ink.

- Blood – Pour hydrogen peroxide or a solution of baking soda and water on the stain.

- Grass – Try a mixture of dishwashing liquid and hydrogen peroxide. If that doesn't work, a solution of hydrogen peroxide, baking soda, and hot water should do the trick.

Buckle up with the best belt for you. Belts aren't just for holding up pants. They're a fashion accessory much like a necklace or a scarf. But not every body type can pull off wrapping a ring around their waist and look stylish.

- A slender woman with a defined waist will look best in a thin or medium-size belt. A thick belt will overwhelm a tiny frame.

- A woman with an hourglass figure can pull off a wide belt in a fun color or texture. But if you don't want to draw attention to your curves, don't slip on a belt.

- Someone with a straight waist – typically a lanky body type with no defined waistline – should wear a medium belt over a loose blouse or dress to give the illusion of fuller hips from the waist down.

- An apple shape – a woman with a big tummy – is better off skipping the belt rack and sporting a bold necklace or a top with frills along the neck and shoulders. This will draw attention away from your midsection.

GREAT IDEA

Easy ways to tackle tie stains

The best way to save a tie from an unsightly stain is to act quickly and wisely. Battle an oily or greasy spot by dabbing it with a clean cloth. Sprinkle it with cornstarch or talcum powder, and set aside overnight. Brush away the powder and check the stain. You may need to repeat the process a few times until the stain disappears.

For nongreasy smudges, dab on a little rubbing alcohol with a clean cloth. Repeat as needed until the stain comes out. Blow dry immediately using a hair dryer to prevent a ring of residue from forming.

Fashion lifesavers at your fingertips. What do a paper clip, a button, and your favorite bottle of wine have in common? They can all serve as fashion lifesavers.

The next time you're trying to fasten your favorite bracelet – the one that's impossible to clasp by yourself – just grab a large paper clip. Open up the clip so it looks like an S, and slide one end into the bracelet link. Hold the other end of the clip in the same hand, and secure the clasp with your free hand.

If you're going on a trip, even if it's only to the gym, throw a button or two into your bag. They make great earring holders. Attach your earrings to the button, and you won't risk losing them. They're a great addition to your jewelry case as well. Keep pairs of stud earrings affixed to your buttons, and you won't have to search to find a match.

Rain boots, fashion boots, cowboy boots — they're all difficult to store without falling over or losing their shape. But if you're a wine lover, you have a remedy right at hand. Simply collect your empty wine bottles, and insert one into the shaft of each boot. Your boots will stay upright and in shape no matter where you store them.

GREAT IDEA

Smart way to shop for shades

Sunglasses are more than just a fashion statement. They're an essential accessory that safeguards the health of your eyes. Without proper protection, your eyes are more vulnerable to cataracts, macular degeneration, even skin cancer on your eyelids.

To protect yourself from these debilitating conditions, shop for sunglasses that block 99 to 100 percent of UVA and UVB rays or with a UV 400 protection label. For added security, try on wraparound styles. They block the sun's harmful rays from all sides and angles. And don't sweat spending a lot of money on pricey, name-brand sunglasses. You can find a good pair of sunglasses at drugstores and optical centers — reasonably priced.

Unique — and cheap — ways to organize your jewelry. You don't need an expensive case or ornate jewelry holder to keep your necklaces, rings, and bracelets in order. Repurpose some old items from around your house, and you'll have a unique organizer without spending a dime.

- A metal garden rake may not be your first thought to hold jewelry, but it has ample room for your necklaces, bracelets, and even scarves. Saw off the metal section with the "teeth" and give it a good washing. Paint it if you like, then hang it on a nail in your closet. Voila – all your jewelry available in an instant.

- A multi-rung pant hanger makes an ideal jewelry holder. You don't have to do a thing – just clasp your necklaces and bracelets around the rungs, and hang it in your closet.

- Use wooden thread spools for an old-fashioned decorative touch. Look for double-ended screws to attach each one to your wall. Secure them with a domed top nut.

- A simple cork board will put all your necklaces at your fingertips. Use thumbtacks or pushpins to hang them. Look for cork boards in different shapes to make your decor more fun.

- A pretty deviled egg plate is the perfect spot for rings and earrings. Just place it on your dresser for quick access to your favorite jewelry. If you prefer to tuck it in a drawer, an ice cube tray will work just as well.

GREAT IDEA

Set knotty necklaces free

When your necklaces tangle into frustrating little knots, use these tips to untangle them. Place your jewelry on a hard surface. Gently tug at the kinks with straight pins. If this doesn't work, sprinkle baby powder or apply a couple of drops of baby oil on to the knots. This will loosen the links and make them easier to untangle with pins.

Spruced up shoes go the extra mile. Wearing shoes is part of your daily routine much like brushing your teeth or savoring your morning cup of coffee. Whether you sport a pair of sneakers, spiffy sandals, or casual loafers, taking care of something you wear daily should be a top priority.

To save your shoes from a rainy day, spray on a water protector like Scotchguard. It will keep water, and any other liquids, from seeping into your shoes. When your shoes get splashed on, allow them to air dry completely before storing. Suede shoes can get extra help from your morning paper. Stuff and wrap them with newspaper — they will maintain their shape and dry out quicker.

You may love the fit and feel of your favorite flats, but you shouldn't wear them everyday. Shoes need a day off to breathe, so alternate them.

Polishing your shoes regularly keeps them looking spiffy on the outside. But did you know the insides need to be cleaned, too? Sanitize with an alcohol wipe or use a drop of tea tree oil, an anti-fungal treatment.

Sweat stinks and wears away the inside of your shoes. Protect them by slipping on hose, socks, or liners as a barrier between your feet and your footwear.

To protect your canvas shoes from getting dirty, spray them with starch. The protective coating will keep them cleaner for longer. If they do get stained, scrub with a toothbrush and carpet cleaner. Allow them to dry, then scrub again with a dry brush.

Slip on snazzy but sensible shoes. When it comes to footwear, you don't have to sacrifice style for stability. Use these tips to learn what to look for and what to avoid.

Run from athletic shoes with bulky rubber soles. The lugs can grab flooring and carpeting, causing you to trip. Look for a walking or running shoe that provides stability if you tend to overpronate — roll your feet inward. Stability sneakers offer cushion and motion control to people who have arthritis in their feet, knees, hips, and ankles. A neutral athletic shoe serves up shock absorption and enough room for inserts or orthotics. To learn if you overpronate, take a worn pair of sneakers to a store that specializes in athletic footwear. A salesperson should be able to help you.

Walk away from shoes with leather or plastic bottoms, which tend to slip and slide on wood, tile, and carpeted floors. And give flip-flops the boot. They offer little stability, and should only be worn by people without foot problems or who don't struggle with balance.

Kick high and low heels right out of your closet. Opt for a shoe with a wedge heel under 2 inches, a thin rubber sole, a spacious toe box, and a closed back or heel strap.

If you're a footwear fashionista, don't think you have to sacrifice style for support. Shop online or at specialty shoe stores for brands such as Born, Clarks, Dansko, Ecco, Naot, Aravon, and Mephisto. These brands combine comfort with flair.

Freshen your smelly boots. If you count a pair of old hiking or work boots among your shoe collection, you may need help keeping them fresh. After all, they carry you through some pretty tough outdoor conditions. Spray a mixture of vodka and water inside the boots, and let them dry. Your boots will be odor-free. If you don't have vodka on hand, try using rubbing alcohol or white vinegar. Mix a 2-1 combination of water to alcohol, or a 1-1 ratio of water to vinegar, and pour into a spray bottle. Spritz the inside of your boots thoroughly, and let dry.

Clutter control

Fresh ways to organize

Start slow to let it go. Are you ever torn between keeping things or giving them away or selling them? There's a simple process that will answer that question for you every time, with complete confidence and no regrets. To get started, you'll need a few boxes, trash bags, and a camera.

Pick an item that, for whatever reason, you can't seem to part with, but you no longer need. Handle it only once while you make a decision about it. Consider whether or not you like the object, if it still works, and when you used it last.

Then, make a decision. Either toss it in the trash, give it to someone who will enjoy it, or store it in a box with the date. If the object is sentimental, take a photo of it first. If you don't use it or miss it after six months, don't take it out. Let it go and move on to the next item.

Play a de-cluttering game. Kids are hard-wired to play "pretend." Adults are not. But if you want to get your clutter under control, a little bit of make believe may go a long way. Just pretend you're moving to a smaller home. Knowing you can't fit everything may give you extra motivation to keep only what you truly love.

Gather five bins or boxes and label them "sell," "give away," "recycle," "keep," and "trash." As you handle each object from a room or closet, ask yourself, "Do I really want to pack this? Will I have room for this in my smaller space?"

When you consider that most people only use 20 percent of what they own, giving items away to a worthy cause or a beloved relative will make you feel good about your decision. Don't focus on the money you spent on an old treadmill you never use. Think of how good someone else will feel using it, or how it might benefit a charity.

GREAT IDEA

Creative way to let go of family treasures

Mae Ryan worked on ceramics for over 40 years. She made hundreds of holiday novelties from Easter bunnies to jack-o'-lanterns to Santas from around the world. Some she gave to her children, grandchildren, and close friends. Many she kept.

When Mae lost her 12-year battle with Alzheimer's, her daughter Linda was left with her mom's collection of over 100 Santas. While she treasured her mom's handiwork, Linda also faced a painful reality — she did not have room to store all of her mom's ceramics. "But they were all very special to me, and I didn't want to give them away to just anybody," says Linda.

As captain of a Walk to End Alzheimer's team for over 10 years, Linda came up with a unique fundraising idea that would support her favorite cause and give her mom's ceramics a new home. "I asked my employer if we could hold a silent auction, and he gave me permission to display my mom's ceramics in our company break room," says Linda. "The next thing you know, we had all these friendly bidding wars going on." In the end, the auction raised more than $500.

"Those bidding wars turned into heartfelt generosity," says Linda. "I've never seen anything like it. And I feel good because, instead of sitting in boxes, my mom's treasures were given new life."

Turn your junk into cash. Are you ready to stop "hoarding" all that stuff around the house? You can turn it into cash or get it removed for free. Here's how.

Take a good look at the stuff that's overcrowding your home, and start tagging the items you no longer want, need, or can't remember why you purchased in the first place. You could start by holding a garage sale or participating in a community yard sale, pricing items dirt cheap. But if a yard sale is too much work, you can move the stuff out without the hassle of a sale and still make money. Try eBay or Craigslist. List your things on either site, and see if you get a bite. Consignment shops will also sell your items for you and split the profit. Or you could donate to charity and take the tax deduction.

If you just want to get rid of your stuff and aren't looking to make a quick buck, check out *www.freecycle.org*. Membership is free. To use the site, list an item, share the details, and wait for someone to respond. Then make arrangements for the person to pick it up. It's that easy.

Go digital for the ultimate file cabinet. Fire up your computer and a scanner – they're all you need to get your piles of papers and file folders in order. With digital files, you can save on space at home and find records easily.

Scan medical forms, real estate records, investment papers, and so forth. Save them into folders on a USB flash drive or CD, and lock it away in a secure spot like a home safe. You can also scan permanent records like birth certificates, Social Security cards, and marriage certificates. Just make sure you lock up the originals.

Or consider using the Cloud for filing at your fingertips. This system of servers saves data on the Internet rather than on your home computer. Services such as Dropbox, OneDrive, Apple iCloud, and Google Drive allow you to store, access, and share your files from your smartphone, tablet, or a friend's computer. Look online for the option that best suits your needs.

No-fuss filing ideas. Ever file something away, then need it, but you've forgotten what you filed it under? There's a way to keep that from happening – and it makes your filing much easier and quicker to boot. Use colored hanging files.

Start by assigning one color to a broad category. For instance, pick green for your financial files, red for permanent records, yellow for insurance papers, and so on. Label your green hanging files with subcategories like "bank" and "retirement accounts." From there pick even smaller categories and alphabetize. For example, your labels might read "bank: checking," "bank: money market," and "bank: savings."

Use clear tabs for your hanging files, and arrange the tabs in a straight line per broad category and color. Affix white, adhesive labels to your file folders. Write legibly on all of your labels with the same color ink, or use a label maker.

To keep your new filing system orderly, place only three file folders in a hanging file, and don't place more than an inch of documents in a hanging file or a file folder.

Smart record-keeping tips. You can organize your financial records the easy way. Use this guide to determine what to keep, what to toss, and where to put it all. For short-term filing, keep:

- ATM receipts and bank deposit slips until you check them against your monthly statement.

- credit card statements and paycheck stubs until you receive your W2.

- expired insurance policies, utility bills, and mortgage papers until the start of a new calendar year.

- loan documents until the loan is paid off.

- investment forms until you receive your year-end statements.

- home improvement records until you sell your home.

You can let go of receipts for minor purchases after you've used them a few times or the warranty has expired. But keep receipts for major purchases. Keep tax returns and tax-related receipts for seven years. After seven years, you only need to hold on to your tax returns. Never get rid of wills, marriage licenses, divorce papers, birth and death certificates, life insurance policies, property deeds, Social Security cards, and military discharge documents.

GREAT IDEA

Know where to dock your docs

You've organized your records. Now you need to know where to store them. Use this guide to help you decide. File originals of the following papers at home in a filing cabinet.

- banking, credit card, and investment statements
- pay stubs
- house-related receipts and warranties
- tax records
- Social Security statements
- insurance policies

File copies of the following at home in a filing cabinet. Store originals in a waterproof, fireproof safe or in a safe deposit box.

- birth, marriage, and death certificates
- divorce decrees
- wills and estate planning documents
- deeds and property titles
- life insurance policies
- Social Security cards
- passports
- passwords
- vehicle titles

Cut out catalog and credit card clutter. Don't send one more catalog to a landfill. The website *www.catalogchoice.org* can help you put an end to unwanted catalogs. Simply log on and create an account for free. Enter the name of a catalog in the search field, and type in the information from your mailing label. If you don't have the label, you can still have your name taken off the mailing list. The website also lists credit card companies, charitable organizations, and data brokers that buy mailing lists from other companies. Cancel just about any piece of unwanted mail.

Simple under-the-bed storage solution

Need more storage space but don't know where to find it? Look no further than under your bed. Attach four casters to an old dresser drawer. Paint and decorate it to match your decor. Then slide it under your bed to stash extra sheets, a blanket, or off-season clothing.

10 smart uses for a shoe organizer. This handy tool can be hung from a door or wall and makes cleaning up clutter a breeze. Check out these ideas for using a pocket shoe organizer in every room in your house.

- kitchen closet — store bottles of cleaners and sponges. Or hang one in full view and display utensils like spatulas and measuring cups.

- bathroom — store toiletries, hair accessories, and medicine bottles.

- bedroom — corral belts and socks.

- garage — put up cans of spray paint and coiled extension cords.

- craft or sewing room — stash skeins of yarn, spools of thread, and rolls of ribbon.

- linen closet — roll up washcloths and hand towels.

- pantry — stock boxes of rice, seasoning packets, and canned goods.

- home office — organize pens, paper clips, and printer cartridges.

- coat closet — round up winter gloves, caps, and scarves.

- garden — plant herbs and flowers in a cloth organizer to provide drainage.

5 simple steps to a tidy bathroom. Tired of losing your favorite tube of lipstick or pair of tweezers under a pile of toiletries? These five easy storage solutions will keep you organized — at little or no cost.

- Place kitchen utensil trays in your bathroom drawers. Divvy up your grooming supplies into each slot. You'll never have to dig through a mountain of toiletries again.

- Repurpose a utensil caddy – the kind you use at a picnic to separate spoons, forks, knives, and napkins. Use it to corral your hair dryer, curling iron, hairbrush, and hairspray.

- Create a decorative display with toilet paper by placing rolls in a tall, glass vase; wicker basket; or a paper towel holder.

- Mount a magnetic strip to the back of a medicine cabinet door. Stick tweezers, nail clippers, and bobby pins to it. Never lose them again.

- Make the most of an empty corner in a cabinet with a turntable like a Lazy Susan. Fill it with bottles of skin care or medicine. Spin for easy reach.

Divide and conquer your linen closet. You want to organize your linen closet but don't know where to start. Start with a stopwatch. Set it for a short amount of time – 15 minutes to 30 minutes max. Pick one shelf and sort through it, setting aside items that are in good condition and tossing out the rest. Only work until the timer goes off. Organizing one shelf a day will make the task less daunting.

As you tackle each shelf, place everyday linens at eye level. Use the top or back of a shelf for beach towels and guest room sheets. Separate sheet sets by room by folding each flat sheet, fitted sheet, and extra pillowcases inside one matching pillowcase. Group towel sets by bathroom, or stack washcloths, hand towels, and bath towels separately. Stash extra blankets in clear plastic bins or cases on the floor. Use over-the-door hooks or organizers to hang soaps, bathrobes, or an extra bath mat.

Make peace with your pantry. You may be surprised how easy it is to organize your pantry. All you need to do is think like a supermarket manager. For instance, divide your pantry into zones, and group like foods together. Keep breakfast cereals, pancake mix, and syrups in one zone. Place dinner kits such as pasta and spaghetti sauce or taco shells and salsa in another. If you really want to get organized, place seven nights worth of dinner ingredients in sturdy bins, one dinner per bin. You'll take the guesswork out of what to cook each evening.

Stack items you don't use often on higher shelves. Place foods that need to be used first in front of those with later expiration dates. Stack foods in tall containers behind short cans and boxes. Label your shelves, and never misplace an item again.

Sort your spices in a snap. Hang a tension rod inside a kitchen cabinet for an instant spice rack. Lightweight yet durable, a tension rod will hold small spice containers that would otherwise get lost in a pantry filled with canned goods and bottles. And you can't beat the price – $2 to $3 at the dollar store. Pick up a few extra rods, and use one under the kitchen sink to hang spray bottles, and the others as dividers in messy kitchen drawers.

Tame mail and magazine piles. Sort your mail, messages, and magazines with a recycled window shutter. The slats make the perfect place to display magazines. And with clothespins, you can clip on postcards, envelopes, messages, photos, and reminders. Paint a shutter to match your decor, and hang it on a wall near a high-traffic zone for easy access. Use a bi-fold door in place of a shutter for an extra-long magazine rack.

Garage storage game plan. Garages are notorious for collecting piles of junk. Deflated soccer balls, broken appliances, and outdated clothing all seem to make their way into a garage's nooks and crannies. Many people can't even park their cars in their garages for all the stuff that's in the way. After tossing out or donating what you don't want, you can take control of what's left with these three simple steps.

- Trade cardboard boxes for clear, plastic bins. If you can see it, you'll use it. And plastic bins are stackable, too.

- Create a sliding storage system on the ceiling. Hang seasonal items that only need to be taken down once or twice a year.

- Designate zones. Store sporting goods in one section, yard tools in another, and cleaning supplies in another.

Nifty, thrifty way to organize your paint

Your garage is overrun with them — gallons upon gallons of paint. Most of those cans contain very little paint, but you need to hang on to them for touch ups. Here's a simple solution — pour your paint into Mason jars.

They don't take up much space, and you can pick out your paint colors lickety-split. Print labels with the name of each color and its corresponding room or project for additional ease. While you're at it, put a few brushes for touch ups in an empty jar, and store with your paints. Never lose a can of paint or paintbrush again.

Feel-good way to knock out clutter. Donating medical supplies is a win-win scenario — you win by clearing out clutter, and the recipient wins by gaining a much-needed piece of equipment. Consider giving away a walker, wheelchair, or a pair of crutches to someone who could not otherwise afford them.

Nonprofits across the nation, including Goodwill, will accept gently used medical equipment. Or you could ask a neighborhood church or local charity. The Afya Foundation in Yonkers, N.Y, and the Second Home Foundation in Cincinnati, Ohio, both accept medical equipment from individuals. Afya sends these much-needed supplies to developing countries in Africa and the Caribbean. The Second Home Foundation will refurbish a piece of medical equipment and pass it along to a local person in need at little or no cost.

Consumer power

How to get what you want & avoid rip-offs

Sharpen your bargaining skills. You negotiate every day — you just don't realize it. From deciding what's for dinner with your spouse to choosing a movie with your grandkids, bartering is a way of life. But how do you haggle with corporate America, be it an online retailer or a financial institution? Here are a few tips to guide you through a negotiation — and help you get what you want.

- Find out what you can about a product or an issue. The more you know about it, the easier it will be for you to make a reasonable offer.

- Be collaborative, not confrontational. Once you allow emotions to get in the way, you've lost. Maintain a calm, friendly tone, and look for win-win outcomes.

- Listen to and acknowledge the other side. This increases your ability to persuade.

- Find common ground. If you and the other person share an interest and spend time discussing it, he will be less likely to argue with you.

- Ask for 15 to 20 percent off a listed price for a used item. For example, if a sofa is selling on Craigslist for $200, offer between $160 and $170. Chances are, the seller will accept your offer. Most tend to price their items at 15 to 20 percent higher than what they really want.

- Never pay full price in a situation where negotiating is the norm. Car salesmen, for example, expect to be offered a lower price.

- Ask for a little something extra. If a company offers you a free shipping voucher to compensate for an error, ask for an additional 20 percent off your next purchase.

Tackle a problem in four easy steps. Most people aren't sure where to start when they have a problem with a service or product. Follow these steps to help you resolve your issue.

- Start by keeping a file. Place all relevant documents in it, and keep a log of phone calls, emails, and letters.

- Contact the seller or service provider. And act quickly. You don't want to wait until it's too late for a salesperson to do anything about the issue.

- Call the manufacturer. They may offer to repair or replace the item.

- If you're not satisfied, file a complaint with local and state consumer protection agencies. And contact the Better Business Bureau.

Put your gripes in writing. A letter will often communicate a complaint better than a phone call. Plus you can address a letter to a senior executive or customer service supervisor. It's unlikely you'll get a higher-up on the phone. Use these tips to write an effective letter.

Be brief and professional. Keep the letter to one page, and use a basic business letter model. Your first paragraph should include the name and serial number of the product, and the date and location of the purchase. In your second paragraph, state the problem or issue you are experiencing with the product.

Tell the company how you would like your issue resolved in the third paragraph. Keep your suggestions practical. For example, "I would appreciate reimbursement for the product," or "I would like for you to send me a replacement." State that you are enclosing copies of records such as receipts, warranties, or contracts – any document pertaining to the purchase. In paragraph four, set a reasonable deadline for a response, and include your contact information. Tell the company you will contact a consumer protection agency if you don't hear from them by your set time.

Make sure to keep copies of all your letters, emails, faxes, and receipts. And lastly, even though you may be angry, resist the temptation to lash out. Maintain a friendly and positive tone for best results. Make the person reading your letter want to help you.

WARNING

Don't get SLAPPed with a lawsuit

In America, you can say what you want when you want without negative consequences, right? After all, the First Amendment protects your right to free speech. But free speech does not cover defamation — false statements that make a person or company look bad in public. So if you're the type who vents their frustrations by writing online reviews, keep these tips in mind.

- Stick to the facts and don't exaggerate. Keep it simple like "My package arrived three weeks late," or "The item was broken when I received it."

- Expand your comments with opinions such as "I was really frustrated that no one returned my calls after leaving multiple messages."

- Don't attack someone's character — that's when you get into big trouble.

- Know your state's SLAPP laws — the Strategic Lawsuits Against Public Participation. These lawsuits are designed to keep consumers from posting negative reviews. But don't be deterred. Many states now have anti-SLAPP laws to protect consumers. Log on to *www.anti-slapp.org* to find out more.

Don't let swindlers steal your identity — and your home.
You can protect yourself from a new form of fraud called "house stealing." Scammers steal your identity and create fake ID cards.

Then they visit their local office supply store to buy forms that transfer property. Next, they file the paperwork with the proper government offices. This gives con artists license to sell the home or property and pocket the profits — all behind the real owner's back. These predators also prey on vacant houses and vacation rentals.

You can take a few steps to protect yourself, according to the FBI. Don't throw away any letters or payment books you get in the mail from a mortgage company. Read the documents carefully, and then call the company. Check your county deeds office regularly to see if any new paperwork has been filed on your home. And check out *www.epropertywatch.com*. This free online service tracks information from your county recorder's office and will alert you if a lien is placed against your property. If you suspect you've been scammed, call your local police immediately.

Guard your loved ones against "ghosting." This form of identity theft brings the dead back to life. Con artists scan obituaries and steal death certificates to assume the identity of a deceased person. They use the information to open fake credit card accounts, apply for loans, and file for tax refunds. Since the deceased can't monitor their own credit reports, these rogues rack up thousands of dollars worth of charges and pocket thousands more in tax refunds. Here's what you can do to protect a loved one.

- When the official death certificate becomes available, request at least 12 copies. You will need these as proof that your loved one has died.

- Thieves scan obituaries looking for information they can use to create an identity. Don't give it to them. Keep your loved one's birth date and mother's maiden name out of the obituary.

- Cancel the deceased person's driver's license.

- Unless you notify the credit bureaus Equifax, Experian, and TransUnion, they will not be aware of the death. Send them copies of the death certificate, and ask them to place a deceased alert on the person's credit reports.

- A surviving spouse or executor of the state may request free copies of the deceased's credit report. Request one periodically and look for suspicious activity.

- Inform the Social Security Administration of your loved one's death. Be prepared to send the SSA a copy of the death certificate.

- Send copies of the death certificate to financial institutions, mortgage companies, insurance agencies, and the Veteran's Administration if the person served in the military.

- Always make copies of all of your correspondence.

GREAT IDEA

End credit card offers for good

Identity thieves love to go through mailboxes looking for preapproved credit cards. Don't let them. Here's a quick and easy way to put an end to credit card offers that come through the mail — and the risk of identity theft that comes with each one.

Opt Out Prescreen is the official consumer credit reporting industry website. Visit *www.optoutprescreen.com* or call 888-5-OPT-OUT (888-567-8688) to cancel offers for five years. Or to stop receiving them permanently, log on to the website and print out the Permanent Opt-Out Election form. Fill it out, and mail it back with your signature.

Whether you call or go online, you'll need to provide personal information, including your birth date and Social Security number. Your information will be kept confidential and will only be used to process your request.

Smart strategies for dealing with a lost purse or wallet.
First of all, don't cancel your credit cards. Instead, call your credit card companies and ask them to issue you cards with new numbers. Canceling your cards could harm your credit score. Here are four other surprising things you must do.

- File a police report and hang on to the paperwork. You may need it in the future to prove your wallet was lost or stolen.

- Call the credit bureaus – Equifax, Experian, and TransUnion – and place fraud alerts on your accounts. Or ask them to place credit freezes once you've ordered new cards. A credit freeze will keep scammers from being able to open new accounts using your name.

- Inform the Department of Motor Vehicles that your license has been stolen. They can flag your file to prevent a thief from using your number.

- Visit your bank to cancel your checking account and any accounts linked to it. Open new accounts, and request a new debit card.

WARNING

Don't let your bank bamboozle you

Smart bank customers check their statements monthly, if not weekly. But banks know there are two times of year when you're least likely to check — August and December. And you may suffer the consequences with sneaky new fees.

Over the holidays and summers, when families are enjoying vacations, many fall out of their routines. According to consumer expert Clark Howard, that's when banks will swoop in quietly, raising fees and changing terms and conditions.

Don't get thrown off guard. Make sure you monitor your statements closely, especially around Christmas and the end of summer. If you see fees added to your statements, call your bank and negotiate. If they won't budge, it may be time to shop for a new bank.

Bank safely from your smartphone. But first, secure your phone. Start with a complex pass code, and enable the auto-lock feature. Make sure the passwords you use for mobile banking are not automatically saved on your phone. Most banks don't keep passwords on phones, but it's best to ask. You can also set up your phone with remote tracking. If your phone is lost or stolen, this feature will purge your personal data.

When banking from your phone, use your bank's app and not the website. Download it from an official app store. Don't save your username on your phone, and don't use the same password you use for other apps. If you lose your phone, call your bank immediately, and ask if it's possible to have your app shut down. Thankfully, if your phone and bank app are hacked, your liability limit is only $50. And most banks waive this charge.

Outsmart a cyberthief with powerful passwords. It's easier than you think. You can create strong, hard-to-crack passwords for all your accounts by following these seven steps.

- Never use words or phrases you can find in a dictionary.

- Never use your hometown's name.

- Use the first letter of each word in a sentence, then insert a number or special character. For instance, the famous musical line "The rain in Spain stays mainly on the plain" can become "tr1Ssm0tp."

- Never use the title of a song, book, movie, or television show.

- Use personal information in an unusual way. For example, just using your anniversary date is a no-no. But something like "0n11/27/82weWed" would challenge even the savviest cyberthief.

- Never use the names of cartoon or fictional characters such as Batman or Cinderella.

- Make it long. The longer your password, the more time it will take a cybercriminal to figure it out. Try a sentence with a number or special character thrown in.

Remember to create solid usernames, too. Use the same guidelines as passwords. The main difference between usernames and passwords are the special characters. You may only use a dot, dash, or underscore in a username. With passwords, you can use math symbols like plus and equal signs.

Get your favorite items on store shelves. Have you ever fallen in love with a product in one store and wished another store would carry it? With a little patience and perseverance, you can make it happen. Approach the store manager first. "A store manager can look through his computer system and see if he can order the item," says Frank Garcia, a supermarket manager in Miami. If the manager says he will get back to you and he doesn't, email the store's corporate office. Most corporate offices will forward a request to a local store fairly quickly.

"If a customer sends corporate a message, and corporate then sends it to me, I am required to respond to both the customer and corporate within 24 hours," says Frank. "A good manager will do whatever it takes to carry the item and make the customer happy."

Demand satisfaction at your salon. Let's face it. Everyone has experienced a bad haircut at one time or another. The question is, what to do about it. If a stylist butchers your hair, don't wait until you get home to complain. If you pay, tip, and leave, your chances of getting a refund are slim. Tell the stylist while you're still sitting in her chair. If the problem is an easy fix like color, she should be able to take care of it.

"I remember one time I asked for soft, caramel-colored highlights for my dark brown hair. I got ugly ashy blond streaks instead," says Annie Walker, a frequent salon customer. "My hair looked like hay. I told the stylist I was unhappy with the color. She agreed that she had not given me the color I'd asked for. She had me schedule an appointment for a few days later. She corrected her mistake to my satisfaction and didn't charge me extra."

What if the problem is not an easy fix – like a hideous haircut? Gently tell the stylist why you don't like the cut, and see if she will make it right. Or, if she gave you a real hack job, speak to the salon owner. Explain why you're unhappy, and ask if another stylist can re-cut it for free. Most salons want their clients to go home happy. If all else fails, ask for a refund or a price break. Fortunately, your hair will grow back.

Beat retailers at their own game. Their job is to lure you into their stores and wipe out your wallet. Your job is to be a clever consumer. Here's a look at how retailers manipulate you and what you can do about it.

What retailers do	What you can do
Provide bigger shopping carts.	Pick up a hand basket or set a time limit.
Lull you with scents, music, and lighting.	Use your head, not your nose.
Place pricier products up front.	Walk past displays.
Sell you a story by combining products.	Shop with a list.
Bait you with coupons.	Don't buy what you don't need to use a coupon.
Create a sense of urgency.	Just say no. If you need it, you'll find it later.
Size clothes smaller.	Step on a scale and be realistic.
Sign you up for a store credit card.	Don't do it. You'll end up spending more in that store.
Boost your confidence in the dressing room.	Get an honest opinion from a friend.

Don't let hidden charges trip you up. Everyone hates those irritating fees merchants tack on toward the end of a transaction, a practice known as drip pricing. Many unsuspecting customers don't even know they've been added until it's too late. But a wise consumer needs to stay alert. To protect yourself, take a few simple steps.

First, ask. Ignorance is not bliss when it comes to drip pricing. Read the fine print, and ask a salesperson to reveal fees up front. This will help you comparison shop before completing a sale. Next, steer clear of companies that play the hidden fees game. And let them know why you won't do business with them. Lastly, if you've been the victim of drip pricing, challenge the charges. Show a manager proof that you were quoted a lower price such as a reservation confirmation or an ad without mention of additional fees. If you charged your purchase, you could request a chargeback or ask your credit card company to dispute the fees.

Don't hesitate to report a company to the Federal Trade Commission for drip pricing. And tell the company you're going to file a complaint. Your actions may change their mind.

Give generously to the right charities. You like the idea of charitable giving but don't want to donate to dishonest causes. You can make sure your donations go to deserving charities and not to a con artist by following these tips.

If you get a call from a charity, ask the caller for the organization's full name. Plus, ask for written materials and a financial statement to be mailed to you. Find out how much of your donation will actually help the cause rather than pay for administration. You can even ask for a breakdown of your donation. For instance, find out how much of it will go toward research, education, food, shelter, or medical supplies.

Ask when a fundraising campaign will end. Some companies will sell products for a certain amount of time to help raise money, but they fail to give consumers the end date. So consumers end up buying items that no longer benefit the nonprofit. Do your homework online. Explore the organization's website, and see if its goals are clear and measurable.

Visit the charity watchdogs online – *www.charitynavigator.org*, *www.charitywatch.org*, and *www.bbb.org/us/charity*. Each site gives potential donors the information they need to make informed decisions.

Guard your home against crooked contractors. You've heard the horror stories. A friend hires a contractor to do work on his home. He pays in full and then never hears from the contractor again. It happens. These shady characters love to scam senior adults. But you can protect yourself if you know what to look for.

Stay away from contractors that request full payment up front. Otherwise, the contractor can disappear at any time and never complete the work. And never make a final payment until the work is finished to your satisfaction. Ask for a contract. The contract should include a start date, end date, total cost of the project, and details of the work that needs to be done. It should also include the contractor's signature, and yours.

Make sure the contractor is insured and bonded. If the company is bonded and it doesn't complete the work, you are protected. Shop around by getting at least three estimates. Plus, don't trust a contractor who says he can do the job quicker and cheaper with leftover materials from a previous project. Or a stranger who knocks on your door selling his services for cheap.

Never hire a contractor whose only means of communication is an answering service. You should be able to contact him as needed. Also, steer clear of a contractor whose only address is a post office box.

A good contractor should share a list of references. Better yet, if you have a friend or neighbor whose home improvement project turned out great, find out who did it. A friend's recommendation may be the best reference of all. Your local hardware store may also have some good suggestions.

Electronics

No-sweat high tech

Take a tip from tech experts. If you don't know much about electronics, but you have to buy a new phone, laptop, TV, camera, or printer, you can slog through hours of reviews – or go to the one unbiased website where they only list the best models. Log on to *www.thewirecutter.com* for a concise "best of" list. Reviewers conduct research and test products, then create a short list of great gadgets at popular prices. They even explain their evaluation process from the number of hours spent reading expert reviews to the number of items tested.

To compare The Wirecutter's findings, check out *www.cnet.com* and *www.pcmag.com* for their take on the latest technology and electronics. CNET gathers information and examines products as soon as they hit store shelves, then gives readers the advice they need to make informed decisions. PCMag tests thousands of products and relays the pros, cons, and bottom line of its top picks. Never again wonder if the TV you're in the market for is a deal or a dud.

Watch TV for free. Tired of watching your cable bill go up? With a digital antenna, you can stop paying for cable and start watching television for free. Simply plug in the antenna to the input on your TV. You may pick up anywhere from a few channels to more than 40, depending on the make and model, your home's distance from TV towers, and where you position the antenna inside your home. You will need a digital tuner, a standard on televisions since 2007. Older models may need a digital converter box.

Prices range from $10 to over $100. Buy from a store with a hassle-free return policy, and test a few models to see which antenna works best for you. And don't worry that your TV will sport outdated rabbit ears. Digital antennas come in sleek and attractive designs.

GREAT IDEA

Boost your brain with video games

Playing video games isn't just for kids. Recent studies show that senior adults who play video games can improve their memory, processing speed, and reasoning skills. Tackling a game that involves strategy improves planning, scheduling, and multitasking abilities. Exercising with a gaming system such as the Wii increases eye-hand coordination and elevates heart rates.

Plus, playing video games leads to one of the best benefits of all — social interaction. Seniors who spend time with friends playing games tend to have less cognitive and physical limitations than those who don't socialize. So go ahead, fire up an X-Box or PlayStation and invite a few friends over — it's a win-win for everyone.

Swap cable for streaming to save big. When you think of a stream, you may envision a gentle babbling brook. But in the world of technology, the word stream refers to the way in which movies, music, and TV shows are delivered to a tablet or television via the Internet. Programs flow continuously in real time versus being downloaded for viewing at a later time.

"Streaming" allows you to drop your high-priced cable and still enjoy your favorite programs. Simply select a service like Hulu, Netflix, VUDU, YouTube, Apple iTunes, or Amazon Prime. Check each service's website to see if it offers your favorite shows. The cost of each channel varies. Some are free with ads while others require a monthly subscription. Others charge by the show or for one- to two-day movie rentals.

In addition to picking a service, you will need a set-top box — a device that streams Internet video to your TV. Popular manufacturers include Roku, Apple TV, Amazon Fire, and Google Chromecast. Prices range from $35 to $100.

To decide if streaming is right for you, consider your viewing habits. Are you a fan of daytime television, live sports, and 24-hour cable news? Then probably not. But if you love watching hours of reruns and hate paying your cable bill, then yes — you're ready to dive into the world of streaming.

3 keys to kick-start your computer

Your computer is acting up and you can't figure out why. Press these three "magic" keys, and presto — your stubborn computer is well-behaved once again. When held simultaneously, the control, alt, and delete keys will restart your PC without shutting it down improperly. Known as the three-finger salute, the key combination will also close a program that acts like it's stuck or suspended indefinitely.

On newer PCs, pressing control, alt, delete gives you an additional option — task manager. This function allows you to end the program that is hung up without restarting your computer.

Play it safe when buying pricey items. Looking at expensive products in a brick-and-mortar store, then buying them online for less money, is a popular way to shop. It even has a name — showrooming. But shopping this way may not get you as good a deal as you think.

Online retailers do not necessarily guarantee that a product works properly or will last for a reasonable amount of time. In fact, read the fine print in an online purchase, and you may be surprised to learn that you're buying the item "as is." If it breaks or fails to work in the first place, the online store may not take it back or refund your money.

To be safe, purchase big-ticket items in a real store. You will likely have an easier time returning it and getting your money back if something goes wrong. Ask the store manager about their price-match policy. Some retailers, such as Best Buy, will match the online prices of major retailers like Amazon or Wal-Mart.

You can also order the item online for in-store pickup. Most retailers will waive their shipping fees and honor their in-store return policies. And check out warehouse clubs like BJ's, Costco, and Sam's Club. They often beat online prices and offer relaxed return policies.

Tips for picking the perfect printer. Before you head to your local office supply store to purchase a new printer, think about how much and what kind of printing you do at home. This will help you decide between an inkjet and laser printer.

A color inkjet printer provides a bounty of great features for any project, from your annual Christmas letter to glossy photos. Text documents are not as sharp, but if you don't do much printing and want something that's cheap and versatile, an inkjet is your best bet.

If you print a lot of text documents and don't need many color copies, go with a laser printer. It costs a little more than an inkjet but delivers faster speeds and higher-quality printing.

While you can still pick up a printer-only unit, all-in-one devices are more popular. They come with a scanner bed on top and the capability to print, copy, and fax. You may not need all of those functions, but these versatile machines are cheap and packed full of value.

Photo printers capture picture images better than any inkjet unit on the market. For anyone interested in preserving family photos over printing reports, consider an inexpensive photo printer. The cost for supplies such as ink cartridges and glossy paper may be a bit high, but the return on quality prints are worth the price.

Smart way to save on ink. The price of ink stinks. So don't make this common mistake that wastes up to 40 percent of the ink in that expensive printer cartridge. Here's what to do instead. When the warning light comes on telling you the cartridge is low, don't replace it right away. Alerts often kick in long before the cartridge is close to being empty. Hold out until the print quality of your documents diminishes, or you need to print a big job. You may get more copies out of your cartridge than you think.

Snap up a camera that suits you. You're in the market for a new digital camera, but with hundreds of models out there, you don't know where to begin. Start by asking yourself a few questions.

Do you want a camera that fits comfortably in your hands and is light enough to take on vacations? If so, today's point-and-shoot devices make it easy to snap good-quality photos without any adjustments to the built-in lens.

Or do you want something that's light but comes with multiple lens options? Check into interchangeable lens models. They offer the ease of point-and-shoots with the ability to swap out lenses, similar to a digital single-lens reflex (DSLR) camera. But they're smaller and lighter than DSLRs because they're mirrorless, which means you view your image directly through the lens and not through a mirrored reflection.

If you want superior photos, nothing beats a DSLR. These cameras serve up speed and quality with a variety of settings and lenses to play with. They're heavier and pricier than other cameras, but their performance is incomparable.

One other surprisingly affordable option is a camera with Wi-Fi, which allows you to snap, edit, and immediately share photos to social networks and store them on cloud services. You can find Wi-Fi on most camera models ranging from low-cost subcompacts to high-end DSLRs.

Cash in on used electronics. Your garage is overrun with them − old electronics. They collect dust and take up space. But you don't need to keep them around any longer. With trade-in programs online and in stores across the country, you can exchange your tech for cash, credit, or gifts cards. As with cellphones, each company will give you a quote based on the make, model, and condition of your device.

The Amazon trade-in program will make you an offer online for anything from an iPad to a GPS tracker. In exchange, Amazon will send you a gift card and a label for free shipping.

Gazelle will also make you an offer online and pay with a check, PayPal, or Amazon gift card. Or you can have your earnings donated to a charity. NextWorth, another online trader, partners with retailers where you can drop off your item. Or you can ship it to them for free and receive payment by check, gift or e-gift card, or PayPal.

Trade-in programs at brick-and-mortar stores like Best Buy, Target, Wal-Mart, and Radio Shack will pay you with their own store gift cards. Take your used electronic to a nearby location, or start the trade-in process on the store's website.

MONEYSAVER

Buy refurbished for rock-bottom bargains

When you're in the market for a new electronic, don't pass up the incredible value of a refurbished product. Refurbished items are generally restored to their original condition, often with newer replacement parts. Plus, they undergo thorough inspections before heading back to store shelves to be sold at a discount.

Other products that retailers may label as refurbished include items returned in opened packages, devices with cosmetic flaws, products that arrive in damaged boxes, recalled items, and floor models. All of them carry discounted price tags.

One word of caution — make sure you ask about return policies and warranties. Only do business with a retailer that will take back a refurbished piece of merchandise in case you change your mind or discover it doesn't work.

Get a grip on gadget grime. Germs — they're everywhere, thriving and multiplying on your tablet, keyboard, and computer mouse. They land on your gadgets by the thousands thanks to sweaty hands, sticky fingers, coughing, sneezing, and food spills.

You don't need to spend much money to get your tech gear squeaky clean. Just make sure you turn off, unplug, and remove batteries from any device before scrubbing.

- To clean your keyboard, turn it upside down and shake it gently. Spray compressed air between the keys. Finish cleaning with antibacterial wipes. Or mix a little alcohol with water, and spray it on a microfiber cloth.

- A computer mouse is a hotbed for viruses. Spray compressed air around the track ball, and use a disinfecting wipe over your mouse and on your mouse pad.

- As with cellphones, you never want to spray glass cleaner directly onto a tablet screen. Opt for a special screen cleaner like iKlear or AM Get Clean. Spray on a microfiber cloth.

- Remote controls are petri dishes for cold viruses. Blast between buttons to blow out dust and dirt, and sanitize with fast-drying wipes like Wireless Wipes.

- Gently dig out crud from ports with a toothbrush, cotton swab, or a cleaning brush made especially for electronics.

Save your tablet from drowning. You drop your tablet in the tub. Don't panic. If you act quickly, these steps could save your tablet's life. First, turn the power off and remove the battery. If it powered down on its own, resist the urge to turn it back on. Next, uncover any openings like the headphone port, remove the SD and SIM cards, and dry the unit with a towel. Use a vacuum cleaner with a small, nozzle attachment to draw out moisture from each port. Finally, submerge your device in a bowl of rice or a box of Rice Krispies, rotating it periodically. Turn it back on after 48 to 72 hours, and watch your tablet come back to life.

WARNING

Tablets a threat to your heart?

Sitting hunched over your tablet all day may give you more than a stiff neck. A recent British study found that use of mobile devices could lead to heart problems later in life.

The hunched-over position constricts breathing and blood flow, forcing the heart to work harder. Essentially, it's more difficult for you to take full breaths when you drop your head and round your shoulders to look at your device. Plus, your ribs struggle to move, which keeps your heart and lungs from performing properly.

But don't feel like you have to pack away your tablet for good. Just spend less time using it, and hold it at eye level when you do. Your heart may thank you.

Go high-tech to preserve your memories. Do you own thousands of slides with images of years gone by? You don't need to store them in a box any longer if you follow this simple idea that will keep your memories alive. Transfer them to a DVD. You'll never have to set up your old slide projector again.

Most stores with photo services, such as Walgreens, offer slide to DVD services for a per-slide price with a minimum order. At warehouse stores like Costco and Sam's Club you also pay a per-slide fee with a minimum order.

Online you'll find an array of options. The website *www.digmypics.com* charges a per-slide fee with no minimum purchase. For a flat fee when you transfer bulk amounts like 250, 500, or 1,000 slides, try *www.fotobridge.com*. Or, to avoid counting hundreds of slides, you could cram as many as possible into a box for a flat fee with *www.homemoviedepot.com* or *www.scanmyphotos.com*.

While you're at it, transfer old negatives and VHS tapes onto DVDs to save even more of your cherished memories. Check with each company or website for details.

Energy savings

Power down your power bills

Find the right replacement for vanishing incandescents.
You can't buy a standard incandescent light bulb anymore. A
Federal law phased out standard incandescent bulbs in 2014
because they required too much electricity. Now you can only buy
more energy-efficient bulbs, like halogen, CFLs (compact fluorescent lights) and LEDs (light emitting diodes). These bulbs can lower
your electric bill, but be careful when you shop. Trying to choose a
bulb by its wattage doesn't work anymore. Here's why.

You can no longer tell how bright a bulb is by looking at the number of watts on the label. For example, grab a 40-watt halogen,
and you'll get the same brightness as a 60-watt incandescent bulb.
You also get 60 watts of brightness from a 14-watt CFL bulb or
10-watt LED. To make things easier, just remember that brightness is measured in lumens. Find the number of lumens on a
bulb's label, and use this chart to decide which bulbs may be right
for a particular socket:

To replace this bulb	Look for this amount of lumens
40	450-600
60	800-1000
75	1100-1200
100	1600 and up

Tips and tricks for choosing the best bulb. Now that you've said so long to incandescent light bulbs, here's how to choose which new halogen, LED, or fluorescent bulb will work best in each room of your home.

Some CFL, LED, and halogen bulbs shine with the same cozy tint as standard incandescents, while others produce a noticeably whiter light. To tell which light a bulb provides, find "Lighting Appearance" on the bulb's label. Lighting tint is measured in Kelvin (K). Here's how to read the number you find.

- 2,700K - 3,000K (Soft White or Warm White) — yellow-tinted light like standard incandescent bulbs. This is ideal for over-head lighting in bedrooms and living rooms.

- 3,500K - 4,100K (Bright White or Cool White) — whiter or more blue-tinted light that appears brighter than soft white. Try this in kitchens and garages.

- 5,000K - 6,500K (Daylight) — the whitest or most blue-tinted light, similar to noon sunlight. This may be too harsh for some indoor locations, but perfect where you want higher-contrast lighting to help distinguish details. You may prefer this light for reading lamps, task lighting focused on a particular area, and overhead lighting in dark basements.

But that's not all because the tint of light isn't the only thing that matters. Consider these questions to make sure you choose the best bulb every time.

- Is the light fixture hard to reach? Choose LEDs for fixtures in hallways, staircases, cathedral or tray ceilings, ledges, and other places where changing a light bulb is difficult.

- Do you need light that shows colors accurately? Some lights don't show the true color of an item as well as halogen bulbs do. That's why they're recommended for lighting bathroom vanities. Just remember, halogen bulbs get hot enough to burn skin or set fire to objects that are too close.

- Will the switch be flipped often? If a light is turned on and off multiple times each day — as often happens in bathrooms — think twice about using CFLs. Frequent "cycling" like this shortens a CFL's life.

- Is the light a nonstandard incandescent? Some nonstandard incandescents, including three-way bulbs, candelabra bulbs, and decorative bulbs like globe lights, are still available in stores.

- Does the bulb work with a dimmer? All halogen bulbs are dimmable, but check the labels of LEDs and CFLs. Most LEDs are dimmable if you have an LED-compatible dimmer, but some CFLs are not. Many LEDs also work with timers or motion sensors, but most CFLs don't.

WARNING

Foil hidden CFL danger

All CFL bulbs contain mercury, a neurotoxin that can be hazardous to your health. When a CFL bulb blows or shatters, don't treat it like a normal incandescent bulb. To prevent mercury contamination of your household and the environment, never throw CFL bulbs in the garbage or vacuum up a shattered bulb. If a CFL bulb shatters, visit *www.epa.gov* to learn how to safely clean it up. Check with your local government for information on how to legally and safely dispose of a shattered bulb.

If a bulb is whole when it stops working, take it to a nearby Lowe's or Home Depot to be recycled.

Stop paying for "phantom" electricity. Up to 75 percent of the power use for many home electronics happens after you turn them off. That's why they call it "phantom power." Discover how to save big bucks with one simple solution — simply unplug items when you won't be using them for several hours and when you leave the house. This could be enough to cut your electric bill up to 10 percent every month. To save time, consider using a power strip or surge protector that fully cuts power to several devices when you flip a switch.

Of course, some items must be reset or adjusted when you plug them in again, and you may need to leave your DVR plugged in so it can record programs while turned off. In fact, whenever you have a cluster of electronics that work together, such as those around a television set or computer, some can usually be unplugged while others must stay plugged in.

This is where smart strips can come in handy. A smart strip is a surge protector that cuts power to items that are shut down or on standby, but the strip includes a few outlets for devices that should always stay on, such as your cable box. Smart strip makers claim you'll save up to $150 a year by using their products – more than enough to cover the purchase price.

MONEYSAVER

Watch TV for less

You might be surprised to discover that one television screen at its brightest can cost $10 or more in electricity every year. Your television and computer screens combined may cost up to $80 annually. To fix this, check the lighting around your televisions and computers to make sure it isn't making the screens appear dimmer. After adjusting the lighting, check the brightness setting for each screen. If it's set to maximum, reduce it to a comfortable level. This can shave $1.25 off your electric bill every month — and those savings add up more quickly than you might expect.

Help your water heater last years longer. Discover the simple, inexpensive part in your water heater you should be replacing every three or four years. It's not the heating element, and you don't have to drain the tank. It's the anode rod. Replacing it regularly could help you delay buying your next water heater for years to come.

The anode rod is a metal rod that hangs inside your water heater's tank. It attracts compounds in your water that would otherwise corrode the tank walls. That's why the rod corrodes while the tank stays untouched.

Eventually, the rod becomes too corroded to protect the tank. If the rod isn't replaced, the tank corrodes until the entire water heater must be replaced. If you replace the rod in time, your water heater will not only last longer, but could double its life span. The trick is to replace the rod before your water heater corrodes.

To do that, you need to know this valuable secret – check the rod every year, even if you rarely need to change it. The life span of an anode rod varies depending on your water's characteristics, the amount of use the tank gets, the water temperature, how well the tank is made, and whether you have a water softener. Some lucky people will discover they can change the anode rod every five to seven years, while others must change the rod more often. Under the very worst conditions possible, some anode rods may last less than a year. Read on to learn how you can inspect the rod and change it yourself.

How to replace an anode rod. You may be able to check and change the anode rod yourself if you are an experienced do-it-yourselfer. Here are the basic steps for doing the job.

- Collect a garden hose, socket wrench with 1 1/16-inch socket, breaker bar, and pipe thread sealant.

- Turn off the water supply and electricity or gas supply to the heater. Close the cold water shutoff valve.

- Using a bucket or garden hose, drain several gallons of hot water from the tank.

- Locate the anode rod, and loosen it with your socket wrench. If it won't budge, ask someone to hold the tank in place while you push harder to free the rod.

- Lift the rod out. Replace it if it's covered in mineral deposits or if the diameter is less than that of a AA battery. Replacements are available at home improvement stores.

- Smear the new rod's threads with thread sealant, insert the rod in the tank, and tighten the rod in place. Restore power and water to the water heater.

Your water heater may require different instructions than what you see here, so consult your water heater manual before you try checking or changing your anode rod. If you can't find your manual, download a copy from *www.manualsonline.com* or your water heater manufacturer's website.

If you don't have much do-it-yourself experience, call your plumber to check and change the anode rod. Even with the extra expense, you'll still save money by helping your water heater last years longer.

MONEYSAVER

Collect a reward for fixing leaks

Just one drip of hot water each second can send up to 138 gallons of water down the drain every month and add nearly $3 to your electric bill. Check your faucets for leaks, and fix any you find. You'll get money back every month.

Lower heating costs and indoor air pollution. Save up to $60 a year on heating bills, avoid furnace repairs, extend the life of your heating system, and even reduce the amount of dangerous toxins in your home. You can do it if you just remember to do these two things.

- Change the filter regularly. Check the air filters on your furnace and return vents every month, and change each filter that either looks dirty or hasn't been changed in the last three months. It takes more electricity or natural gas to push air through dirt-laden filters than clean ones. Dirty filters may also lead to more repairs and may force you to replace your furnace earlier. Worst of all, mold and mildew can grow on dirty filters and release toxic chemicals into the air. Clear the air, prevent repairs, and preserve your heater by changing those filters regularly.

- Schedule regular maintenance checks. Even fairly new furnaces can corrode and leak dangerous gases like carbon monoxide. To help prevent that, arrange for maintenance visits every six months. Routine maintenance helps your furnace run more efficiently and survive longer, so you keep more money in your pocket.

Easy fix to a chilly problem. That mystery draft that chills your legs on a gusty winter day could be coming from an electrical outlet. This may be the one place in the house almost nobody thinks to insulate, but insulating electrical outlets and switch plates may save up to 20 percent on your heating and cooling bills for years to come. Even better, it's easy to do. For each outlet and switch plate, you can buy a foam gasket perfectly shaped to insulate that spot. Check online sellers as well as local stores to make sure you get the best price.

To install the gaskets, cut power to the room from the circuit breaker, and make sure the electricity is off. For each foam gasket, remove the cover plate with a screwdriver. Push the gasket in the outlet or switch slot so it fits securely, and put the cover plate and its screws back in place. When you have insulated all the switch plates and outlets in a room, restore power.

For added savings, install child safety plugs in the electric sockets you're not using, and close all your closet doors so you won't pay to heat or cool those spaces.

Keep your windows from leaking dollars. Windows can be responsible for up to 25 percent of heating and cooling losses in a home. That means you pay to heat more air in winter and cool more air in summer. Use one or more of these methods to put a stop to that and gain more control over your energy bills.

- For temporary insulation on windows that are oddly shaped or rarely used, cut Bubble Wrap to fit each window. To apply, spritz the glass with water, and press the bubble side of the wrap against the window surface. You may be surprised at how long it stays put.

- Blackout curtains that block light can put a big dent in heating and cooling losses and are available at your local discount department store. For smaller windows, consider blackout shades.

- Use thick curtains to keep heat in and winter out, or line thin curtains with fleece or another heavy material if you can sew.

- Install storm windows, or coat windows with either plastic or insulating inserts. You can even buy low-emissivity window films you can apply to windows yourself.

12 ways to slash utility costs. You can save more money on your power and water bill than you think. To put the most money back in your pocket, don't forget these practical tips.

- Shower instead of taking a bath. Baths can use up to 70 gallons of water a day or more than 2,000 gallons every month.

- Switch from using your clothes dryer to using a clothes line or rack. This can really make a difference because the clothes dryer uses more energy than almost any other appliance in your home.

- Turn down the thermostat, and dress more warmly in winter. You can add two to three degrees of warmth just by putting on a sweater.

- Install a low-flow shower head in your bathroom.

- Only run your dishwasher or clothes washer when you have a full load.

- Wrap your old water heater with an insulation blanket to conserve heat, and save up to $20 a year. Many new water heaters don't need extra insulation. In fact, adding insulation can void the warranty. Check the tank and your manual for information or warnings about whether extra insulation can be added. Follow the manufacturer's instructions.

- Install aerators in your kitchen and bathroom faucets.

- Turn off the water while washing your hair, and turn it on again to rinse. You'll save over 100 gallons of water every month.

- Replace a broken lamp with a three-way lamp that lets you choose dimmer light when brighter light isn't needed.

- Insulate your attic yourself if it doesn't have enough insulation. You can do it for as little as $200.

- Humid air feels warmer than dry air, so use energy efficient humidifiers to help warm rooms in winter.

- Caulk and add weather stripping around all exterior doors and windows to reduce your heating and air conditioning use by up to 20 percent.

Help your fireplace save heat. Everyone loves the warm, cozy glow of a wood-burning fireplace, but don't mistake it for an energy saver. It won't shrink your heating bill and may even increase it. Whether a fire is burning or not, the same system that pulls smoke out of the fireplace also pulls air out of the house through the chimney. That's air you've paid to heat, so you actually may be paying more to warm your home. When you use the fireplace, close all doors to the room and turn down the thermostat. Installing glass doors and a heat exchanger can help reduce your losses even more.

Close the damper when you're not using the fireplace, but keep in mind that it may still leak some air. During long periods of nonuse, a chimney pillow may help. This inflatable device blocks air from leaving your chimney. It's simple to install and can easily be removed when you want to start using your fireplace again. Manufacturers claim this remedy could save you $200 or more each year.

MONEYSAVER

New switch lowers your lighting costs

A new kind of light switch makes sure your lights will go off when a room is empty, even if someone forgets to flip the switch. These occupancy sensor switches have a motion detector that sees when a room is empty. If the room stays empty for a set amount of time, the switch will automatically turn off the lights. You can install the switch yourself, and the manufacturer claims it will shave about $25 off your electric bill each year. Visit *www.amazon.com* to see your options, or look for them at your local home improvement store.

When shopping, check whether the switch is compatible with your CFL, incandescent, LED, or halogen bulb, and how many square feet the motion detector covers. Also, if the light can be turned on by two different switches in the room, make sure you buy a three-way switch.

Save $200 this year with better seals. You may be paying up to 20 percent more in heating and cooling costs because your heated and cooled air is escaping through leaky air conditioning or heating ducts. Ironically, this happens because duct tape does a poor job of sealing ducts. Fortunately, resealing these leaks isn't hard.

Start with ducts in areas that aren't heated or cooled such as your attic, garage, crawl space, or an unfinished basement. Repair both leaky areas and any points currently sealed with duct tape. First, run your hand alongside the ducts to feel for leaks. Tag these spots. To seal leaky holes and duct-taped spots, remove old duct tape if it's there, wipe the area with a damp cloth, let dry, and reseal with foil tape. Experts suggest this could save $200 or more every year.

Make the most of your household fans. If you're trying to save money by using fans instead of your air conditioner, experts say that's not always the best choice. Learn better ways to save money and stay cool with these do's and don'ts.

- Don't choose fans over air conditioning if the temperature inside your house is 95 degrees or higher. At those temperatures, fans won't prevent heat-related illness and may make you hotter. Instead, turn on the air conditioning, set the thermostat higher than usual, and run your fans. Fans can make you feel up to 8 degrees cooler. Besides, even if you only set your thermostat 2 degrees higher than normal, you'll reduce your cooling costs by up to 14 percent this year.

- Do set up box fans so they draw cool air from the shady side of the house or room into the warmer rooms on the sunny side.

- Don't place your box fan in a window if rain is possible. Box fans aren't protected against rain like window fans are. But if you're expecting a dry night, and the outside air is cooler than the air inside, place your box fan close to an open window with the blade facing toward the room. This pulls cool air in from the outside. Just remember, you shouldn't try this if you have concerns about the safety of leaving your windows open at night, or if you don't want pollen, humidity, and dust to come in from outside.

- Do check your ceiling fans to make sure they blow air downward. Adjust the fan to full speed and stand beneath it. If you feel a stiff breeze blowing on you, the fan is properly adjusted. If not, turn off the fan, and let the blades come to a full stop. Check for a direction switch on the side of the fan. It may not be labeled. After you change the switch position, turn on the fan, and test again.

- Don't leave fans on when you're not at home. Fans don't lower humidity or air temperature. They just help move hot air away from you so you stay cooler.

Cut costs with warm-up water

Stop paying for water that goes down the drain without being used. Slip a bucket in the shower while you wait for the water to warm up. Use that water to flush your toilet so you won't have to pay for extra water. It's easy. Just dump the bucket water in the toilet bowl, and the toilet will flush itself. But don't stop there. Use smaller containers to collect water in your kitchen and bathroom sinks while you wait for the water from those faucets to warm. You can use that water to soak stubborn food off dirty dishes, give your houseplants a drink, or help clean your bathroom or kitchen.

12 ways to save money on outdoor watering. The average household uses as much water outdoors as indoors, so you can make a big dent in your water bill by limiting the water used in your yard. Start with these tricks and tips.

- A lawn measuring just 32 feet by 32 feet can require more than 600 gallons to water 1 inch. Reduce the size of your lawn, especially in areas where grass struggles to grow. Replace the grass with native and drought-tolerant plants that need less water.

- Water your lawn once a week, instead of daily. Place an open tuna can nearby, and give the grass a good, slow soaking. When an inch of water has collected in the tuna can, turn off the water.

- Mulch trees, shrubs, and beds so they'll lose less moisture to evaporation and won't require as much watering.

- Use drip irrigation around trees and shrubs.

- Fertilize your lawn less, and use slow-release fertilizers.

- Attach a pistol-style sprayer to your hose so the water won't run continuously.

- Collect water from your gutters with a rain barrel, and use it to water your flowers and grass.

- Adjust your mowing height to 2 inches, and leave clippings on the grass instead of bagging them. Your grass will retain more moisture and need less water.

- Sweep your patio and driveway with a broom instead of hosing them down to clean them.

- Water during the early morning when winds and temperature are lower and the water is less likely to evaporate before your plants can drink it.

- If you wash your car at home, don't turn on the hose until you are ready to rinse.

- Avoid planting grass on steep inclines that are hard to water.

GREAT IDEA

Stop slaving over a hot stove

Cooking with your stove or oven on a hot summer day can turn into an exercise in sweaty misery. So when you cook in summer — or any time you only cook for one or two people — use your toaster oven instead of the regular oven. A toaster oven uses up to 50 percent less energy, and it won't make you feel like you're the one being cooked. You can also keep your oven from heating the kitchen and raising your cooling bill by cooking outdoors. Or try cooking the food in your oven during the coolest part of the day and reheating it in a toaster oven or microwave just before you serve it.

Choose the right water heater. Shopping for a new water heater may lead to a model that saves money every month, offers better features, or does a better job than your old water heater. But you may have to sort through dizzying rounds of sales pitches and lingo before you buy. To help cut through the sales hype and choose wisely, use these tips.

- Water heater capacity is often measured by the size of the tank. In general, a 50- to 60-gallon tank is appropriate for one or two people, and an 80-gallon tank can usually supply three or four people. But don't just look at gallons, find out the first-hour rating (FHR). This is the amount of hot water in the tank plus the incoming cold water it can heat in the first hour. The higher the rating, the more hot water available at peak demand times. Talk to a professional or use an online calculator to find the right FHR for you.

- Check the energy factor (EF) rating to help determine how cheaply you can run the water heater. Higher numbers are better.

- Direct vent water heaters release exhaust gases into surrounding air, but power vent models reroute exhaust to another location.

- Bigger water heaters require more space around them, and those setups that already have power vents may need a bigger vent size. Even if you want the same size water heater, ask about new regulations that may require more space.

- Gas heaters are cheaper to run but cost more. The savings pay for themselves over time if you already have natural gas service.

- The more years in the warranty, the better quality found in the water heater, says a *Consumer Reports* buying guide. Check whether the warranty covers labor costs.

Reconsider an oil-fired heater

Replacing an old oil-fired water heater with a newer model may not be your best choice because oil-fired heaters are so costly. Many people choose an electric water heater, instead.

Futuristic water heaters you can buy now. New technologies have produced water heaters that are even cheaper to run than highly efficient standard models. If you expect to buy a water heater soon, you need the lowdown on hybrid, solar, and tankless heaters.

A hybrid model is an electric water heater with its own heat pump. The pump pulls warmth from surrounding air to help heat the water. This can save up to 60 percent over a regular electric heater, and the savings may not take very long to pay for extra starting costs that come with the hybrid. Hybrid heaters require:

- extra space above the water heater.

- a condensate pump or place to drain water.

- a space of at least 1,000 cubic feet that remains between 40 and 90 degrees year round.

Solar hot water heaters collect the sun's heat to help raise the water temperature. As a result, they may save up to 80 percent on water heating costs. Yet, they can't get by on sunlight alone, and the amount of savings varies with available sunlight and time of year. The savings from solar heaters take at least 10 years to pay for the extra costs of installing and buying the water heater.

A tankless water heater rapidly turns cold water hot as the water passes through the heater, so no tank is needed. To determine the tankless heater size you need, look at its temperature rise combined with gallons-per-minute or flow rate. Typically, you'll see a rise of 70 degrees per five gallons for gas models or 70 degrees per two gallons for electric units. Salesmen promise you can't run out of hot water, but you can come up short in some rooms if you have too many things demanding hot water at once. So choose your size accordingly. Tankless gas heaters can save up to 50 percent every month.

Both gas and electric tankless heaters may last 20 years, but they cost more to buy and install and require yearly maintenance. Run the numbers before you buy.

MONEYSAVER

Wash your way to an extra $70

You can make your clothes last longer and save $70 or more in yearly energy costs if you use cold water for most laundry loads. If you'd like, you can add special cold-water detergent. Reserve warm water for unusually dirty clothes, and only use hot water for severe stains. This strategy can do more than just save money. Hot water sets protein-based stains like dairy foods, mud, clay, blood, human waste, and baby food, so you can't get them out. If you rarely wash in hot water, you're less likely to set stains like these and more likely to enjoy laundry savings.

Spend less on your shower every day. Trimming your shower by just two minutes can save up to 150 gallons of water every month. What's more, if each person in your household showers in seven minutes or less daily, you may save more than $100 a year. To persuade the rest of your family to shorten their showers, master the art of the seven-minute shower yourself to set an example.

To make this work, you need a way to track your time in the shower. Placing an egg timer just outside the shower may be best. The trick is to use it the right way. Don't set your timer to ring when the shower should end, or the timer may go off while you're still shampooing or using the soap. You may rush to finish, but you're already too late to reach your goal.

To fix that, set the timer to ring at the halfway point. Hurrying to finish will become much more effective, and you'll gain a clearer idea of how to pace yourself to reach your seven-minute goal. When you think you've got the timing down, set the timer for the full seven minutes to make sure you're on target.

Hunt down your hidden energy hogs. Some energy hogs, like clothes dryers, are easy to spot, but others are much tougher to discover. Don't let that keep you from making your energy bills as low as they can go. Try one of these strategies to ferret out your energy hogs.

- Find out how much electricity your plug-in appliances and other electronics use with outlet checkers like the Kill-A-Watt. You can buy one at your local discount department store, or you may be able to check one out from the library. To test any device, plug your monitor into an outlet, and plug your device into the outlet monitor. You'll soon know which appliances and electronics demand the most electricity. Just remember, some items that don't require much electricity can still become energy hogs if you use them enough.

- To monitor all the energy your home uses at once, buy a power monitor, or see if your library has one to loan out. These devices continuously monitor your home's power use by plugging into an outlet or your electrical panel. Some can also connect wirelessly to your electric meter. To learn how to lower your energy use, experiment with turning things off or unplugging them. Some people report spending up to 30 percent less on electricity after using these devices.

- Open a free account at *www.myenergy.com*. Once you link your utility company accounts, the site helps you track your energy use and find ways to reduce your bills. People who have tried this service report good savings on their annual energy bills.

- Ask your electric and gas companies if they offer free energy audits. These audits may help uncover energy-hogging leaks or find other home improvements to help save energy and money.

MONEYSAVER

Reduce your energy bill painlessly

Turn your thermostat down just 1 degree, and you could cut your heating bill 2 to 5 percent every month. You can save just as much by raising the thermostat 1 degree during warm weather. If a 1-degree change doesn't bother you after a few days or weeks, consider experimenting with a 2- or 3-degree change. Turning the thermostat up 3 degrees during hot months and down 3 degrees during winter may save you over $70 each year.

Switch to a thrifty thermostat. If you get sticker shock when your heating bill arrives, you may be missing some opportunities to make money-saving adjustments to your thermostat. Imagine how much money you could save if your thermostat automatically turned itself down every time you left the house or went to bed. Or how about if it checked the weather on the Internet to make sure it used no more energy than needed to reach the temperatures you want? That's what the Nest Learning Thermostat does.

During your first week with the Nest, you teach this "smart" thermostat your habits by adjusting it each time you leave the house or go to bed. It will also sense when the house is empty and adjust temperatures accordingly. Figures from the EPA and Nest's manufacturers suggest this thermostat can save 20 to 30 percent on your heating and cooling bills, which may help offset its higher-than-normal price tag. Fortunately, many programmable thermostats cost much less and can also help save on cooling and heating.

Instead of adjusting automatically, programmable thermostats must be set to change to different temperatures at certain times of day.

For example, you might program the thermostat for a cooler temperature when you leave for work or go to bed, adjusting to a warmer temperature when you return home or get up in the morning. During winter, program your thermostat to reduce the temperature by 5 degrees for the eight hours you're at work, and experts say you'll save up to 15 percent every year.

Make a new window AC save more money. Your old window air conditioner finally gave up the ghost, but don't assume your new one should be the same size. In fact, you may not even want to place it in the same window.

If your old air conditioner sat in an unshaded window that faced south or west, the unit was forced to use more electricity to counteract the extra sunlight and heat it received. Check whether you can cool the same room or space by putting your new air conditioner in a window that faces north or east or is better shaded. If so, the new air conditioner may use up to 10 percent less cooling capacity to get the same results as the old unit.

Also, be careful to select the right size cooling capacity. Choose an air conditioner with too much, and you'll use more electricity than needed. Cooling capacity is measured in British thermal units (BTUs), and the number of BTUs you need is determined by your room's square footage. So before you shop, measure your room, and calculate its square footage. According to *www.energystar.gov*, you need:

- at least 5,000 BTUs for a 100-square-foot room.

- a minimum of 6,000 BTUs for a room 150 square feet or larger.

- around 7,000 BTUs for 250 to 300 square feet.

- 9,000 BTUs for rooms ranging from 350 to 400 square feet.

Heavily shaded rooms may get by on up to 10 percent less BTU capacity, but a room that is regularly full of people may need at least 600 extra BTUs.

Simple way to keep AC operating costs down

To make your old air conditioner unit more efficient, check the manual to learn how to clean or replace the air filter. In many cases, you'll find the filter behind the front panel and can simply clean it with soap and water. Just make sure the filter is dry before you put it back in the air conditioner. During the months when the air conditioner is in use, clean or replace the filter every four weeks. It's an easy way to help control electricity costs.

Pay less to use your computer. You don't have to cut back on using your computer to reduce its electricity costs. You can save money painlessly with just a couple of changes.

Turn off your computer when you're not using it. Don't believe the old myth that claims you must leave a computer on to extend its life. That was true for old mainframes but no longer applies to today's desktops. According to *www.energystar.gov*, you can save up to $36 a year by turning off your computer on nights and weekends, especially if your machine is Energy Star qualified.

To save even more, stop using your screen saver. Contrary to popular belief, your computer doesn't use less power while the screen saver is on. Cut costs by using the sleep mode or power management settings instead. Sleep mode puts your computer in a state of very low power use until you wake it up again. Power management settings allow you to choose additional ways to save power. You can find them in the System Preferences on an Apple computer or the Control Panel on a Windows PC.

And here's a bonus tip. When the time comes to replace your desktop computer, consider switching to a laptop. Laptops use up to 90 percent less power than a desktop.

Extra income

Surprising sources of get-it-now cash

A job market that loves to employ seniors. Not only is this job market one of the fastest growing in the U.S., it also employs thousands of workers over age 55 — and will be hiring even more with each passing year. So what is it? It's a variety of jobs for direct care workers such as personal care assistants and home health aides. These workers assist older adults and people with disabilities or chronic illnesses, but they may do it in different ways.

Personal care assistants are more likely to help with tasks like cooking, cleaning, or running errands, while home health aides help mostly with tasks like bathing, dressing, meals, and doctor's appointments. Some direct care providers visit people's homes to do their jobs, while others work in hospitals, adult day care, or nursing homes. These jobs are low-wage, come with a higher-than-average injury rate, and can be physically demanding. Yet, they are also a great way to assist people who genuinely need help, and you can usually work part time. Training and education requirements vary by state, so check what's required before you apply.

Handy moneymakers you can do in your spare time. The best and fastest way to make an extra $300, $500, or even $1,000 a month is to start a business based on skills you already have, suggests author Loral Langemeier in her book, Put More Cash in Your Pocket. These skills can come from your job experience, hobbies, volunteer work, or even chores. For example, if you already have skills and experience in:

- Calligraphy. You can be paid for work on wedding invitations, party invitations, and more.

- Transcription or speedy typing. You can be hired to transcribe locally from tapes or videos or from material provided online via the Web.

- Bookkeeping. If you're also certified as a CPA, small businesses may pay you to do their bookkeeping.

- Cooking. You may offer classes to neighborhood children, high school kids, or college students. If you have extra skill with baked goods or cake decorating, you can consider a side business in treats like decorated cakes and cookies, pastries, or specialty breads.

Be smart and choose wisely. If you want to quickly turn your skills into cash, Langemeier suggests you shouldn't waste your time on these ideas:

- introducing an innovative product or service that is new to customers and hard to understand

- starting a business that requires you to borrow a lot of money

- launching a business based on skills that are new or unfamiliar to you

Play a pretend patient for real rewards. If you live within easy driving distance of a medical school or teaching hospital, contact them and ask how to apply for their Standardized Patient (SP) program. As an SP, you play the patient in a simulated doctor's office visit that helps train medical students. You won't need any acting experience to qualify, but a good memory and the ability to think on your feet helps.

You could be assigned the role of a fictional patient with severe knee pain. Like an actor, you'll have lines to memorize, and you may even be trained on how to play some parts of the role. The medical student must ask you the right questions and perhaps do a little poking and prodding to make the right diagnosis. After the office visit, you fill out a checklist to evaluate things like the medical student's bedside manner and communications skills.

In exchange for these patient performances, you'll get hidden extras like free medical information and contacts, and you'll learn what to look for in a doctor and how to recognize the difference between good medical practices and bad ones. Your experiences also teach you how to work with your doctors – helpful questions to ask and what they may look for during an office visit. If all this makes you want to become a standardized patient, plan for a work day between two and six hours and pay rates around $10 to $25 an hour.

Part-time jobs that improve your health. You can get paid to grow healthier during retirement. Today's retirees can work part-time as dog walkers, child care workers, crossing guards, housecleaners, and tour guides. Jobs like these often provide health-building exercise on every working day. That's important because exercise comes with plenty of good side effects. Don't be surprised if it helps:

- boost your endurance

- control your blood sugar and weight

- give you energy

- protect your brain and memory

- ease arthritis and back pain

- lower your risk of hip fractures

In fact, studies show sustained exercise is linked to better health, even if you start exercising late in life. So check with your doctor to find out what exercises are safe for you. Then look for part-time jobs that require plenty of doctor-approved exercise. A job that requires lots of walking may be a good choice. You win two ways – when you start working in a job that requires exercise, you'll boost your bank account and your health at the same time.

Transform unique skills into gold

Sometimes the key to making extra money is to put your more unusual skills to work or use common skills differently. Here are several ideas you can try.

- Offer sewing skills with a twist. Find out which doll is the most wildly popular among today's kids, and take orders to make clothes for those dolls. You can also offer to make matching outfits for doll owners.

- Turn repairing electronics from a hobby into a career. Buy and repair broken electronic items, and sell them for a profit.

- Consider selling bagged lunches to friends, busy parents, and large families, especially if people compliment you on the lunches you make for your family.

- Become a garden sitter. Tend and water the gardens and plants of vacationers and business travelers while they're away.

- Transform your years of experience into a DVD or series of booklets you can sell if the physical demands of a service job, like landscaping or hairstyling, have become too much.

Start a specialty cleaning business for more perks.
Housecleaning can be a good way to earn extra income. But before you start a housecleaning business, check how many companies you'll compete against and what they charge. If you'll have to charge ultra-low prices because so many businesses already compete for the same customers, consider a specialty cleaning business instead. Organic or green housecleaners only use nontoxic cleaners and cleaning methods.

This kind of cleaning business could mean you face fewer competitors and can charge higher rates. What's more, you won't need to spend a lot of money to get started, and you might even have an opportunity to work part-time so you can enjoy more leisure during your retirement.

Make more bucks on a garage sale. Get creative when you plan your garage sale. Use these insider secrets from garage sale gurus to boost your profits.

- Ask your neighbors to hold their sales the same day as yours. Advertise a streetwide or neighborhood sale, and you'll all get many more customers.

- Group your merchandise into departments like a store would, and you may double your sales. Clean each item so it looks its best, and display it with the original box.

- Place your most exciting items and any products that appeal to men close to the street. More people will stop at your sale.

- To boost sales even higher, tack a large sign marked "Free" to one box, and fill the box with things to give away.

- Advertise in your local newspaper, but also advertise for free on *www.craigslist.com*. If you have plenty of goods in a particular category, advertise with a theme like Christmas in October, kitchen-wide clearance, or book bonanza.

- To dramatically increase clothing sales, show off the clothes on racks. Display everything else on tables or bookshelves. Borrow extra tables, shelves, and racks if you don't have enough.

- Make extension cords and batteries available to prove electronics still work.

- Instead of guessing at prices, know what your wares are worth. To find used-good prices, check neighborhood yard sales, thrift stores, *www.eBay.com*, *www.craigslist.com*, and online price guides from *www.satruck.org* and *www.goodwill.org*. Price each item a little higher than its average selling price, so you'll have room to negotiate. For more expensive items, attach a printed page from *www.amazon.com* showing what the item sells for new. That way, customers can compare it with your lower price tag, or you can simply attach a "make an offer" sign instead of a price tag.

Supercharge sales with super signs

Eye-catching yard sale signs may more than double the money your yard sale makes, claims one expert. But before you get creative, check your local ordinances to learn the rules for yard sale signs.

To make an attention-grabbing sign, think big. Make each sign from large, neon-colored poster board glued to a sheet of cardboard. In case of rain, write with waterproof ink, or cover with clear packing tape.

But don't stop there. Use large, bold letters to make the sign easy to read. Include the date and time of your sale and big arrows to guide people to your location. And, if local ordinances allow, attach balloons or plastic streamers to help your signs get noticed. Post signs at major routes nearby, and direct shoppers to your sale location using additional signs. To test the first sign you make, post it at a major route, and try to read it as you drive by.

Make a fortune on the junk in your attic. You want to sell all the junk in your attic, but you don't feel comfortable having people come to your home for a yard sale. Fortunately, the answer may be as close as your computer. Just sell your stuff on eBay, and you could make good money. One woman reported making more than $1,500 in one year, mostly from selling items she already owned. Some people also say you'll make more money selling certain goods on eBay than you would by selling them in a yard sale. These include electronics, quality clothing, shoes, kitchen appliances, and select household goods.

To get started, visit *www.ebay.com*, and review their tutorials and advice for sellers. Then register for an eBay account, and choose "casual account" to get 50 free auction listings every month. eBay is famous as an auction site, where people bid on an item offered for sale. For each item you sell by auction, you'll pay roughly 10 percent of the sales price to eBay. You can choose to sell at a fixed price instead, but you'll pay additional fees.

Before putting an item up for sale, check eBay's completed sale listings to see what prices similar items have sold for. Compare that price to the total cost of shipping your item and paying the eBay fees to sell it. Only sell items that can fetch a higher price than those costs.

When you put an item up for sale, write a clear, accurate description including the item's condition, and plenty of high-quality pictures. This will help you sell your items and start making money.

Boost consignment shop profits on your stuff. Earn more money from selling your used clothes, furniture, and other things to consignment stores. Start by choosing the best store for your merchandise. Check your local phone book or go online to see which stores are available. Choose several stores to visit, including any that specialize in the items you want to sell. Stores that specialize in a particular type of clothing or in particular categories like furniture or sporting goods may offer more.

When you visit, notice which stores are busiest and which ones sell the items you want to offer. Ask questions about what goods they accept and how the sale process works. Narrow your list, but don't pick just one store. Instead, set appraisal appointments with several stores; show them your clean, used items in good condition; and see what each one offers. This helps you sell each item to the store that offers the most for it.

Clever way to sell things you make. You may be able to get shelf space for crafts, jewelry, clothing accessories, or other things you make at a consignment or thrift store. To help you persuade the store owner, try this first. Find several school or church events where you can set up a table or booth to sell your stuff. Once you get the hang of selling your wares and have several successful events under your belt, you'll be ready to approach a store manager about shelf space.

Visit several consignment or thrift stores to see which one you'd like to approach about a shelf-space agreement. Ask whether the store will allow you to reserve shelf space in exchange for some of the profits. If they're interested, you can show them samples of your products and tell them about your sales. You may discover that if you provide the goods, they'll do the selling for a cut of the profits, and you'll have extra money to take home.

GREAT IDEA

Great reasons to become a resort baby sitter

Here's a new way to use your baby-sitting and childcare experience if you live near a destination city or popular vacation spot. Look into signing up with a professional baby-sitting agency or a hotel that provides baby sitters to vacationers and business travelers. The qualifications and the job requirements can vary widely, so ask plenty of questions.

A potential employer may require a background check; CPR and first aid certifications; or you may need to qualify to be licensed, bonded, or insured.

But once you are hired, you'll be able to choose when you work and how often. Pleased families might ask for you specifically every time they come to town.

Free-time fun

Easy ways to enrich your life

Beat the just-retired blues. During the first year of retirement, you may feel stir-crazy, bored, or even depressed as your social ties from work fade away. Spend time with your former coworkers when you can, but start building your retirement life, too. Think about all the things you would have done while working if you only had the time. For example, get more involved with your church or with other organizations that promote values or causes that are important to you. You have time for that now. You also have time to develop new skills, interests, or hobbies you've only dreamed about during your working life.

And, of course, you can always do things just for fun. A good way to find fun activities — as well as ways to develop skills or interests — is to pretend you are visiting your town on vacation. Check your local newspapers and bulletin boards, and see what's available from your Chamber of Commerce. Visit your library or go online to research local activities, clubs, and events. You may be astonished by all the wonderful things you've been missing.

Frugal way to learn a new hobby. Spend less learning more about your favorite pastime or taking up a new hobby. For example, if your first love is cooking, visit your local Williams-Sonoma store and ask about their classes. You may discover several free classes you like. Just be sure to confirm that they're free before you sign up. If you have Internet access, check out *www.Epicurious.com* for great cooking lessons. If cooking isn't your thing, check with your favorite hobby stores to see if they offer free classes, demonstrations, or workshops. Also, check *www.youtube.com* and websites dedicated to your hobby. You may find free videos, lessons, or classes there.

Mingling tip for shy people. Conversation can be difficult when you meet new people, but here's a great way to solve that problem. Volunteer to help at parties and social events, or work as part of a team at charity events or work parties. These are great ways to meet new people and turn acquaintances into friends. It works because volunteering keeps you busy. You can enjoy short conversations, but you'll rarely need to keep a conversation going for long. Instead, you'll just excuse yourself by politely explaining that you are helping in the kitchen or serving food and drinks. When you do charity work or similar volunteer jobs, most of your conversation will be about the tasks you're doing, so you probably won't have to think of things to talk about. Casual conversation will happen naturally, and you'll end up making new friends.

Ways to socialize despite chronic health issues. Conditions like hearing loss, chronic pain, or COPD (chronic obstructive pulmonary disease), can make socializing difficult or nearly impossible. But many people with chronic conditions say you don't have to go it alone.

- Join a support group for your condition. To find one, ask your doctor, or contact the national organization for your health issue. If no local support group is available, start your own, or look for one online.

- Ask your doctor what forms of exercise or activity can help your health problem. If he suggests one, ask if you can safely take a class or join a club that does that kind of physical activity.

- Do whatever volunteer work you can for your church, a charity, or any other organization that helps people or animals.

- If you have Web access, take up social networking. Some people with chronic conditions say this has made a big difference in their lives.

Meet people easily in your new neighborhood

Break the ice the simple way. Just get outdoors and strike up conversations with your neighbors when you see them. Sit on your porch, walk the dog, or weed your yard. Take walks throughout your neighborhood, and visit outdoor common areas as often as possible. When you see someone, mention that you are new to the area.

Ask questions about the neighborhood, learn where to get a good price on gas and what traffic hazards to avoid, or find out whether a neighborhood association is available. While you're at it, you may also learn a few things about your neighbor, and perhaps even get advice on what to do with all those leftover moving boxes.

Claim more senior discounts. The next time you go to an outdoor craft fair, a fast food restaurant, or even the Goodwill store, ask about a senior discount. You will probably get one if you meet the age requirement. Other surprising places where a senior discount may be available include your cellphone service provider, greeting card stores, major and minor league baseball stadiums, outlet malls, fitness centers, amusement parks, theaters, zoos, beauty salons, museums, rental car services, and stores where you fill your prescription for eyeglasses. Just remember, many of these places won't give you the discount unless you ask for it, so be sure to speak up.

Books for a buck — or free. Some people swear by their local Goodwill store as the best place to find books for a dollar or less. Other thrift stores may also offer top-flight books at bargain basement prices. Want more options? Watch for yard sale signs, and you may find paperbacks for a quarter or hardback books at deliciously steep discounts. But that's not all these sellers have to offer. If you are willing to dig a little at yard sales and thrift stores, you may uncover great reads and timeless treasures you just can't find in regular stores.

You'll discover treasures much closer to home if you start a small neighborhood library. In fact, you may have already seen this at work in other neighborhoods. The wildly popular "little free libraries" often resemble charming, super-size birdhouses, but you'll find books inside if you look closely. These boxes are also a great way to protect books from the elements.

To start a neighborhood library, check local ordinances, and work with your neighbors to decide where to put the box and who will care for it. For information on how to buy or build a library box, and instructions on starting and maintaining your neighborhood library, visit *littlefreelibrary.org* on the Web, or talk to someone in a neighborhood that already has a library. The website also offers useful information on finding sponsors who may help pay for a box. To kick off your library, ask everyone in the neighborhood to donate a book. This should offer enough books to expand everyone's reading options for weeks or months to come.

Find a better deal than online book swaps. Your friends rave about online book swapping sites like *www.paperbackswap.com.* Such sites are often free if you register with a valid e-mail address. But although PaperBackSwap users get books for free, they must pay the cost of mailing books to someone else. If you don't have a computer or just want to avoid the cost of mailing a book, nose around your area for a used bookstore that allows you to trade in books and get store credit toward new books. If you can't find a used bookstore near you, check your newspaper or library to learn whether a local paperback swap is already available. Otherwise, consider organizing an annual swap party at your home or church, or talk with a librarian about starting a swap club that meets at your local library.

Super alternatives to pricey gyms. The high price of a gym membership may seem smart during January snows, but always consider your options. You might save a lot of money.

- Check with your local hospital, community center, or senior center and you may discover exercise rooms, classes, or fitness programs available to the public. Ask about prices to see if the cost is less than a gym. Don't forget to include the expenses of gas and parking when you compare costs.

- Find out if your church or a friend's church offers free or inexpensive workout rooms, a gym, or exercise classes. Some churches allow nonmembers to take classes or use equipment for a small fee.

- Your cable television company may offer on-demand videos of fitness classes. Find out whether your cable provider offers this service, and ask if it costs extra or is already included in your current cable subscription.

If you need something more specialized, such as tennis courts or an indoor pool, check nearby colleges, high schools, or universities to see if you can use their facilities at a discount.

High-tech way to save money on music. Instead of paying for CDs or downloads of your favorite tunes, try Internet radio for free. You can listen on your computer, tablet, or smartphone, if you have a connection to the Internet. Even better, getting started is easier than you think. For example, if you decided to try the Internet radio service, Pandora, you'd create an account. Then you would pick your "radio stations" by choosing an artist, group, song, or type of music. You can find everything from the latest hits to golden oldies. What's more, you can start streaming music to your listening device almost immediately.

But choose wisely. Be sure to select the free version of an Internet radio service, and make certain it's compatible with your smartphone or other device. Also, if you stream to your smartphone, track how much data you use so you won't go over your cell plan's data limit. To learn more about your Internet radio options, visit these sites:

- Pandora at *www.pandora.com*

- iTunes radio at *www.apple.com/itunes/itunes-radio*

- Spotify at *www.spotify.com*

Groceries

Bright ideas to help you buy, prep & store your food

Save hundreds by never tossing out food. The average family of four wastes up to $2,275 of food annually. That means you could save hundreds of bucks a year if you avoid tossing out food. To help you start, try these handy "keep it fresh" tips.

- Place a paper towel in the plastic bag with your carrots to keep them fresh for up to several weeks.

- Keep milk on your refrigerator's top shelf behind your carton of eggs, instead of storing both foods in the refrigerator door. The door temperature is warmer, so moving eggs and milk to the shelf preserves them better and saves them from an early grave.

- When you store bread or other foods in a resealable bag, press all the air out of the bag before it goes in the refrigerator or freezer. You'll be surprised at how much longer that makes foods last.

- To give lettuce as much as an extra week, forget storing the whole head. Rinse and dry completely. Chop the lettuce, place in an airtight container, and store in the refrigerator. Tuck a paper towel over the lettuce to draw moisture away, and replace the paper towel daily.

- Line your vegetable crisper with paper towels, and your vegetables may take longer to spoil. Replace the paper towels once a week.

- Make celery last up to four weeks. Trim the ends, and wash and completely dry each stalk. Wrap the celery in dry paper towels. Store in a plastic bag in your refrigerator's crisper drawer.

- Store whole tomatoes at room temperature with the stem end down.

- To extend the life of cottage cheese or sour cream, close the tub, make sure the lid is on firmly, and slip a rubber band around it to secure that lid. Keep the tub upside down on a paper towel in the refrigerator.

GREAT IDEA

New ways to use an old ice cube tray

Freeze lemon juice or orange juice in your ice cube tray today, and use it to flavor your water, tea, or favorite recipe later. You can also freeze coffee creamer in the tray for cubes that are just the right size to cool down steaming coffee. Some people even make ice cubes out of the coffee itself, so the cubes won't dilute their iced coffee.

If you're an avid cook, use an ice cube tray to freeze chopped herbs like rosemary or thyme for your recipes. Partially fill each cup with the herb, and top it off with olive oil or melted butter. Stored this way, your herbs can last up to one month.

Ice cube trays are also great for freezing broth, salsa, puréed vegetables for smoothies, pesto, tomato paste, and other leftover sauces.

Keep berries fresh for a week. Love fresh berries, but hate that they can go bad or get moldy in just a few days? Here's an easy way to make them last more than a week in your refrigerator.

In a large bowl, mix 3 1/2 cups of water with three-fourths cup of white vinegar. Drop the berries in the bowl, and swirl them around to wash them. Drain them in a colander, and rinse under cold, running tap water.

Spread the berries out on a paper towel spaced well apart. If possible, place the paper towels on racks or screens before spreading the berries across them. Let the berries dry for one to two hours. Be careful to dry the berries thoroughly, or you will taste vinegar when you eat them. Store your berries in a loosely covered container lined with paper towels, and place that container in the refrigerator. Most berries will last at least one week. Try it and see for yourself.

And to make sure you're getting the freshest berries, sniff that basket of strawberries before you buy it. The ones that smell the best will also taste best.

5 surprising foods that last for months in the freezer.
Freeze these foods before they go bad, and you'll have plenty of time to find another use for them.

- Eggs. Break eggs into a bowl. Add either one tablespoon of sugar or one-third teaspoon of salt per cup of eggs, and stir until the yolks and whites are blended. Measure three tablespoons — the equivalent of one egg — into each cup of an ice cube tray. This makes your frozen eggs a great size for baking. Let the mixture freeze solid, slip the egg ice cubes into a freezer bag, and keep in the freezer for up to six months. Thaw in the refrigerator before using.

- Avocados. Peel ripe avocados, remove their pits, and mash them. Add one-half to one tablespoon of lemon juice per avocado. Freeze in a container with a little air space. These keep up to five months.

- Cheese. Hard or semi-hard cheeses like provolone, mozzarella, cheddar, and Swiss freeze well enough to work in recipes. What's more, they last four to six months in the freezer and can rescue you from unsavory encounters with moldy cheese. To freeze, cut into blocks up to 1 1/2 pounds, wrap tightly in plastic wrap, and put in a freezer bag. Thaw in the refrigerator, and use within a day. The cheese may be too crumbly to add to your favorite sandwich, but it will taste delicious in your favorite recipes.

■ Buttermilk. Freeze buttermilk in small paper cups, a muffin pan, or an ice cube tray. You can freeze in sizes up to a half cup if you use paper cups or muffin pans, but use the ice cube tray for portions of one or two tablespoons. Wrap each cup in plastic wrap after it freezes. Store cups or ice cubes in a freezer bag in the freezer for up to two months. Thaw in the refrigerator or microwave. Freezing may cause solids and whey in the buttermilk to separate, so whisk, stir, or run through a blender before using.

■ Nuts. Freeze in an airtight container, or place them in a freezer bag, and press out the air before sealing. Use within six months. You can chop them or toss them whole into a recipe right from the freezer, or thaw them in the refrigerator first.

MONEYSAVER

Uncover the best days of the week to grocery shop

Schedule your grocery shopping for Wednesdays if you want a great deal. A large number of stores start their weekly sales on that day but also honor the previous week's sales specials. You get double the deals you would on other days, and that makes bargain shopping twice as nice.

But some supermarkets take a different approach. Because their managers know many people only have time to shop on weekends, these stores offer their best deals Thursday through Sunday. Check your local grocery stores to find out which ones prefer weekend deals and which ones offer the Wednesday double-dip.

Use this restaurant steak secret at home. Uncover the real reason steaks taste better at a restaurant, and discover how you can get the same results at home without buying more expensive meat.

While your restaurant steak may come with all sorts of specialty seasonings or exotic sauces, it may also come with something any-one can buy from the grocery store – butter. To make the perfect culinary butter for your steak, mix two tablespoons of fresh parsley with a stick of butter. Store the seasoned butter in the refrigerator until needed.

When the steaks are done, remove them from the grill. Scoop out 1 1/2 teaspoons of butter, and drop it in the center of the first steak. Repeat the process for each one. After the last bit of butter melts, serve your delectable steaks, and prepare to enjoy compliments from all your guests.

GREAT IDEA

Peel ginger with ease

Don't use your vegetable peeler or a knife to peel ginger root. That's doing it the hard way. Instead, turn the bowl of a spoon toward the root so you can gently scrape the skin away with the spoon's edge. You'll be done before you know it.

Rescue apples from rapid browning. The moment you cut into an apple, you know you're on borrowed time. The fruit may not turn brown instantly, but you won't have to wait long. If you need to save the apple for later and want to keep the dreaded browning at bay, try this easy tip.

First, find a clean elastic-style headband or another type of elastic band. Slice your apple into four to eight equal sections around the core. Don't throw out the core because you'll need all parts to fit tightly back together after cutting. Why? Your apple turns brown because air reaches its edible surfaces and causes oxidation, a process similar to rusting. The longer you shield your apple's flesh from contact with air, the longer that ugly browning takes to set in.

To keep your fruit fresh, reassemble the core and other apple pieces so they make an entire apple. Secure the parts together with the headband. Loop the headband two or three times around to make sure the parts fit snugly together. As long as air can't reach the surface of the apple slices, they'll stay as perfect as when they were first cut.

Speed shop thru the grocery store

Shopping in the same grocery store each week gives you a benefit you may not have thought about. You know exactly where everything is. Take advantage of this when making your grocery list, and write down the items in the order you will pick them up in the aisles. Put your coupons in the same order. To save even more time, shop when the store is less crowded. You'll be amazed at the difference in time small changes like these can make.

Save these foods with a slice. Your brown sugar has not only dried out but turned into a solid brown brick that's harder than the Hope Diamond. But don't fret. If you slip a slice of bread in the brown sugar container before you go to bed, your sugar will be soft by morning.

Throw another slice of bread in the cookie jar to keep your chewy cookies from becoming hockey pucks. Check the bread and cookies each day, and replace the bread if needed. The cookies should stay soft for several days — if they aren't eaten sooner.

Cakes don't get hard the way cookies do, but they can dry out. Add a slice of bread to the cake container to keep your cake moist, and check the bread every day. Replace the bread if it becomes dry and hard.

GREAT IDEA

Flavor up a grilled cheese sandwich

Thanks to an unusual restaurant named Jafflechutes, people in Melbourne, Australia can order a grilled cheese sandwich online and have it delivered by parachute. But you don't need a special delivery system to get a better-tasting version of this popular sandwich. Just try seasoning your grilled cheese with flavorful options like garlic or other herbs and spices. Add tangy tomatoes or sweet peppers, or spread on a layer of guacamole or salsa. You'll be amazed at just how good your grilled cheese sandwich can be.

5 smart ways to throw out less food. Use more of the food you buy so you won't spend as much at the grocery store. These tips can help.

- Store foods in clear containers so you can see exactly what you have in your refrigerator and pantry. You're less likely to lose track of leftovers and ingredients when they're easy to spot, so they shouldn't spoil before you can use them. When clear containers are not enough, use labels. Either plaster a label where you can clearly see it, or put up a flag. Stick a label on a toothpick or half a straw, and tape it to the side of the package so your label stands high enough to be seen – like a flag on a flagpole.

- Use a permanent marker, a label maker, or a date stamp on food packages to mark down when your food went in the refrigerator, freezer, or pantry.

- Portion out your leftovers and stick them in the freezer if they haven't been eaten in several days. Assign them a "use by" date so they won't overstay their welcome. Visit your library or *www.stilltasty.com* to determine which leftovers you can freeze, how to do it properly, and how long they will keep. Your research may also turn up delicious and clever ways to use those leftovers.

- Designate one spot in your refrigerator as the Last Chance Cafe, the place where you put leftovers and other foods nearing the end of their shelf lives. Place a brightly colored tray or the bottom half of a shoe or pizza box in that location to contain those foods and remind you they need to be eaten. Use those foods first, and far fewer of them may spoil.

- Every time you throw spoiled food away, write down the name of the food and why it never got eaten. Come up with several ideas for how you could have prevented that waste and what you will do next time. Over time, you will get better at using food before it spoils, and you'll end up spending less on groceries.

GREAT IDEA

Creative ways to prop up your cake cover

You arrive at a potluck dinner and discover the plastic covering your cake or casserole has collapsed, sticking to the food's surface like shrink-wrap. The toothpicks you inserted were supposed to prevent this problem, but they just poked through the plastic wrap. Fortunately, you can make sure this won't happen again.

For cakes, replace plain toothpicks with cocktail umbrellas or mini-marshmallows mounted on toothpicks. Protect your casseroles and other savory dishes with pastry cones, corn cob holders, or with toothpicks topped with raisins, dried cranberries, or olives. If you don't want your plastic-wrap props to be seen, remember to remove them before you serve the dish.

Solve kitchen problems with a paper towel. A paper towel may seem like little more than an expensive, disposable replacement for dish rags, but it can also be a vital kitchen tool. Try these ideas to see how paper towels can earn their keep.

- Keep frozen bread from thawing into a soggy mess. Just slide a paper towel in the bag before you freeze the bread, and you'll get great results.

- Wipe down a corn cob with a wet paper towel to remove all the silky strands.

- Dampen a paper towel, and spread it out beneath your cutting board. It will prevent the board from slipping around on the countertop while you chop or cut.

- Use a damp paper towel instead of plastic wrap to cover your microwave dishes. It will keep food from spattering but won't melt into the dish.

GREAT IDEA

Keep fruit from bruising while it's cruising

Delicious fruits like plums, peaches, and nectarines are tough to bring to work or anywhere else because they bruise so easily. The next time you need to take delicate fruit somewhere, nestle it in a layer of cushioning material like Bubble Wrap, or carry a single fruit in a rubber or foam drink "coozie." Tuck smaller fruits in the protective cups of an egg carton.

Food fraud — what you need to know. Some bottles of 100-percent olive oil may contain soybean oil. Even worse, some honey may include corn syrup, and some milk may be watered down. These are just a few examples of food fraud.

Such cases include incidents where:

- food is tampered with.

- ingredients are replaced or removed.

- fillers are added.

- packaging or advertising is misleading.

More than 800 new cases of food fraud have been found since the beginning of 2011, and the numbers keep rising. Some foods seem more prone to this problem than others. A 2012 study in the *Journal of Food Science* suggests the most common foods afflicted by fraud include milk, honey, coffee, orange juice, apple juice, olive oil, vanilla extract, maple syrup, and saffron.

At the least, this means you may not be getting the food you're paying premium prices for. Even worse, food fraud may boost your odds of eating expired foods, toxic additives like melamine, or an ingredient you may be allergic to. To help avoid tainted foods, take steps like these.

- Buy from local producers when you can. Good places to try include farmer's markets, local farms, pick-it-yourself orchards, local beekeepers, and co-ops. When you can't buy locally, choose foods that are not imported.

- Grow or process your own. Start a backyard garden to grow some of your own fruits, vegetables, nuts, or herbs. Instead of buying juices, juice your own fruits and vegetables. Buy coffee beans instead of ground coffee, and grind the beans yourself.

- Buy well-known brands made by companies that have a reputation to protect.

- Visit the Food Fraud Database at *www.foodfraud.org* to check their fraud reports.

- Read the ingredient list on packaged products to be sure it contains what you think it does.

Join community garden and save. If you have no space at home for a garden, join a local community garden. This can be a cheap way to get space to grow vegetables, fruits, herbs, flowers – whatever you want. At some community gardens you can rent your own small plot, maybe 8x10 feet, for less than $100 each growing season. The cost may also include water and expert gardening advice.

In an established garden, you may get a bed with good-quality soil that's already built and prepared, so you won't need to replace native dirt. Some community gardens even provide soil testing. Check the website of the American Community Gardening Association, *www.communitygarden.org*, to find a community garden near you. With more than 18,000 community gardens across the United States and Canada, there's likely one nearby.

Slash food spending with a grocery price book. You may be surprised at how much you can save by writing down and comparing grocery prices. Even if you don't spend much time on it, a price book can help you:

- recognize which bulk discounts save the most money and which ones don't.

- spot pricing trends and recognize regularly recurring sales you can count on seeing again.

- avoid the frustration of stocking up at one sale only to find a better sale a few weeks later.

- uncover which store offers the cheapest price on an item.

Some people have even discovered that sales with seemingly big discounts really saved less than a nickel.

To see what a price book can do for you, start with the high-efficiency version. Pull out your grocery receipt, and choose the top seven items you want to save money on. Circle or highlight these products.

Get a pocket-sized tablet or notebook, and divide it into food categories such as meat, dairy, beverages, fruits and vegetables, and so on. Write each of your seven items in the appropriate category. Include the purchase date, the price, and the store where you bought it. If possible, calculate the unit price, and write the unit size nearby. Otherwise, take a calculator with you when you shop, and add the unit price then. Finally, leave space for future entries because you will write down a lower price the moment you find it.

As you shop, check the prices on each of your seven items at each store you visit. Update the price book when you find a better price than what you paid in the past. You'll soon find you don't need to look at your price book very often because you'll already remember the best prices. Not only will you avoid overpaying for your seven items, you'll know when to stock up so you can save the most money.

For even bigger savings, add seven more products to your price book, and start saving on those, too.

3 new ways to use your box grater. Your box grater isn't just for shredding cheese anymore. See what else it can do for you.

- Zest a lemon. Gently rub a washed and dried organic lemon against the side of the grater to make your own fresh lemon zest. Be careful to only grate the peel and not the flesh beneath.

- Melt cold, hard butter with amazing speed. Using your grater on the butter can give you smaller pieces that melt right away.

- End the struggle to cut fresh ginger root or mince garlic. Just grate what you need instead.

Also, try your grater on nutrient-rich vegetables like radishes, carrots, and squash for perfect-sized pieces to add to soups, salads, or your favorite dishes.

Use more of the eggs you buy

You hate throwing out eggs that might still be good, but you're wisely afraid to take chances. To find out which eggs must go, try this test. Pour two teaspoons of salt in a container. Fill the container with cold water until the water is twice as deep as your tallest egg. Stir until the salt dissolves.

Place your uncooked egg very gently in the water. The amount of air in an egg increases as it gets older, so old eggs are more buoyant. If an egg floats so that even a little of the shell is above the water's surface, throw it away without a second thought. If the egg sinks to the bottom and rests on its side, it is still safe to use.

Shop smart when your health changes. If you've developed a health condition like gout, diabetes, or celiac disease, your doctor has probably prescribed changes to your diet. That means your next trip to the supermarket will be a whole new ball game. Fortunately, you can make that trip far easier with these tactics.

- Ask your doctor where to get more information about your new diet, how to eat, and where to shop. Also, ask about magazines, websites, and support groups for your health condition.

- Before you make your grocery list, look for recommendations on those sites for foods and recipes you can eat. You may also discover coupons and other ideas for discounts.

- Make a list of foods and ingredients you need to avoid, and take it with you to the supermarket.

- Shop when the store won't be crowded, so you can take time to read ingredient lists and check labels. Carry reading glasses or a magnifier to help read small print on packages. Also, arrange to shop without toddlers or other distractions.

- If you have a friend or family member who is familiar with the guidelines for your diet, ask that person to help you shop a few times until you get the hang of what to buy.

GMO food controversy — how to play it safe. Some say genetically modified foods are like Clark Kent turning into Superman while others argue these foods are a case of Dr. Jekyll becoming Mr. Hyde. If you've wondered what all the fuss is about, and what it means for you, here are your answers.

Scientists create genetically modified organisms (GMOs) from normal food crops. For example, a scientist can make a food crop more nutritious or better at surviving insects by inserting a gene from another plant into the cells of the food crop plant. The altered plant is a genetically modified organism.

Although the National Academy of Sciences found no hazards from GMO foods, critics point out that the long-term health effects of these foods aren't known yet. As the controversy rages on, some have decided to play it safe by trying to limit or avoid GMO foods and foods with GMO ingredients. If you want to do the same, remember these points.

- No food certified as organic can contain genetically modified organisms. If you're shopping for non-GMO produce, look for a sticker with a 5-digit code that begins with 9. These products are more likely to be organic.

- Genetically modified foods and ingredients are not required to be labeled as GMOs, but if they are, the product code usually begins with an 8.

- Look for the non-GMO Project Verified Seal. Products with this seal have undergone a voluntary certification process proving they contain no more than 0.9 percent GMO ingredients.

- Avoid cooking with oils or oil blends that contain corn oil, soybean oil, vegetable oil, or canola oil. It's a good bet these are made with GMOs.

- More than 60 percent of processed foods may contain GMOs, so choose whole foods instead. When you can't avoid processed foods, limit or eliminate foods that contain corn, high fructose corn syrup, corn-based ingredients, soybeans, or soybean-based ingredients. Corn and soybeans are among the most common genetically engineered crops.

5 questions to ask before joining a food co-op. Food co-ops can be a great way to get discounted foods, fruits and vegetables fresh from the farm, organic foods, or items your grocery store doesn't carry. But before you join, ask these questions to see if the co-op is right for you.

- Do I have to join to get bargains? Co-ops are owned by their members, which includes both the farmers who grow the food and the people who buy it. Some co-ops allow nonmembers to buy from the co-op, but only members get discounts. Other co-ops sell only to members.

- Is every member expected to volunteer? To join the co-op, members may be required to pay a fee, volunteer part time at the co-op, or both. If you work, you may prefer a co-op that does not put demands on your time.

- Will I save money? Some co-ops claim to save as much as 40 percent off your grocery bill, but savings may vary from one co-op to the next. If the co-op requires a membership fee, make sure you can save more money than the fee costs. Also, check each product's prices and unit prices to see how co-op discounts compare to prices at other places where you shop.

- Do I have to buy in bulk? Ask if your co-op only offers discounts on bulk orders or if you can get price breaks on smaller orders, too. If you must buy in bulk, determine whether you have enough cash for the bulk buy, whether you can use the food before it spoils, and whether you can make space to store or freeze it.

- How do I shop at the co-op? Some co-ops are open most anytime you need to buy, while others have limited hours or require you to shop or pick up your order within a limited time. Find out how your co-op wants you to buy and whether you can be available at the right times.

MONEYSAVER

Find a food co-op near you

You may be living right on top of a food co-op and not even know it. Ask at local food stands or farmer's markets to see if they know of any food co-ops in the area. If you have a computer, you can go online to *www.coopdirectory.org* for more information and to find the closest food co-op.

Squeeze more value out of your freezer. You finally got that chest freezer you always wanted, so make sure it earns its keep.

- Before you fill an empty freezer, prepare it so just-added food freezes quickly, and you'll avoid issues with ice crystals. Either set the temperature control to -10 about 24 hours before you add food to the freezer, or use the quick freeze setting.

- Each time you add a new load of food to the freezer, avoid adding more than 2 to 3 pounds of food per cubic foot of storage space. Also, leave space between the foods while they are freezing. Following these rules helps foods freeze more rapidly. After the foods freeze completely, pack them closer together. Fill any unused space in your freezer with water-filled milk jugs.

- To prevent foods from spoiling before you use them, start a list of the foods in your chest freezer, and include the date they were frozen. Tape that list to your freezer, and strike through any foods you remove.

And remember, to protect against food poisoning, never thaw foods on the counter. Instead, thaw them in your refrigerator overnight so they'll be ready for use the next day.

Buy a chest freezer for less. Check newspaper ads or *www.craigslist.com* for used chest freezers and you may be pleasantly surprised. People often sell their chest freezers when they move out of town, so you may find a great price on a used freezer.

While you're in the market, measure how much space you have available for a chest freezer, and determine what size freezer you need. Chest freezers range from compact models around 4.7 cubic feet in size to larger models offering 25 cubic feet. Industry experts suggest you need 1.5 cubic feet of space for each person in your household. Or plan on 1 cubic foot of space for every 35 pounds of food you'll freeze from bulk buys or other sources. For more information about what to look for in chest freezers, visit your local library or *www.consumerreports.org*.

How to tell when stocking up is a good deal. Whether you're at the supermarket or the warehouse store, nobody wants a bulk buy that doesn't save money. Follow these steps to be sure you only buy bulk deals that are worth your while.

- Check the unit price. Is this price better than the per-unit price at all the other places you shop? If the item is nonperishable, can you get a better deal and free shipping online? Bigger savings may be available in a smaller package.

- Find the expiration date if the product has one. Calculate how often you must use the item to finish it before it spoils, and consider whether you're likely to use it that often. If you can't use the entire product in time, can you split the cost and the food with a friend or family member? If any of the product will be wasted, don't buy it.

- Determine whether you have enough room to store the item in your refrigerator, freezer, pantry, or root cellar. To make this easier, check your storage spaces before you shop. Clean out any foods that have spoiled, and note how much storage space you have left. If you don't have space in the refrigerator or pantry, can you freeze part of the item until space is available? Is there room for it in your freezer? Don't buy anything you have no room to store.

- Don't stock up on a product you have never bought before. If you try the product and hate it, you'll have paid for a large amount of a product you won't use. Also, think twice about products you don't use often, especially if they are perishable.

Enjoy tastier, more nutritious corn

Buy corn in the husk, and leave it unshucked until cooking time, and you'll get corn that stays fresher for longer. But don't boil that corn. Boiling leeches nutrients out of the corn and into the boiling water, so you end up with depleted, low-nutrient corn. That's like turning your corn from a Charles Atlas strongman into a 98-pound weakling.

To keep your corn pumped up with nutrients, grill or microwave the ears in their husks. If you use the microwave, cook the corn for three minutes, let cool, and then peel off the silks and husk. You'll be surprised at how much flavor you've been missing.

Make chocolate cake healthier. Cook up a delicious chocolate cake that has fewer calories and less cholesterol and fat. You won't believe how good chocolate cake can taste when you replace two-thirds of the butter in the recipe with all-natural avocado purée. Use this chart to help you make the change without doing a lot of math. Simply replace the total butter called for in the recipe with the combined amounts of butter and avocado.

Total butter	Butter	Avocado
1/4 cup	1 T and 1 t	2 T and 2 t
1/3 cup	1 T and 2 1/3 t	3 T and 1 2/3 t
1/2 cup	2 T and 2 t	5 T and 1 t
3/4 cup	1/4 cup	1/2 cup
1 cup	1/3 cup	2/3 cup
1 tablespoon	1 t	2 t
1 teaspoon	generous 1/4 t	generous 1/2 t

Clever recipe substitutions to try this week. You count out the eggs for your cake recipe but you're one egg short. Instead of rushing to the store, try replacing the egg with three tablespoons of peanut butter, two tablespoons of mayonnaise, or one-fourth cup of applesauce. If you're short on something else in the kitchen, one of these substitutes may help.

- Replace one cup of corn syrup with two tablespoons of water and seven-eighths cup of sugar.

- Substitute one cup of crushed, rolled oats for one cup of sifted all-purpose flour.

- Replace one small garlic clove with one-eighth teaspoon of garlic powder. Use this same amount of garlic powder to replace one-half teaspoon of garlic juice.

- Substitute one-half teaspoon of vinegar for one teaspoon of lemon juice.

- Replace one cup of buttermilk with one cup of regular milk and 1 3/4 teaspoons of cream of tartar.

- Use an equal amount of granulated sugar in place of brown sugar.

- To replace one small, fresh onion, rehydrate one tablespoon of instant minced onion.

- The recipe calls for beer or champagne, but you don't have either one in the house. Substitute ginger ale instead.

- Replace ground cloves with allspice.

- To make a milder version of a recipe with cayenne pepper, replace the cayenne powder with paprika. To keep things spicy, use chili powder instead.

- When baking, you can replace each ounce of unsweetened chocolate with three tablespoons of cocoa and one tablespoon of fat.

MONEYSAVER

Claim the discount you've earned

Check your grocery store's website, or ask the supermarket staff if the store offers a senior discount or a senior rewards club. Find out the minimum age for the program and how to go about getting your discount. After all, you don't want to miss out on the savings you deserve.

Prep part of your meals a day or more early. When you can't do all the cooking on the day a meal will be eaten, use these ideas for doing part of the work ahead of time.

- Peel garlic cloves for multiple uses. Either freeze them whole in freezer bags, or chop them and wrap snugly in plastic before freezing.

- Parboil carrots, green beans, broccoli, or butternut squash. Boil until crisp-tender, dunk in chilled water, drain, and store in plastic in the refrigerator. When you cook them the next day, they will be done quickly.

- Make soup early and freeze it, but leave out the cream, milk, pasta, rice, and any grain ingredients. Add these when you warm the soup before serving. Just make sure the pasta, rice, and grains are cooked before you add them.

- Always cook more brown rice than needed. If you'll use the extra rice the next day, store it in the refrigerator. For use further in the future, let the rice cool, and freeze one-cup servings in plastic containers or freezer bags.

- For salads, switch from regular tomatoes to cherry or grape tomatoes. You can use them whole or chop them a day ahead of time. Chop romaine or iceberg lettuce, dry thoroughly with a salad spinner or paper towels, and store separately from the tomatoes. Cover the lettuce with a dry paper towel and plastic wrap, and replace the paper towel daily to keep the lettuce from wilting. Combine the lettuce and tomatoes with dressing and other salad ingredients shortly before serving.

- Peel and cut potatoes the day before. Drop into a bowl, cover with water, and store in the refrigerator.

- Chop vegetables – like onions, carrots, celery, broccoli and peppers – a day or two early, and store in the refrigerator.

- Marinate beef in an oil-based marinade in a resealable bag in the refrigerator. Use the beef the next day. Don't marinate overnight if the mixture contains vinegar, lemon juice, or other acid ingredients.

Beware unit pricing traps. Be careful when you compare unit prices. Make sure both prices are based on the same size unit. For example, one bottle may be measured in liters while another is labeled in fluid ounces. To help solve this problem, carry a calculator with you to the grocery store, or use the calculator in your cellphone. You can also copy this quick reference to help convert prices based on different units.

- 1 liter = 33.8 ounces or 1.06 quarts

- 1 fluid ounce = 2 tablespoons or 29.57 grams

- 1 gallon = 3.78 liters or 4 quarts or 128 fluid ounces

- 16 fluid ounces = 1 pint or 2 cups

- 1 dry ounce = 28.35 grams

- 1 pound = 16 ounces or 453.6 grams

Many people automatically assume the economy-size version of a product is always cheaper. Don't make that mistake, especially if you're shopping at a warehouse store. Whip out your calculator, and check the unit price to find out whether bigger really is better — or if the product is cheaper at another store.

GREAT IDEA

Make frozen broccoli healthier and tastier

Some experts say frozen broccoli isn't as healthy as fresh because it can't produce cancer-fighting compounds like sulforaphane. But new research from the University of Illinois suggests you can easily fix that problem by mixing a small amount of certain foods into your broccoli. Try adding spicy mustard, raw radishes, watercress, horse-radish, cabbage, wasabi, or arugula. These foods help restore frozen broccoli's ability to make cancer fighting compounds — and they'll add some zing to your broc-coli's flavor.

How to freeze leftover mashed potatoes. Contrary to popular belief, you can freeze mashed potatoes. You just have to learn the best way to do it. Line a baking sheet with parchment or waxed paper, and place scoops of mashed potatoes on the sheet. Freeze solid, and store in resealable plastic bags.

To revive your frozen mashed potatoes, reheat one or more portions in a dish without its lid, either in the oven or the microwave. Leaving the lid off allows water to evaporate so the final product won't be watery. Mix the mashed potatoes with butter, sour cream, yogurt, or buttermilk to refresh their flavor before eating. Or you can use your defrosted mashed potatoes to replace one-third of the flour in a recipe.

WARNING

Don't let nutrients escape

You buy nutritious foods to help you stay well, but those foods may lose plenty of nutrients by the time they reach your plate. Use these techniques to retain more vitamins and minerals in your dishes.

- Steam or microwave your produce instead of boiling. If you don't have a steamer, cook your vegetables in a pan with only a small amount of water. Less water and shorter cooking times help preserve nutrients.

- Keep milk out of strong light. More light means less vitamin B2.

- Don't add baking soda to green vegetables to keep their color. It destroys vitamins.

- Boiling pulls nutrients out of vegetables and into the cooking water. Take advantage of that nutrient-filled water — refrigerate it, and use it to make soup later on.

- Eat both cooked and raw produce. Cooking may reduce the amounts of B and C vitamins but can increase nutrients like lycopene, beta carotene, and minerals.

Make nut chopping easier. Chopping nuts with a knife is not only difficult, but bits of nut often fly off and have to be thrown in the trash. To prevent that, only chop nuts with a knife when you need finely chopped nuts or have a small amount of nuts you want to chop coarsely.

To handle nut flyaways, place a baking sheet beneath your cutting board before you chop. The sheet catches your wayward nut pieces, so you can bring them back into the fold.

For efficient, chef-style chopping, use a large knife. Hold the hilt with one hand. Place the blade of the knife on the cutting board, and use your other hand to brace the tip from above. Keep the tip in one place, and move the handle from side to side while chopping.

If you have a large amount of nuts to chop coarsely, leave your chopping knife in the drawer. Instead, pull out a large, resealable bag, and fill it with a single layer of shelled nuts. Seal the bag, lay it on the cutting board, and pound the nuts with a rolling pin or kitchen mallet until the nuts are chopped to your satisfaction.

4 secrets to preparing dinner even faster. You may be an old hand in the kitchen, but you can still speed things up with tricks like these.

- Heat your pans while you prepare your ingredients by putting the cookware on top of the stove or in the oven while it pre-heats. Your dish will cook faster if the pan is already hot when food goes in it.

- Designate a small bag or bowl for garbage if your trash can isn't nearby. You'll save more time than you think possible.

- Practice what they teach in culinary school – *mise en place*. That's French for "together in place." It means you should prepare your ingredients and cooking equipment as much as possible before you start cooking – almost as if you were demonstrating a recipe on a cooking show. *Mise en place* is particularly helpful for recipes that require you to combine ingredients quickly or when you have several dishes going at once. Simply measure the ingredients into individual containers, and place near your cooking area. If you don't have enough measuring cups or small bowls, get creative with plastic drinking cups, coffee filters, cupcake liners, muffin pans, or empty egg cartons. Don't forget to prepare your pans, utensils, and other cooking tools so they are ready to use as well.

■   After your next meal, make notes about what kept you from cooking at top speed and how you can fix those problems. For example, if you have trouble getting to ingredients or utensils, rearrange your pantry, refrigerator, or kitchen cabinets. If chopping, grating, or peeling seems difficult and slow, consider whether you should sharpen or replace old knives, peelers, or graters.

MONEYSAVER

End red sauce stains forever

You stored your pasta sauce, curry sauce, or chili in a plastic container as usual, but now the orangey-red stains won't come out of the plastic no matter what you do. To spare your unstained containers from this horrible fate, spray the inside of the container lightly with nonstick cooking spray. If you don't have cooking spray on hand, coat the container with a thin sheen of olive oil or any cooking oil that won't spoil the flavor of your sauce. After that, simply pour the sauce in the container, and store as usual.

Use a similar trick before pouring sticky ingredients like syrup or honey into your measuring cups and spoons. Spray your measurer lightly with cooking spray, and the sticky ingredients slide out easily. No fuss, no muss.

Give leftovers a second chance. You may not be thrilled about having tonight's leftovers again tomorrow, but what if they didn't look or taste like the original meal? Give your leftovers a tasty makeover, and you won't need to throw them out. If necessary, you can dice, purée, or chop the ingredients so they'll easily fit into other dishes.

- Use part or all of the leftovers as ingredients in a wrap sandwich, a soft or hard taco, or a yummy burrito.

- Turn them into pizza or nacho toppings.

- Mix them into a hearty stew or soup, a spicy chili, a flavorful stir-fry, or hot casserole.

- Toss them into a fresh green salad, antipasto salad, or pasta salad.

- Serve the leftovers over rice or mashed potatoes, or combine them with pasta sauce and serve over pasta.

- Dress up your leftovers with one or more spice blends, garlic or other herbs, balsamic or flavored vinegar, or lemon juice. Or try sauces like barbecue sauce, hot sauce, marinara, gravy, soy sauce, Worcestershire, salsa, cocktail sauce, or sweet and sour sauce.

- Blend fruit or vegetable ingredients into a smoothie.

Plan meals that save money and time. You could save up to $25 a month, prepare meals more quickly, and avoid food waste just by cutting back on the meat in your meals. Here's how to do it in the most delicious way.

Start the week with dishes where meat plays a starring role. Enjoy foods like steak or baked chicken during the first few days after your trip to the grocery store, when the meat is freshest. After that, switch to low-meat or no-meat meals.

Low-meat meals can include shepherd's pie, casseroles, stir-fries, soups, and other dishes where meat plays a supporting role instead of being the star. Using meat as a side dish or as an ingredient in a larger dish is a great way to lower your grocery bill.

When the meat is gone, switch to meatless dishes. These recipes get their protein from cheese, beans, eggs, nuts, grains, and seeds. Good examples include cheese pizza with vegetable toppings, scrambled eggs, quiche, three-bean chili, oatmeal topped with raisins and nuts, or even peanut butter and jelly sandwiches. Best of all, these alternate proteins are often cheaper than meat and may take less time to prepare.

MONEYSAVER

Time your shopping for extra savings

Drop by your grocery store in the evening, and you may find that morning's fresh baked breads marked down drastically. This is known as a manager's special, a sale that happens when perishable items won't last much longer. Keep an eye out for these sales, and learn what time of the day or week they are most likely to happen. If you can shop at the right time and use the product right away, you may pay a lot less for that food than everyone else does.

You can get even more bargains right after a holiday. For example, find Christmas baking ingredients at deep discounts on December 26, buy turkey and canned pumpkin on sale after Thanksgiving, and stock up on bargain-priced mustard, ketchup, and other barbecue foods right after July 4.

Find the bargains others miss. The next time you're at the grocery store, count how many times you see someone pick up an item from a bottom shelf. You probably won't see it often, which means most people are missing a golden opportunity. Supermarkets put more expensive products where you can easily see and reach them. So if you're debating about getting a pricey item, check the bottom shelf. You may find a substitute that costs less.

Another bargain people miss is the unadvertised special. To catch these fleeting opportunities, check the prices for items you regularly buy or expect to need soon, even if they're not on your grocery list. You may discover an unadvertised special you can use to stock up at a cheaper price than usual. Items that are nonperishable or freeze well are usually your best bets for saving money this way.

To find even more hidden bargains, get to know the supermarket staff. They can clue you in how the store works and when fresh shipments come in. Over time, you'll glean other bits of insider information that may help you nab money-saving opportunities most people miss.

GREAT IDEA

Keep foods warm while waiting to serve

Entertaining, holiday dinners, and other food-centered events means you need to keep a lot of food warm until you can serve it. Fortunately, you may have more warmers available than you expect. Consider trying these ideas.

- Put all your covered dishes in the oven together, and set the oven to 200 degrees. Remove all items after 35 minutes.
- Use your toaster oven and slow cooker as chafing dishes.
- Keep sauce or gravy warm in a thermos.
- Keep foods toasty inside your gas grill, but be careful to use a low setting, and place the food in covered, heat-safe dishes.

To avoid inviting food-poisoning germs to your party, keep all foods above 140 degrees, and don't leave any food at room temperature for more than two hours.

Uncover your grocer's money-saving policies

Ask the supermarket staff or the store manager how you can get a copy of the store's policies. This document can tell you whether the store matches prices charged by other supermarkets, if it will honor coupons from other retailers, and whether you can get a rain check if the store runs out of a sale item. It may also reveal other hidden opportunities to lower your grocery bill.

Freeze bulk buys from the farmer's market. You can't believe the amazing deal you've found at the farmer's market — until you realize you must buy in bulk to get that deal. But if you can freeze part of your bulk-bargain produce, you can enjoy spectacular savings. Use these tips to help.

- Be careful to select produce that's not too ripe for freezing. If you must accept some overly ripe items, use them right away, and freeze the younger produce.

- Make sure you have enough freezer space before you buy, and invest in some high-quality freezer bags to store your produce.

- Check with the seller, the library, your local cooperative extension office, or online sources to determine whether you must blanche your produce before freezing, and for how long.

- Label each freezer bag with the name of its contents and the purchase date. Use your frozen produce within six months. Mark a deadline on your calendar just to be safe.

If the vendors are only offering small amounts of fruits and vegetables, don't be afraid to negotiate to see if you can get a bulk deal for the items you want. You have nothing to lose and potential savings to gain.

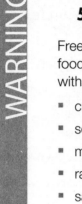

5 bulk-buy foods you cannot freeze

Freezing part of your bulk buys is a great way to keep food from spoiling before you can use it, but don't try it with foods like these. They don't freeze well.

- cream cheese
- sour cream
- mayonnaise
- raw potatoes
- salad vegetables like cabbage, celery, cucumbers, lettuce, parsley, and radishes

Keep your cookbook on the right page. Open your cookbook to the page you want, and use one of these handy ideas to keep it open until you're done cooking.

- For lightweight, paperback cookbooks or single recipe sheets, grab a sturdy hanger and two extra-large binder clips. Hook the hanger over one of the knobs on your upper cabinets. Clip the binder clips around the bottom rung of the hanger, and use them to grip the top edge of your open cookbook so it hangs where you can read it. Another option is to use a skirt hanger.

- Pull the napkins out of your napkin holder, and place your open cookbook in it instead. Shift the book to the right or left as needed so you can read the entire recipe.

- If your cookbook is small enough, slide it into a gallon-size or pint-size resealable bag. For best results, make sure the thicker side of the book is near the open end. Press the air out, seal the bag, and set the open book on your counter.

- Rest a clear glass casserole dish or clear cutting board on top of your open cookbook. Read the recipe through the glass.

GREAT IDEA

Put leftover green tea to work

Your leftover green tea can make meat healthier and more tender. A recent study found that beef marinated in green tea for six hours forms up to 75 percent fewer cancer-causing compounds during pan-frying.

Use unsweetened green tea to marinate either beef or chicken. If your leftover tea was sweetened with sugar, it will make an ideal marinade for barbecued meats and steak.

Keep reusable bags germ-free. Researchers have found a number of illness-causing bacteria on reusable bags, but a few smart habits can help protect you from getting food poisoning or other bugs from these bags.

- Wash your bags after each shopping trip. Check the care label to find out whether the bag is machine washable or must be hand washed. Let each bag dry thoroughly before you store it.

- Wipe insulated bags with a disinfecting or sanitizing wipe, especially the nooks and crannies.

- Designate a particular bag for meats, another for seafood, and a third for produce. Label these bags accordingly, and do not use them to carry anything else. In fact, never put nonfood items in a reusable grocery bag used to carry food items.

- Put raw meat in a plastic bag before placing it in a reusable bag.

- Storing the bags in the trunk so you won't forget them may seem like a good idea, but don't do it. The temperature and humidity in a trunk can be a great environment for bacteria to grow in.

Prepackage for crunch times

Cook faster during busy weeks by doing some clever prepackaging. Store recipe ingredients together in a tray, box top, or basket in your pantry or refrigerator. Instead of hunting for individual bottles, bags, and packages, you'll simply grab and go.

Measure out the dry ingredients for recipes into a resealable bag and label it. You'll get the convenience of a mix without the painful price tag.

Love your morning smoothies? Pre-chop the ingredients you'll need for each day, and freeze each serving in its own bag or container.

Spend less on milk, juice, and soda. Forget "no pain, no gain." You can save money on milk, juice, and soda without feeling deprived.

First, stop using fresh milk in cooking. Buy less-expensive nonfat dry milk to use instead. To replace one cup of skim milk in a recipe, mix one-third cup of nonfat dry milk with seven-eighths cup of water. To replace one cup of whole milk, use one cup of reconstituted dry milk.

You can also use nonfat dry milk to stretch the milk you drink. Mix up the nonfat dry milk according to the package directions. Fill your glass with three parts fresh milk and one part of the dry milk mixture. Gradually work up to equal parts fresh milk and dry milk. You can even try drinking the dry milk mixture on its own, but chill it first for best results.

Some veteran skim milk drinkers say they save money by watering down 2 percent or full-fat milk so it tastes like skim milk. But keep in mind, this may also affect your intake of calcium, vitamin D, protein, and other nutrients, and it only saves money if higher-fat milks are the same price as skim milk.

Stretching juice and soda is easier than stretching milk. Just start by mixing the beverage with a small amount of water. Gradually increase the amount of water over time, while reducing the amount of juice or soda. If you don't like the combination, replace the water with another beverage that is less expensive than the soda or juice. You may discover a delicious new flavor combination – and you'll still save money.

Clever new ways to use kitchen tools. Discover how your pizza cutter, ice cream scoop, and other tools can do more to make your kitchen work easier and faster.

- Use your pizza cutter to cut waffles, pancakes, finger sandwiches, brownies, French toast, quesadillas, cooked pasta, pitas, and sheet cakes. You can also use it to cut sliced cheese, sliced deli meat, or lettuce into strips for salads or tacos.

- Let your ice cream scoop do double duty by using it to scoop out sandwich fillings like tuna salad.

- Scoop seeds out of foods like winter squash, hot peppers, cucumbers, or apples with your melon baller.

- Drain canned foods with your colander to save time. Just put it in the sink and let the food drain while you get other things done. If you need to save the drained juices, put a bowl beneath the colander first.

- Tongs are remarkably versatile. Use them to pull toast out of the toaster. If they're metal, make sure you unplug the toaster first. You can also use them to fish food out of a hot pot or pan on the stove. And they make a surprisingly great juicer. Bring your orange, lemon, or lime to room temperature, roll it on the counter, and slice it down the center. Then simply plunge your closed tongs into the center, and twist them back and forth to extract the juice. Strain out the seeds, and your fresh juice is ready for your favorite recipe.

4 ways to make money-saving food choices. Get the ingredients and foods you need for less just by visiting a different part of your grocery store. It's easier than you think, and you can experiment with techniques like these to see which ones you like.

- Replace expensive ingredients with cheaper substitutes. For example, try switching from cardamom to equal parts ground cinnamon and ground cloves, or use canned salmon when recipes call for fresh or frozen salmon. You can even replace part of the meat in a recipe with cheaper ingredients like beans or oatmeal. For more tips, check the cookbooks in your local library or log on to *www.foodsubs.com*.

- Buy fresh fruits and vegetables when they're in season. For out-of-season produce, compare the price of the fresh version with canned or frozen options. Buy the one that's cheaper.

- Choose the most natural and least-processed version of the food. Buy whole meats, cheeses, fruits, and vegetables instead of pre-sliced or precut versions. Skip prepackaged salad greens in favor of washing and chopping your own. Choose rolled oats instead of instant oats. Some people even make their own condiments, mixes, snacks, and sauces from scratch, and claim to save hundreds every year.

- If you buy organic produce, you may have another option. According to the Environmental Working Group, fruits and vegetables with the least amount of pesticide residue include avocados, pineapples, cabbage, onions, corn, asparagus, mangoes, papayas, kiwi, cantaloupe, eggplant, grapefruit, cauliflower, and sweet potatoes. Consider buying conventional versions of these foods instead of their pricier organic siblings.

Find a hidden opportunity for savings. Take this test the next time you go shopping. Make a grocery list of what you need. When you return from shopping, compare your grocery list to your supermarket receipt. Notice which items appear on your receipt that were not on your list. A couple of these may be things you simply forgot to list, but the rest may be impulse buys. Add up the cost of your impulse buys to see how much money you can save on future grocery trips. Take this test every time you shop, and you'll be surprised at how easy it becomes to resist impulse buys.

Go on a treasure hunt for food bargains

The price you pay at your supermarket may not be the best price you can get. You may find bigger bargains at sellers like farmer's markets, warehouse stores, dollar stores, ethnic markets, and hard discounter stores such as Aldi's. You can also check for salvage grocery stores near you by visiting *www.extremebargains.net*.

When you visit these stores, read labels carefully and check expiration dates and product quality to make sure you buy a product that's just as good — and as safe to eat — as the one at your regular grocery store.

Spend less time on coupons to save more. Coupon queens report massive savings on every trip they make to the supermarket, but those savings may require hours of time spent hunting, reviewing, and organizing coupons. Use these three rules to get the most savings for the least amount of work.

- Only cut out coupons for items you planned to buy anyway. Otherwise, your coupons may cost more than they save. To find the right coupons more easily, glance over the packaging of products you regularly buy. You may find one hidden behind a label.

- Don't clip a coupon unless it can save more money than buying the store brand. In many cases, your grocery store's house brand may be cheaper than buying a name brand item with a coupon.

- Aim to use your coupon when the item is on sale or when you can combine a store coupon with a manufacturer's coupon. Look for store coupons in the store's weekly ad flyer and manufacturer's coupons in the Sunday paper. It should tell you at the top of the coupon which one it is. Just be sure to ask whether your store allows them to be used together before you try this trick.

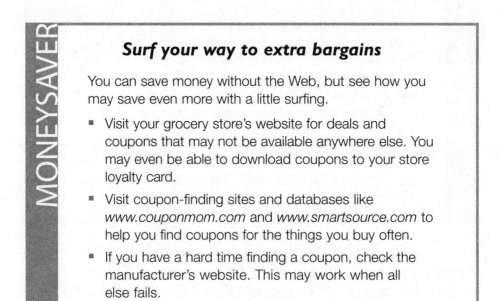

MONEYSAVER

Surf your way to extra bargains

You can save money without the Web, but see how you may save even more with a little surfing.

- Visit your grocery store's website for deals and coupons that may not be available anywhere else. You may even be able to download coupons to your store loyalty card.

- Visit coupon-finding sites and databases like *www.couponmom.com* and *www.smartsource.com* to help you find coupons for the things you buy often.

- If you have a hard time finding a coupon, check the manufacturer's website. This may work when all else fails.

Turn tough meat tender with a Chinese secret. Buy tougher cuts of meat for less, and use a Chinese cooking technique called velveting to transform the meat into tender morsels for stir-fry dishes. This technique is similar to the ones used by Chinese food restaurants.

Slice one pound of beef into small pieces, cutting across the grain. Season with salt, if you want. In a separate bowl, mix one large egg white with one tablespoon of cornstarch. Coat your beef pieces with this mixture. Before marinating, you can also add flavorings such as soy sauce, rice wine, dry sherry, or sesame oil.

Place the beef in a sealed container, and let marinate in the refrigerator for 20 to 30 minutes. While you wait, prepare a colander or
paper towels for draining the beef after it cooks. You have two ways
you can cook the beef. Choose the one most convenient for you.

- Heat two cups of vegetable oil or peanut oil in a wok until the
  temperature reaches 275 degrees. Remove the beef from the
  refrigerator. Cook small batches for 30 seconds, using a wooden
  spoon to separate pieces so they cook properly. They will float
  to the surface when cooked. Remove the beef and drain it.

- Choose a pot large enough to cover the beef in water. Fill with
  water and bring to a boil. Reduce the heat to medium, add the
  beef, and cook for two to three minutes while stirring. Remove
  the beef and drain it.

Cook the beef along with the rest of your stir-fry ingredients, and
be sure to toss or stir the meat to make certain it's thoroughly
cooked. Even with the extra heating time, the meat will come out
unbelievably tender.

GREAT IDEA

Soften beef with just two ingredients

Consider this alternative to traditional velveting if you're
short on ingredients but long on time. Slice meat thinly
against the grain. Put a half cup of cornstarch per pound
of meat in a bowl or plate. Coat the meat with cornstarch,
and add water or soy sauce to make a paste. Mix the
beef thoroughly in this paste, and marinate in the refrigerator for four to five hours. After marinating, drain off any
excess liquid, and follow your usual process for adding
the beef to a stir-fry.

Holidays & special occasions
Creative ways to celebrate

Unlikely source for gift-giving discounts. Warehouse clubs may be the best kept secret for snagging a good deal on presents. They sell everything from jewelry and flowers to movie tickets and gift cards at below-retail prices. Where else can you buy a gift card for less than its face value?

Costco leads the pack with a wide array of offerings, but Sam's Club and BJ's aren't far behind. Buy tickets to special events like Cirque du Soleil or travel packages to places like Alaska. Live plants and floral bouquets, golf passes, and gift certificates for local attractions also make for great holiday, birthday, or anniversary presents.

You'll find some items in-store, but others are only available through the store's website, often with free shipping. So start shopping for gifts through your warehouse store a little early to be sure they arrive on time.

Score huge savings by shopping online. The Internet can be a bargain shopper's dream. It's bursting with coupons and special deals that could save you hundreds of dollars on all sorts of gifts. You just have to know how to find them.

Start by signing up for Facebook (*www.facebook.com*) or Twitter (*www.twitter.com*). Besides staying in touch with friends and family, these websites can be a gateway to crazy coupons and secret deals.

Visit the Facebook page of a brand or retailer and "like" it to receive coupons or alerts about special sales and offers. Open a Twitter account and "follow" the same brand or retailer to qualify for super discounts.

Or let websites like *www.bradsdeals.com, www.retailmenot.com,* and *www.mybargainbuddy.com* do the legwork for you. These scan the Internet all day, every day for deals on everything from clothing and coffee to computers and jewelry. Another website, *www.restaurant.com,* specializes in discounted gift certificates to local restaurants. Simply type in your location to see all the available offers.

As the holidays approach, specialty websites pop up to help you track sales. Try *www.bfads.net* to see Black Friday store ads weeks before they are published on Thanksgiving Day. You can also search ads for the best deal on a given item and organize your Black Friday shopping list.

You can even find free shipping from almost any store, any day of the year, at *www.freeshipping.org.* This website lists current code words you can type into a retailer's website during checkout to score free shipping on your purchase. Or simply put off buying your Christmas gifts until Free Shipping Day. One day a year, hundreds of retailers offer free shipping on online purchases. To learn this year's date, visit *www.freeshippingday.com.*

Simple trick to stick to your shopping budget. It's so easy to lose track of how much money you've spent on holiday gifts, even if you pay with cash. Don't run out of money before buying your last present. Figure out at the beginning how much you can afford to spend this year on gifts. Then write that amount in the balance column on a blank page in your check register. Each time you buy a present, write down the recipient's name in the description column and the amount spent under the withdrawal or debit column. Subtract this from your remaining balance, and you'll easily be able to see how much money you have left. No guess work and no unpleasant surprises when the holiday bills roll in.

Credit card perk saves you money. Some people prefer shopping with a credit card for convenience or safety. If you're one of them, make sure you take advantage of a valuable but often overlooked credit card perk – price protection, or price rewind. Many credit cards promise that if you use them to buy an item now and you find it cheaper at a later date, they will refund the difference. This may be especially helpful if you do your holiday shopping in advance. No more worrying that your gifts will go on sale later on.

You may have to jump through some hoops to claim your refund, such as documenting the lower price and submitting it to the card company along with proof of your original purchase. And some items aren't covered, like jewelry, closeout specials, or online purchases. But spending a few minutes untangling the red tape could earn you a fat refund. Check your card's benefits for details.

MONEYSAVER

Simple guide to the best discounts

Just because something is on sale does not mean it's a good deal. Retailers know how much people love markdowns. They set the price of goods like clothing artificially high, so they can then offer big discounts and still make plenty of money.

When is a sale truly a good deal? According to the website Shop It To Me, clothes that are at least 42 percent off are actually good deals in November and December. Expect even bigger discounts after the holidays, in mid- to late-January. You'll get around 46 percent off.

Never forget another birthday gift. Designate a drawer, bin, or shelf in your closet to store gifts you buy throughout the year. Then, when you see a great item on clearance or score a super deal with a coupon, snatch it up and put it in your presents pile. For really good finds, consider buying two or three of the same item and setting them aside when you need a gift to give on short notice. The same goes for cards. Grocery and drug stores occasionally offer coupons on cards for special occasions. When that happens, stock up. The next time you forget a friend's upcoming birthday, you'll be ready.

Share the fun — and cost — of giving. Split the cost and double the fun of homemade gifts and accessories. Call a couple of friends over for a present party. Only, instead of swapping gifts, you'll be making them. Decide together what sort of homemade gifts to give this year. Cookies? Preserves? Scented bath salts? Then pool your money and go shopping. Share the cost of everything – the ingredients, plus the jars, gift baskets, ribbon, or greenery you'll wrap them in. If you're each good at making a different goody or craft, then make batches large enough to divvy up among you. Spend a few hours with your friends making and wrapping your presents together. You'll save money, have a blast, and make new memories.

Give new life to old baskets. Make the most ordinary gifts seem special by grouping them in a woven basket wound with leftover ribbon. Keep your eyes open for inexpensive baskets at garage sales and thrift stores throughout the year. Weave lengths of ribbon between the slats along the sides of each basket or around the handle. Crumple tissue paper in the bottoms to keep gifts upright.

Fabric-wrapped gifts in 4 simple steps. Tired of wrestling with tape and wrapping paper? Use scarves or scraps of fabric for an elegant, creative solution. The Japanese call it furoshiki, and it's a brilliant way to use up leftover fabric cluttering your sewing room.

Start with a square-shaped gift, since these are easiest to wrap. You'll need about 1 square yard of fabric to wrap a gift the size of a shoe box. Cut the fabric with pinking sheers, if needed, to keep the cloth from fraying.

Lay it diagonally on your sewing table, print-side down, with the box in the center. Pick up the corner closest to you, pull it over the box toward the opposite corner, and tuck any extra fabric under the box. Now grab the corner on the far side, and pull it toward you and over the top of the box. Grasp the right and left corners, bring them to the center of the box, and tie them together in a simple, overhand knot.

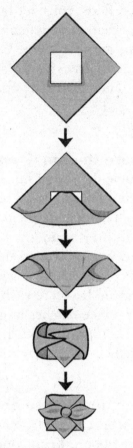

You can try variations of this, too. Instead of folding two of the corners over, tie them together in the center, followed by the other diagonal corners. This is known as "yotsu musubi," or the four-tie wrap. Pin a brooch to your knot for added zing.

If tying knots is hard on your hands, don't worry. Simply gather the corners at the top of the box, and wrap a ribbon around the neck of the fabric.

Give the love of your life the best present ever. Being married for many years can sometimes take the shine off love. Get your relationship gleaming again with a special gift for your spouse. Start a diary titled, "The Reasons I Love You." Every day for a month, write down at least two things you love about your partner. They can be as simple as making the coffee early each morning so it's ready when you wake up, or making you feel loved and safe.

Intersperse photos or drawings between your comments to make it even more meaningful. Wrap it up for the next big occasion, and be prepared for the hug of a lifetime.

Follow these rules for regift success. Regifting is something of an art form. It's hard to know when it's appropriate, and it can make for an awkward situation if you get caught. The experts at Money Management International, the force behind the how-to website Regiftable.com, say that in many cases there's nothing wrong with giving a gift you got from someone else as long as you follow a few guidelines.

- Only give items that are new and still in their original packaging. If you've peeled off the wrapper, you probably shouldn't give it as a gift.

- Never, ever regift something handmade or otherwise unique, including monogrammed or autographed items.

- Think carefully about who gave you the item in the first place. Don't regift it to someone they are likely to bump into.

- Only give it to someone whom you really think would like it. Remember, regifting is not an opportunity to clear the white elephants out of your closet.

So what items make for good candidates? Nice, unopened bottles of wine; unused gift cards; CDs or DVDs still in the original wrapper; and books with crisp, clean pages and uncracked spines are just a few.

Spring for nice wrapping paper and a new name tag. After all, it's not as if you had to pay for the thing to begin with. Better yet, crochet gift bags for these twice-loved presents, so your recipient gets something truly unique.

And don't feel bad about regifting. Do it well, and your gift will be enjoyed just as much as if you bought it yourself.

Transform tightwad gifts into treasures of love. The most treasured presents are sometimes free. If you've hit a year where you can't afford to buy anything, consider it an opportunity. Have you been meaning to bequeath an heirloom to someone in the family? This may be the year to do it. Wrap it with love, write a heartfelt note about what it meant to you, and give it with good cheer.

Food is a crowd-pleaser when budgets are tight. Make a friend's favorite dish for her birthday. Wrap ribbon around jars of your homemade jam, and give them at Christmas to friends and family. Use tins from past holidays to hold fresh-baked cookies. Tasty treats like these, given with a warm note telling someone how much you appreciate them, are as good as any gift money can buy.

Slash shopping time with themed gifts. Want to make holiday shopping a breeze this year? Pick a theme for the gifts you'll be giving. Decide in advance that everyone will get something sweet from the candy store, or something new for their kitchen. Then you can do all of your shopping in one store and avoid the madness of multiple trips to the mall to find the right size or perfect color.

Take themed gift-giving to the next level by personalizing it. For instance, grab a few picture frames the next time they go on sale at the arts-and-crafts store. Raid your photo albums, and insert special images into the discount frames. Give your daughter a photo of your mother as a little girl, or a friend a picture of the two of you on vacation. They'll appreciate the gifts, and you'll finish your shopping in record time.

Turn throwaway paper into one-of-a-kind wrap. Any piece of paper with a pretty drawing or interesting image can be turned into custom gift wrap. So save the fold-out maps that come with your National Geographic magazine. Gather together old cards. Raid your sewing room for patterns you no longer need. Wrap a CD for the music-lover in your life with old sheet music. Cover presents for a nature-loving friend in maps of hiking trails. Pick up used children's books at the thrift store, carefully tear out the pages, and use them to wrap your grandkids' gifts. Ideas like these not only make use of what you would otherwise throw away — they add excitement to the opening of any gift.

Pretty packages from pine cones and twine. Create elegant, rustic bows with pine cones from your own backyard. Loop ribbon or raffia into bows and secure with twine or hobby wire. Then attach the pine cones to the center of the bow, using either hot glue or wire. Tie the bow onto the gift with twine for a natural look, or with matching ribbon. Spruce up your gift even more by substituting a few sprigs of greenery like cedar twigs in place of the bow. Wire the sprigs and pine cones together, then tie to the package with twine.

Organize twisted ribbons. Tangled ribbons or missing rolls make your crafting projects take longer. Put an end to that frustration. Use a leftover length of roof gutter to neatly corral all your rolls of ribbon in a dispenser. To put your gutter to work, attach end caps and mount it on the wall above your workspace. To jazz it up, decorate with stickers, stencils and paints, or rubber stamps before mounting.

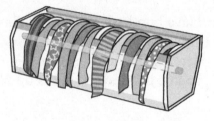

After you mount the gutter, add a small, expandable, tension curtain rod from your local discount department store or home improvement store. Thread your ribbon rolls on the tension rod, drop this row of rolls into your gutter, and expand the rod so it rests gently against the inside of the gutter's end caps. Let the end of the ribbon from each roll hang over the gutter's edge. The next time you need some ribbon, simply pull out the length you need and snip.

Same ribbon problem, different solution

To easily organize ribbons without using a gutter, mount an old kitchen paper towel dispenser above your workspace, and thread your ribbon rolls on it. Place any remaining rolls side by side in a shoe box, poke holes in one of the long sides of the box, and thread one ribbon through each hole.

Wrap lights fast for easy storage. Ever notice that garland comes wrapped around a piece of cardboard? Why not try the same idea with strands of holiday lights? Cut a piece of cardboard about 10 inches long and 8 inches wide. Then cut a notch in each end on opposite sides to hold the lights in place. Slide one end of the strand through a notch and begin wrapping it around the cardboard. When you reach the end, slide it through the other notch. Make one holder for each strand, and stand them on their sides in a sturdy box.

Have hundreds of feet of lights to wind? Cheat by wrapping them around an old hose reel. Admit it – you stopped winding your garden hose on it a long time ago, so put it to good use. Use the reel's handle to wind the lights up fast.

Store fragile ornaments in everyday containers. Don't fret if you threw away the box that housed your breakable ornaments. Put plastic cups, egg cartons, and seedling trays to work storing these fragile items. Start with a large, sturdy box or plastic storage bin and a package of plastic cups. Place a medium-sized ornament into each cup in the bottom of the box. Once you fill up the bottom row, lay a piece of cardboard over the cups and start the second row. Store smaller ornaments in egg cartons or seedling trays. Super-sized ornaments can go in the pockets of a six-pack bottle carrier. Wrap particularly precious or fragile keepsakes in tissue paper or Bubble Wrap for extra protection.

Keep gift wrap corralled and crush-free. Store your wrapping paper where it won't get in the way or get crushed – the ceiling of the closet. Hang an extra section of wire shelving about 4 inches below the ceiling. And instead of running the shelving lengthwise, hang it perpendicular from the front of the closet to the back. This creates a shelf across the top of the closet, where you can slide rolls of wrapping paper up and out of sight.

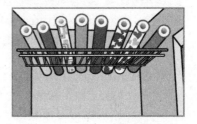

That may be too high to reach if you're on the short side. In that case, stand your rolls along the inside of the closet. Anchor screws in the back and front of the closet about 4 inches from the corner and 10 inches above the floor. Then anchor another set about 10 inches above these, one in the back wall and one in the front. Connect the screws in the back wall with those in the front with twine or wire. Simply slide wrapping paper rolls between the wall and the wire.

Keep the paper from unraveling with an empty roll of toilet paper. Cut the empty tube lengthwise, and slip it over the rolled-up gift wrap. Now your paper is neat, tidy, and ready to go.

Store your tree in 10 minutes or less. Remember this storage trick the next time you're tempted to leave your artificial Christmas tree up year round just to avoid taking it down. Have a helper lift the tree off the stand and lay it on the ground. Fold the limbs up to make the tree as slim as possible. Measure its length, and head to your local hardware store. Look for a concrete form tube or large PVC pipe wide enough and long enough to hold the tree. When you get home, simply slide the tube up the folded tree from the bottom. Store it standing in the closet or garage for easy access next year.

Fashion a wreath for all seasons. One wreath form can serve all four seasons with just a few tweaks. Start with a foam form, florist's picks, straight pins, and hobby wire.

- In summer, use florist's picks to attach whole citrus fruits like oranges and limes. Start with the largest fruits, then fill in the gaps with the smaller ones and with large, glossy leaves from a shrub in your yard. Attach hot peppers with straight pins for an added pop of color.

- Follow the same pattern in fall with seasonal apples or pears. Attach large fruits with florist's picks and smaller ones, like cranberries, with straight pins. Add a cluster of pomegranates to give your wreath an exotic flair. Wire on pine cones for a touch of fall.

- For a winter wreath that's sure to wow, wire together clusters of evergreen sprigs from your yard, then wire them onto the form. Hide the wires by pinning on seasonal goodies such as clementines and small winter squash.

- In spring, use florist's picks to attach small grapefruits to the foam wreath. Space them out more or less evenly, then attach a scattering of kumquats with straight pins. Add natural greenery by using straight pins to attach clusters of seasonal legumes such as snow and snap peas still in the shell.

Indoor "tree" changes with the seasons. Dress up your table or mantel for any holiday with branches from your own back yard. Find a fallen branch with an interesting shape and several twigs sprouting from it. You'll use these to hang ornaments. Brush it off and bring it indoors, then decide whether to spray paint the wood or leave it natural. For holidays like Christmas, spraying it white or silver creates a lovely winter wonderland-look.

Next, display it in a decorative bowl or vase. Fill the bowl with sand or floral foam to keep the branch upright. Hide the foam with Spanish moss or glittery garland. Use fishing line, yarn, or ribbon to hang seasonal ornaments from the twisted twigs of your indoor tree — plastic Easter eggs, small Christmas ornaments, or whatever else strikes your fancy. You can reuse your "tree" year round, changing out the decorations with each season.

DIY ornaments in under a minute. It's the world's easiest way to make your own ornaments. Pick up a package of clear ornament globes at the craft store, pop off the tops, and fill them with whatever you like — tinsel, pine needles, tissue paper and glitter, or anything you can imagine. Hang them from your tree with colored ribbons for one-of-a-kind decorations.

Special jar celebrates holiday blessings. Everyone needs to be reminded of their blessings sometimes, and Thanksgiving is the perfect time to do that. Help your loved ones reflect on their good fortune with a blessings jar or gratitude wreath. Cut orange and yellow construction paper into 3-inch by 4-inch pieces and set them by the door, along with markers. Set a large mason jar on the table, or hang a plain wreath made of twigs or vines on the door.

Ask each guest who shows up for Thanksgiving dinner to write down one thing they are thankful for as they come in the door. Have them drop their notes into the jar or slide it between the twigs in the wreath. At the end of dinner, bring the jar or wreath to the table, and read each note aloud. Save yours and reread it when you need a reminder of your own blessings.

Eye-catching way to display cards. Standing holiday and birthday cards on the mantel is boring. Find a new way to show them off. Drape a length of garland or festive beads along your banister. Punch holes in the top of each card, and use ribbon or yarn to hang them from the strand. Don't have a stairway? Hang the cards and garland across the front of a mirror, mantel, or window, instead.

WARNING

Candles could be making you sick

Your sore throat or cough could be caused by the candles you're burning. Experts say some people with indoor allergies or lung irritation may actually be reacting to candles made from paraffin, a byproduct of petroleum.

Burning paraffin candles can contribute to indoor air pollution and expose you to cancer-causing chemicals. Burning the occasional candle probably won't hurt, says South Carolina State University (SCSU) researcher Amid Hamidi. "But lighting many paraffin candles every day for years, or lighting them frequently in an unventilated bathroom around a tub, for example, may cause problems."

Ruhullah Massoudi, professor of chemistry at SCSU, agrees. "For a person who lights a candle every day for years or just uses them frequently, inhalation of these dangerous pollutants drifting in the air could contribute to the development of health risks like cancer, common allergies, and even asthma." Avoid these problems altogether by burning soy or beeswax candles. They cost a little more, but they do not release indoor air pollutants the way paraffin candles do.

Design a simple but stunning centerpiece. No need to buy a fancy candelabra for your table or fireplace mantel. Make your own candle centerpiece at home using mason jars or clear glass tumblers. Fill half of the glass container with small seasonal nuts or acorns from your own yard. Then set a votive or tealight candle in the center. Do this for as many jars as you like. Line them up in a row along your mantel, sideboard, or table. Place a runner beneath them for color or weave a ribbon between the glasses.

Put old lamps to work in new ways. Give old hurricane and kerosene lamps a new job to do. Remove the glass covers and set them on your mantel or fireplace. Then coil short strands of white Christmas lights in the bottom of each glass, leaving the plugs hanging out. Cluster the glasses together or line them up in a row. Plug the end of each light strand into the one next to it, and the final one into an outlet, for a unique display of holiday cheer.

Streamline and simplify holiday decorating. Holidays should be joyous and fun, not stressful and exhausting. Don't knock yourself out decorating your whole home. Focus on just three areas — say, the mantel, the Christmas tree, and the dining room table. Choose the three you and your guests spend the most time in or that have the greatest visual impact when you first enter the house. Simplify even further by throwing a tree-trimming party. Turn decorating into an excuse for visiting with close friends. You supply the food and decorations, they supply the helping hands to get your home ready for the holidays.

Take a plain bowl from ordinary to extraordinary. At Christmas, fill clear glass containers such as bowls, jars, or snifters with something shiny, like glittery ornaments or jingle bells. Keep it looking elegant by following a basic design rule — fill the glass with items that are similar shapes and colors but a variety of sizes, or similar sizes and shapes but in different colors. What if you don't have clear glass? A solid-colored bowl or even a cake stand can make a gorgeous centerpiece. For deep bowls, fill the bottom two-thirds with sand and the top one-third with shiny jingle bells or ornaments to hide the sand. Skip the filler for shallow containers, like cake stands. Nestle candles of different sizes amidst the baubles, and place on a table or sideboard.

Make fallen trees into custom candle holders. Create one-of-a-kind pillar candles with a drill and a fallen tree. Save a few logs the next time you or a neighbor has a tree taken down. Find a limb or trunk at least 2 inches wide, if you plan to light taper candles, or wider if you prefer votive candles. Cut a relatively straight piece of the wood into a variety of lengths, as short or long as you like. Try to make your cuts straight, so that your logs end up with flat tops and bottoms. With a spade (boring) bit, drill a hole in the top center of each log. Use a bit the same width as the base of your candles.

Stand up your logs and drop in your candles. For the most eye-catching effect, choose trees with interesting bark, like birch, and cluster your candle logs together in groups.

Free help with holiday planning. A clever idea called Christmas Countdown can help you stay on top of holiday preparations, from shopping to tree trimming to cooking. It's a free, six-week system that starts in late October on the website Organizedhome.com. Its goal — to get you organized so you can enjoy the holidays with less stress. Each week of the countdown features a different theme.

One may focus on getting your holiday budget in order, while another tackles your Christmas card list or meal planning. You can print ready-made checklists and planning forms for each week and sign up for daily inspirational emails with recipe and craft ideas. Just visit the website *http://christmas.organizedhome.com/christmas-countdown* to get started.

WARNING

Wash hands after handling this holiday staple

Christmas lights are pretty, but they may harbor a hidden danger. Four out of five sets of holiday lights contain lead, according to research, mostly around the base of the bulbs. Half contain enough lead that they need a warning label when sold in California.

"Lead is in the PVC jacketing that connects Christmas lights to each other," explains Joseph Laquatra, professor of design and environmental analysis at Cornell University. "Because of this, strings of Christmas lights should be handled carefully."

You can still enjoy their warm, cheerful glow as long as you take some common-sense precautions. Wear gloves while hanging lights on your tree or home. Wash your hands thoroughly if you handle them bare-handed. Look for lights that claim to be RoHS (Restriction of Hazardous Substances) compliant. These should contain little or no lead.

Most importantly, don't let children handle Christmas lights, and keep pets away from them. "Very small amounts of lead can cause serious health problems, especially in children," Laquatra warns. "There is no known safe exposure level to lead."

Turn topiary forms into twinkling displays. Put the topiary forms collecting dust in your shed to work as holiday decor. Stand them beside the fireplace or on your front porch and wrap them with twinkling strings of lights. A lighted topiary can even double as a Christmas tree when you don't have the time or energy to put up a regular one. Potted topiary forms add festive flair, too, as climbing vines lend a touch of green in winter. Move the pot, plant, and topiary indoors and wrap with lights for instant holiday cheer.

Hang holiday garland with ease. Don't worry about trying to weave a long garland of fresh greenery or tinsel through the rungs and rail of your banister. Do it the easy way. Stretch greenery along the top of the banister, and tie it on with hobby wire. For tinsel garlands, drape them in swags down the side of the banister, tying the top of each swag to the rail with wire. Either way, wrap ribbon around the garland to hide the wire.

Dress up Easter eggs beyond plain dye. Wow guests at your next Easter luncheon with elegant, one-of-a-kind egg decorations. Raid your fabric chest for scraps of lace, or cut up an old lace tablecloth. Wrap it tightly around a boiled egg, gather the loose ends, and tie them together with wire, yarn, or a rubber band. Use the fabric ends to dunk the egg in a dye bath. Afterward, untie the fabric to reveal a delicate, lacy pattern on the shell. For a glitzy look, skip the lace in favor of glue and glitter. Boil then dye your eggs as usual. Once they dry, squirt small dots of glue all over each one, then sprinkle glitter on the glue.

Quick and easy pumpkin carving. You don't need a pumpkin carving kit to make scary-good jack-o-lanterns. Chances are, you have all the tools you need in your garage right now. Use a drywall saw to cut through the thick pumpkin rind. It's perfect for removing the top of the pumpkin and carving the eyes and mouth. For perfectly round eyes, mouths, or noses, turn to the drill. Use regular bits for small holes, spade bits for medium ones, and a hole saw for large ones.

Help your pumpkin last through Halloween with a little lemon juice. Rub down the inside of your carved-out pumpkin with half a lemon. Squeeze the juice from the other half and brush it on any cut areas, like the insides of the eyes or mouth. The juice's acid will slow down the rotting process and inhibit mold.

Dress up your dinner table. Add a touch of class to your next dinner party with fancy, folded napkins. The classic fan can be arranged three ways — standing on the plate, slipped in a wine glass, or tucked into a napkin ring.

1. Flatten the napkin on the table and fold the top half over to the bottom.

2. Begin pleating the napkin from either the right or left side, and stop when you have about 2 inches left.

3. Fold the napkin in half again, this time bringing the bottom half up to the top.

4. Grasp the top corner of the unpleated piece, fold it downward, and tuck it inside the pleats. This creates a stand to keep the napkin upright.

5. Now unfurl the pleats, and stand the napkin on a plate for a beautiful fan.

You can tuck it into a glass or napkin ring, too. Simply pleat the entire napkin rather than leave 2 inches for a stand. Once pleated, fold the entire napkin in half, and place in a wine glass or slide into a napkin ring.

Turn scrap fabric into fantastic table linens. Nice table linens don't have to cost a fortune. You can make them yourself from throwaway fabric in the remnant bin at your local craft store. Cut your pieces to size, and trim stray threads from fabric edges. If you sew, attach a line of bias tape over the edges to finish them.

If not, try one of these three no-sew methods for making scrap fabric look finished.

- Cut along the edges of the fabric with pinking shears to limit fraying.

- Fold the raw edges of the fabric under and "hem" them with bonding tape and a warm iron.

- Fold the edges under and iron them flat to hide them from guests.

Look for upholstery fabric for place mats and sturdy linen for napkins and tablecloths. Keep in mind how washable the fabric is, since it's likely to need laundering after big family gatherings.

Foolproof techniques for a fabulous buffet. Hosting a holiday dinner party doesn't have to be a lot of fuss and muss. Buffets can take some of the work out of hosting, but don't fret that the serve-yourself style is too casual for nice occasions. Not so. Dress up your buffet as fancy as you please with everyday items from around your home.

Take a tip from designers, and stage foods on the buffet table at different heights. Stack cereal boxes, books, and overturned pots along the table, and cover everything with a large tablecloth. Or create risers that don't need to be hidden using hat boxes, overturned flower pots, or an upside-down cake stand, bowl, or wine glass. Anything that gives you a sturdy, solid base can hold a dish. Set some serving dishes on the raised platforms and others in the valleys between them. Add depth to the table by placing short dishes in front of taller ones.

Create colorful contrasts by serving foods in dishes that offset their colors. For instance, put yellow rice in a purple bowl or pink salmon on a blue plate. If all your dishes are white, add color with fabric. Place a purple napkin under the bowl of rice, or a piece of blue fabric beneath the fish platter. Play with fabrics of different textures or patterns to find what makes the best impression.

Finish your buffet display with a string of white Christmas lights wound between dishes. It adds light and eliminates the danger of a guest burning themselves while reaching over a candle. Hide the light cord with greenery and silk flowers.

3 clever uses for ribbon remnants. Random, leftover pieces of ribbon can amp up the wow factor at any party. Here's how.

- Tie a different colored piece of ribbon around the stem of each wine glass to help your guests tell which glass belongs to them.

- Tie ribbon around small sprigs of seasonal flowers or greenery, and lay a sprig on each plate for delightful place settings.

- Swirl a wide ribbon in a serving bowl or clear vase, fill it with ornaments or unshelled nuts, and artfully weave the ribbon among them.

Fun, fruity ice cubes without a lot of fuss. Dress up party punch and pitchers of plain water with decorative, fruity ice. Chill punch in a large bowl by freezing ice in a bundt pan or gelatin mold. Fill it with 1 inch of water then add layers of sliced fruit. Orange slices, grapefruit wedges, or pomegranate seeds work well and will look pretty. Choose fruits that go well with the flavor of the punch. Add sprigs of mint for a refreshing kick and a dash of green.

Pop the pan in the freezer until frozen. Then remove it and add another 1 to 2 inches of water to fully cover the fruit. Freeze again until you're ready to bring out the punch. Run warm water over the bottom of the pan until the ice releases, and place it in the bowl.

Use the same technique with a muffin pan to chill a pitcher. For normal-sized ice cubes, place a whole, small strawberry, leafy green top and all, in each compartment of an ice cube tray. Fill with water and freeze for a fun way to cool your drink on a hot, summer day.

GREAT IDEA

Party survival tips for the shy

Holidays can be hard on introverts. The social whirl starts around Thanksgiving and doesn't let up until after the New Year. Keep yourself sane while fulfilling your obligations with a few hints.

First, arrive on time. Most people show up to parties "fashionably late," but wait until then and you may have to face a crowd. Get there earlier, and you may be one of only a handful of people present, making it easier to have a relaxed conversation.

Second, pace yourself. Step outside for a few minutes if you need a break at a gathering, or excuse yourself to the restroom. If you're truly having trouble handling all the people, leave a bit early. You shouldn't feel bad about doing so if you were among the first to arrive.

Last, limit the number of functions you agree to attend right from the start, so you aren't exhausted and over-whelmed by the time the holidays finally arrive.

Home & auto insurance

Get the right coverage for the best price

Compare home insurers before you shop. Save yourself from bad home insurance companies and super-inflated prices. To see which home insurers may be worth considering, investigate the two R's — rates and reputation. Start by checking your Yellow Pages or local library for the phone number of your state's insurance department. Or find its website by searching on *www.usa.gov*. State insurance departments often provide information about the typical rates charged by major insurance companies, so you'll soon know which rates are in the right range and which ones are unusually high.

Don't forget to look for each company's rate of consumer complaints. If you can't find it, check the National Association of Insurance Commissioners' educational website at *www.insurance.insureuonline.org*. Look for a link to its Consumer Information Source, where you can find complaint rates for individual companies.

Insure your home for the right amount. Surveys suggest up to 61 percent of homeowners don't have enough insurance to rebuild their homes after a disaster. This may happen to you if your insurer based your policy amount on the real estate value of your home. Unfortunately, the price tag for rebuilding your home could be much higher than the price it would sell for today.

To fix this problem, tell your insurance agent you want the structural limit of your home insurance policy to be based on a rebuild estimate for your home rather than its market value. Your insurer can provide that rebuild estimate. Some experts recommend you also check with local contractors to verify what it would cost to rebuild a home like yours. Recent disasters have revealed that insurer estimates of replacement costs are sometimes too low. You can also get estimates for a reasonable price from a website like *www.accucoverage.com*.

Be prepared for what home insurance won't cover. Don't call your home insurance agent if a sewer backup damages your house. Most home insurance policies don't cover that. They may also exclude damage caused by power outages, mudslides, termites, pets or other animals, mold and mildew, dry and wet rot, war, terrorism, nuclear accidents and explosions, earthquakes, floods, and sinkholes. And that's not even the whole list.

Read your homeowners insurance policy carefully to find out what's excluded and what is not. In some cases, you may even find good news. For example, some policies include limited coverage for mold, and in Florida, sinkholes are always covered. To cover things that are excluded, you need to purchase riders or endorsements from your insurance company or specialty insurance from another insurer. Focus on the coverage gaps that are a big risk in your area or can cause tremendous damage.

For more specific information about floods and earthquakes, see the box on renters insurance, *Avoid a costly insurance mistake.*

Make renters insurance an even better value. If a fire rages through the apartment or home you're renting, the landlord's policy won't cover your personal belongings, but you can insure them with renters insurance for just pennies a day. What's more, those pennies really work hard for you. They can insure $20,000 to $30,000 worth of your stuff against damage from burst pipes, fire, lightning, windstorms, hail, theft, or vandalism. That's why experts recommend renters insurance as a good value.

But if disaster happens, the only way to replace what you've lost is to provide your insurer with a detailed list of every item and its replacement cost. Try naming all the items in your kitchen from memory, and you'll see how this could be a problem. So before a disaster happens, make a home inventory video showing every item in your apartment or rental house. While filming each item, describe it, and estimate how much it cost. When you finish, store a copy of the video with a friend or family member, or upload it to a cloud storage site like Google Drive or Dropbox.

WARNING

Avoid a costly insurance mistake

Renters in earthquake country or flood-prone zones may be in for a nasty surprise sooner or later. That's because renters insurance, like home insurance, doesn't cover floods, earthquakes, or damage from earthquake-caused fires. Fortunately, you can usually still get coverage. Earthquake riders are available for your insurance policy. To find companies that offer flood insurance, visit *www.floodsmart.gov* or call 888-379-9531.

Alert your home insurer after a car break-in. Your car insurance doesn't cover the loss of items like newly bought clothes if they're stolen during a car break-in, but your homeowners insurance does. Surprisingly, home insurance covers some items that aren't inside your home, including personal possessions in your car. Most people are covered for losses equal to as much as 10 percent of their total personal property coverage.

So if your coverage is $100,000, up to $10,000 in stolen possessions may be covered, but check with your insurance agent to be sure. To file a claim for the stolen property, you'll have to meet a deductible and file a police report. Meanwhile, call your car insurance agent as well. If you have comprehensive coverage, that covers damage to your vehicle from the break-in.

3 car insurance discounts you may be missing. Three little-known discounts — advance renewals, life insurance bundling, and working in certain professions — could save you up to 10 percent on your car insurance. Advance renewal means you renew and pay your yearly premium a week or two early, saving you an average of 8 percent. Buying your life insurance from the same company may reduce your car insurance premiums even more. You may even be eligible for a profession-related discount if you are a teacher, engineer, or an employee of certain companies.

These discounts may not be widely available yet, so it pays to ask about them. Also, be sure to check on other common price breaks like:

- driving less than a set amount, such as 10,000 miles, each year.

- sticking with the same company for several years.

- driving a car with safety features like a theft prevention system, airbags, or antilock brakes.

- being over age 55 or having an AARP membership.

- buying your home insurance or disability insurance from the same company.

- having a clean credit record.

- taking a defensive driving course, being a good student, or being married.

- keeping a clean driving record over several years. This may also lower your deductible.

Score a better deal on car insurance. People save an average of $386 a year when they switch car insurers, says a recent survey from J.D. Power and Associates. But you may get a better deal without switching. Take a page from your cable or phone service, and see what happens if you tell your agent you're thinking about changing carriers. You may be pleasantly surprised by what you're offered — and how much you can save.

Of course, you need to shop around first. That will help you find new opportunities for savings and spot where your coverage needs adjusting. Get estimates from other companies for coverage similar to the coverage you want. Show the lower estimates to your insurance agent, tell him you're considering a switch, and ask what kind of deal he can give you.

Resist the temptation to actually change companies unless the benefits greatly outweigh the disadvantages. Switching may come with early termination fees. You may also lose your loyalty discount, accident forgiveness, and any discounts you get from buying two types of insurance from the same company. Plus a new company may not offer the same level of coverage, quality of service, or record of paying claims.

Choose a cheap add-on that can really pay off. You've just been injured in a car accident by a driver with no insurance. You could be stuck for major medical bills unless you have a special type of coverage on your own policy. Uninsured motorist coverage is one of the cheapest kinds of car insurance you can buy, and it could save you a bundle in the long run, experts say.

One out of every seven drivers on the road has no car insurance, and this coverage will pay the medical costs if one of them injures you or your passengers. It may also pay if you're the victim of an underinsured driver who doesn't have enough insurance to fully cover the medical costs. Experts recommend you buy uninsured motorist coverage if you don't already have it. Talk to your auto insurance agent to learn more.

Can driver monitoring save you money? Yes, say some insurers. You may save up to 50 percent on your car insurance if you install a "black box" device in your car that records your driving habits. But actual savings vary depending on what your insurance company measures, the kind of driver you are, and several other factors. That's why it pays to ask questions and learn as much as you can about your insurer's program. Here's where to start.

When you sign up for one of these programs, you agree to provide information on your driving habits to your insurance company so they can evaluate your driving. Whether you get the discount and how deep it is depends on how well you meet your insurer's definition of a low-risk driver.

Some programs mostly look at how many miles you drive, while others may also record your speed, the times of day you drive, where you drive, how hard you accelerate or brake, and how you take corners. Of course, you can't win the discount game if you don't know the rules your particular insurer uses, so ask questions like these before you sign up.

- What does the device record besides mileage?

- What driving habits help me get a bigger discount?

- What driving habits would lower or prevent my discount?

- If my spouse or someone else drives my car, how does that affect my discount?

- Can I lose any of my other discounts due to information the device provides?

GREAT IDEA

Be ready if the unthinkable happens

You can't think straight right after a car accident. That's why you should have expert help on hand to help you report the accident for your insurance claim. Ask your insurance agent for an accident form to keep in your car and fill out at the scene of the accident. If your insurer does not provide a form, visit *www.insureuonline.org* for a form you can print out.

If you have a smartphone or iPad, apps are available to help you through the reporting process. For example, USAA offers an app for the iPad, and Nationwide has one for your Android phone or iPhone. Check with your insurance company to find out whether they offer their own app for accident reporting.

Win a fair payout for your totaled car. Your car may have been declared a total loss, but you can still take steps to avoid a low payout check. Confirm the exact make and model of your car, its age, and its mileage. Visit the library or the Web to check sources like Edmunds (*www.edmunds.com*), the Kelley Blue Book (*www.kbb.com*), and the National Auto Dealers Association (*www.nadaguides.com*) for estimates of the market value of your car just before the wreck.

Print or make a copy of your findings, and average the figures from all three sources. If you have the receipts, add the price of any customizations or extras installed after you bought the car – including the dealer-installed ones.

Because you'll have to pay the sales tax, registration, title and other fees for a new car, insurance allows you to add those figures to your payout. So call your state's department of motor vehicles or visit its website to learn what fees and taxes you'll pay for a new car with the same value as your old car.

Add that to your car's value and subtract your deductible to get your final payout number. If the amount your insurance agent offers is significantly lower, show her your findings and calculations, and campaign for an estimate closer to yours. She may agree to cut you a bigger check.

Home & personal security

Insiders' secrets you need to know

Schedule a free home security check-up. "Many home-owners suffer from a victim mentality, believing that there is little they can do to deter a determined burglar. This isn't the case," says Michael Fraser, former host of BBC's *Beat the Burglar*. "Most burglaries are committed because an opportunity has arisen." To make sure your home won't present opportunities for burglars, call on the experts – the police. Ask your local police department if it offers a free home security audit. Many police departments do. This means you can make an appointment for a police expert to walk through your home, point out the weak spots that put you at risk, and explain how to fix them. It's that simple, and it could make all the difference.

Know what to do when a stranger knocks. Experts warn that some door-to-door salespeople may be burglars. For example, someone may pose as a home security system salesperson so he can enter your house and "case the joint" for a later burglary. To help prevent robberies and other crimes, don't open the door when a stranger knocks or rings your doorbell. Instead, ask who it is and what they want. Or, if you have a peephole, check to see who's there. If the person claims to be:

- a repair worker, meter reader, or employee of a business, utility company, or government agency – ask the person to stand by. Look up his employer's phone number, and verify that he works for them. Don't use a phone number the person gives you unless it matches the number you look up. Only open the door if the person is legitimate and can show you a photo ID, preferably a company ID card.

- a delivery worker – ask who she is delivering to. If she can't tell you, look up her employer's phone number and call to be sure she works for them.

- a security alarm salesperson or any other door-to-door sales-person – call his employer to verify that he works for them. If he does, ask him to leave his office contact details and company information outside the door, so you can research the business and decide whether to schedule a sales appointment.

If the person wants to call 911, a roadside assistance service, or a family member, offer to make the call. Con artists and criminals may quickly vanish after you make this offer, but people with a legitimate problem are likely to stay.

Tricks to brighten your home in a blackout. Don't worry if you don't have enough flashlights when the power goes out. You may have other lights available, and some won't even need matches or batteries. For example, if you have solar landscape lights, bring them inside at sunset. Drop each one into its own tall mason jar or drinking glass, and place them wherever you need light. Put them back outside to recharge the next morning. If you don't have solar lights, leftover glow sticks from a recent kids' party are good substitutes – and they're cheap.

If you can't come up with other lighting, use this trick to get more light from your flashlight. Turn the flashlight's narrow beam into a wider glow by filling a milk jug with water. Rest the flashlight so the lighted end is pressed against the flat outside surface of the jug. The light shining into the jug will be reflected by the water so you get a pleasantly lighted area several feet wide.

Defend against car burglaries. Thieves who break into cars love readily visible goodies, so keep your car from offering a showcase of loot. Always hide your new purchases, purse, electronics, and other valuables so a potential burglar can't see them. Yet be aware that some thieves spy on parking lots to catch people putting purchases or valuables into a hiding place. Here's how you can frustrate them.

Any time you leave your car, lock your trunk and all your doors, and close all your windows. When you can't avoid keeping valuables or new purchases in your car, either pull over and hide them in your trunk before you reach your destination, or plan your shopping so you don't need to hide things before you're ready to leave.

If you must offload purchases to your car and do more shopping, move the car to another section of the lot, preferably a well-lit, busy area far from your original parking spot. If your car has no trunk for hiding things, stash your items under the seat, or cover them completely.

Of course, your best bet is to avoid keeping valuables and purchases in your car for any longer than necessary. Always unload them at home as soon as possible.

Check security features at overseas hotels. Don't assume hotels in foreign countries come with the same security and safety features that are standard in the United States. Experts say that sticking to American chain hotels in foreign nations may help, but you still need to do a quick safety review when you arrive. Aim to think like James Bond, and know how you can protect yourself. Check for secure locks, fire extinguishers, alarms, and fire escapes, and don't assume the balconies are as safe as the ones you're used to. Also examine the windows and doors to see how secure and safe they are.

For added protection, count the doors between your room and the nearest exit. Do the same for an alternate exit. This will help you leave quickly during a fire or any other danger, even if smoke or darkness makes it hard to see.

WARNING

Keep your room number secret

When the hotel clerk tells you your room number, he is broadcasting it to everyone within earshot, even if he doesn't mean to. Take steps to prevent that security lapse. When you check in, tell the clerk you'd like to keep your room number confidential. Ask him to write the number down so no one can overhear it. If strangers are nearby, you can even ask him to fold the paper before handing it to you, so no one can see the number.

Give your home an extra layer of protection while you're away. Call the police before you go on vacation, and ask if they offer a vacation home check program. These programs arrange for police officers or volunteers to either drive by participating homes or perform a walking check of the house while a homeowner is away. And many towns offer the program for free. Simply tell the police when you will leave and return from vacation and what you would like them to do. Some people prefer not to have their house checked as it may tip off potential thieves that they're away. Once you've signed up for a vacation home check, you'll probably enjoy your vacation even more thanks to this extra layer of protection.

Prevent garage door break-ins.
The next time you're locked out of the house, ease a coat hanger through the tiny gap along the top of your garage door. Then you can release the emergency latch and open the garage door from the outside — just like burglars do.

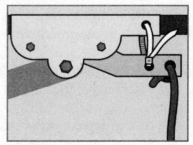

Of course, if you can get in, thieves can, too. But don't worry. You can make your garage door more secure with just a couple of plastic cable ties, also known as zip ties.

Remember, all automatic garage doors have an emergency release you can trigger by pulling the handle. Typically, you'll find the release beneath the door track that runs along the center of the garage. Thread a zip tie through the holes in the release mechanism and its handle so both are tied in place and the emergency release can't open the garage door. If you need to open the door manually, a hard yank should snap the fastener so the emergency release can work again. But play it safe. Keep a tall step stool and scissors in the garage or nearby, just in case you need to cut the zip tie.

What to do if you're stranded in a winter storm.
Thousands of Georgia drivers were stranded on interstates for up to 22 hours during a 2014 winter storm. Two weeks later, the same thing happened to thousands of drivers in Raleigh, N.C. Here are five things you can do if this happens to you.

- Stay with your car. Only leave to go for help if that help is available within 100 yards.

- Make sure everyone else can see your vehicle. Tie brightly colored cloths on your antenna and side mirrors, and turn on the dome light at night.

- Check that nothing is blocking your tailpipe. To save gas and prevent carbon monoxide poisoning, only run the engine and the heater for 10 minutes out of every hour. Also, roll down the windows facing away from the wind just a little to keep carbon monoxide from building up.

- Move your arms and legs vigorously from time to time, but don't leave the car.

- If you have a cellphone, call for help.

To avoid getting stranded in winter storms, always pay close attention to the weather and road conditions before going out on the road and while you're traveling.

Warning — you may be inviting a robbery. You wouldn't tell a thief when you're going on vacation – or that you just got a new diamond pendant or big screen television he can steal. But you may be sharing this information with thieves or other troublemakers even if you don't mean to. It's so easy to share sensitive information in a public place without realizing it. For example, you could be overheard while:

- walking down the street with a friend as you chat about when your new work schedule will keep you away from home.

- talking over the sound of a blow dryer at a hair salon as you describe the expensive new birthday present you just received.

- speaking loudly into your cellphone in a public place because the other person is having trouble hearing you. If you're making an appointment by phone, you may even give out your phone number and other personal information.

Sometimes you don't even have to speak. You can tempt a home invader just by posting vacation photos on social media while you're away from home.

So be careful about what you say or type when you're in any place that may not be private. Don't mention your schedule, travel plans, expensive or rare possessions, account numbers, or personal information unless you're sure no one can overhear you or read your lips. Also, watch out for places that may seem private when they really aren't, such as public restrooms, your yard, a street, parking lot, restaurant booth, city bus, or subway. If you absolutely must speak about sensitive information in public, lower your voice and cover your mouth.

3 crime prevention tips for people who live alone

Keep strangers from realizing you live alone, and you may protect yourself from home invasions and other dangers. Use tricks like these to help.

- Call out a good-bye to your dog or cat or just yell "Bye, honey" every time you leave the house. Shout "I'll get it" whenever the doorbell rings unexpectedly.

- When you leave home, leave the television on, or turn on the radio and tune it to an all-talk or all-news station.

- Invite a friend or two over whenever you're expecting a repairman, salesperson, or other stranger to visit your house.

Avoid a worn-out rental car. You'll find higher mileage on rental cars these days than in the past, *The Wall Street Journal* reports, and that means more rental cars develop car trouble while on the road. Don't let your rental car die out on you while you're traveling. You might get stranded in a dangerous place. Before you leave the rental car lot, do some safety checks.

- Check the tires for under-inflation and wear, and take a good look at the tread. If the tires seem worn, ask for a different car.

- Open the hood, and examine the battery terminals for corrosion buildup.

- Find the controls for the windshield cleaner fluid, and test the wipers.

- Check the headlights to make sure both bright and dim settings work.

- Test the turn signals, and confirm that the check engine light, check oil light, and any other safety indicator lights are not lit.

- Take a brief drive around the parking lot to test the steering and brakes. Make sure you can stop suddenly if you need to.

If one of the car's systems or safety features isn't working properly, return to the rental office, and ask for a replacement.

Hand sanitizer could make you sick

Ever since you heard about the outbreak of the norovirus stomach bug on cruises, you've been using hand sanitizer regularly to protect yourself. But that may not be such a good idea. A recent study found that people who used hand sanitizer instead of washing their hands were much more likely to contract norovirus than frequent hand-washers were. That's because the alcohol in hand sanitizers is not effective against the norovirus, even though it does help fight the spread of colds and flu.

To protect yourself against norovirus — both when traveling and at home — don't depend solely on hand sanitizer. Instead, the Centers for Disease Control and Prevention (CDC) recommends you wash your hands with soap and water, and only use hand sanitizer in addition to hand washing or when soap and water aren't available.

Smart routine if you live by yourself. Schedule a daily check-in with another friend or relative who lives alone. That's what Jane Sullivan did. She asked her friend, Margaret, to be her safety partner. Every day at 10 a.m. Jane would call Margaret. If she wasn't able to reach her after a few minutes, Jane would go to Margaret's house to check on her. If Margaret didn't hear from Jane by 10:30, she would go to Jane's house to make sure she was all right.

You can set up a similar arrangement if you live alone, but you're not limited to your phone. Some people text each other with their cellphones or use instant messaging on their computers. Others may use Skype to video chat with a webcam and computer. You might even use social media, but only if you can set limits to make sure no one but your friends and family can see and respond to your posts.

For added protection, choose more than one safety partner. You might want to check in with one partner in the morning and another right after dinner. This is a cheap, effective way to make sure help is never more than a few hours away.

Schedule extra check-ins when traveling solo

You might be tempted to shed your responsibilities and skip your daily safety check-ins when you travel. But if you travel alone, you should protect yourself by checking in even more often than usual. For example, when Laura goes to Florida on vacation every year, she uses her iPad to send her daughter-in-law regular updates about her plans and locations throughout the day. You may prefer to call or text instead, but be sure to include all the information your contact would need to help you or find you if trouble were to happen. You may also want to include your route and roughly when you expect to reach your destination or provide your next update. Remember, the more often you check in, the safer you'll be.

Useful oddities to add to your emergency kit. Outdated and frivolous items can become surprisingly useful during a disaster. Consider adding these to your emergency kit.

- An old phone. If you keep an old cellphone charged, you can still use it to call 911 during an emergency, even without a contract. That could come in handy if your current cellphone dies and you have no power for your cordless home phone. An old-fashioned corded phone is also helpful during a blackout. Unlike cordless phones, your corded phone will still work if the electricity is out.

- Paper maps. GPS units, smartphones, and computers may be useless after a disaster when power may be out and you can't connect to the Internet, but paper maps never need electricity. Include paper maps of your local area and your state in your emergency kit so you can use them if you have to evacuate or travel locally after a disaster. You'll know why you need them after the third time a detour sign, downed tree, or other problem forces you to turn around and hunt for a new route.

- Glow bracelets. Use these to mark door knobs, stair rails, tripping hazards, your phone, vital supplies, and other important things during the pitch-black nights that come with power outages.

Plan for disabilities and medical needs. Planning ahead for disaster may save your life. Start your plan with these tips.

- Ask your doctor how you can manage your disability during a power outage or disaster.

- If you need regular medical treatments, such as dialysis from a hospital or clinic, or if you depend on frequent home health care visits, ask your service provider what to do during a disaster.

- Notify your power company if you depend on electricity to run vital medical equipment like a battery-operated wheelchair or oxygen concentrator. Also, ask what alternatives are available during a blackout. Keep extra batteries or manual versions of equipment for emergencies.

- If you need a daily or weekly supply of medicine or other treatment items, ask your doctor and pharmacist how you can keep from running out during a disaster.

When good news is really bad

Sometimes fake officials deliver welcome news instead of threats. You may hear that you have won a government-supervised sweepstakes or that you have a tax refund coming. But if the good news depends on your ability to wire money or give out personal information, this may be just another impostor scam. Hunt down the organization's phone number, and call to confirm the official's identity and claims — just as you would for a threatening call.

Beware of fake police and other impostors. Your phone rings and your caller ID displays your local police department's number. The caller claims to have a warrant for your arrest. But he promises you can avoid criminal charges if you pay the fine by immediately wiring money or paying with a pre-loaded debit card.

Don't rush to obey. Scammers can falsify the caller ID information you see, and they can find personal information about you that may make the call seem genuine. The Better Business Bureau named this Arrest Warrant scam as one of its top 10 scams of 2013. And it's not the only impostor scam you may face. You could also get threatening calls, text messages, visits, or emails from fake officials who claim to be from the IRS, Medicare, Social Security, the FBI, your utility company, or the courts. The emails, calls, and credentials may seem official, and visitors may even sport uniforms or badges.

If anyone demands money or personal information, don't give it — especially if the person asks you to wire money or pressures you to act immediately. No government agency will ever call or email to ask you to wire money or provide a Social Security number, credit card number or other personal information. So look up the phone number of the organization the "official" works for, and call to confirm the person's identity and whether their demands are legitimate.

4 ways to charge your cellphone during a blackout. Your cellphone may be vital for getting help or emergency information when the power goes out. For those who have given up landline service to save money, it may be even more important. Fortunately, you have several options for phone charging during a lengthy power outage, especially if you plan ahead.

- Laptop. If your laptop is almost fully charged, you can probably plug your phone charger or a USB cable into one of the laptop's USB ports. This transfers power from your laptop battery to your phone.

- Car charger. Newer cars may offer an AC outlet port you can use with your regular phone charger. But if your car doesn't have that, a car charger can plug into your car's cigarette lighter or charging port and use power from your car's battery. If you didn't get a car charger with your cellphone, you can buy one. Or, if you're really stuck, ask a neighbor if they have one that fits your phone. Just remember, if you turn on your car's engine to charge, pull your car out of the garage to avoid carbon monoxide poisoning.

- Cranking charger. Some emergency radios include a hand crank to generate power and a USB connector port for charging your phone. You can also buy a hand-crank phone charger without the radio. These may not be as cheap as a car charger, but you can probably buy one for under $50.

- Battery-powered charger. You can pick up a charger that runs on AA batteries for less than $15, but be sure you always keep plenty of AA batteries on hand. You may also need a charging cable that has the proper connectors for both your phone and the charger.

GREAT IDEA

Keep one credit card in protective custody

Take two credit cards with you on vacation, but only carry one with you while sightseeing. Lock the other one in the hotel safe as soon as you check in — for its own protection. If someone picks your pocket, you won't be stuck without a credit card. You can simply retrieve the second credit card from its "protective custody" in the hotel safe. Just be sure you contact your other credit card company right away to report and cancel the stolen card.

Drive safely in any weather. Roads aren't just slippery when wet. They may be oily, too. During the first hours of rain, freshly fallen water combines with hard-to-see oils already on the roads. This can make driving conditions much slicker than you may expect. That's one reason rain contributes to more than 1 million weather-related car accidents every year. Follow these rules when you encounter bad weather.

Reduce driving speed by one-third when roads are wet, and cut your speed in half if the road is snow packed, but not icy. For example, if the speed limit is 60 miles per hour (mph), drive 40 mph on wet roads and 30 mph on snowy roads. If the roads are icy, avoid driving, pull over if you're already driving, or slow to a crawl, and drive very cautiously. Also, don't forget to drive more slowly in fog or darkness when you can't see as far as usual. Research shows that if you brake suddenly at 60 mph, your car will travel at least 271 feet before stopping. If you can't see that far ahead, you can't stop in time. Slowing down just might save your life.

Uncover roadside assistance options you didn't know you had. If you're shopping around for the right roadside assistance program or would like to find a better one, don't forget to check the options hiding in policies you already own.

- Car warranty. Review the terms of your car's warranty or extended warranty to see if it includes roadside assistance. Many do, but they only cover one car. Also, make sure your warranty hasn't expired.

- Cellphone plan. You may discover a roadside assistance fee buried in your cellphone bill. If not, find out if a roadside assistance option is available as an add-on to your plan.

- Credit card agreement. Look for a roadside assistance package in the terms. Most credit card packages charge you only when you use their services, and the price for basic services and towing will probably be cheaper than paying out-of-pocket. Other packages may pay a portion of the cost for each use until you pass the annual limit on service calls.

When reviewing roadside assistance plans like these, be sure to check:

- whether you must pay extra to add other family members.

- the average response time to service calls.

- whether limits are placed on the number of service calls or which repair shops your car can be towed to.

- the percentage of costs covered and whether you must pay upfront and be reimbursed later.

- whether towing after an accident is covered.

Practice answering machine safety. Robbers sometimes call your home pretending to be phone surveyors or claiming to have called the wrong number. Their goal is to find out whether you're home. That's why you should be careful about the answering machine message you leave. Never give your name or say you're not there. Instead, record a message that includes the number the caller has reached and say, "We can't come to the phone right now." That's right. Say "we" instead of "I" even if you live alone. If you're a woman living alone, ask a male friend or relative to record your message for you. If you have a cellphone, ask your cellphone provider about the cost of forwarding your home phone calls to your cellphone. If you can do that, callers won't know when you're not home.

GREAT IDEA

Turn ceiling lights into motion detectors

Make that dark garage, basement, or attic a safer place. Just unscrew the light bulb in your ceiling fixture, and screw in a motion-sensing light socket. When you're done, screw the light bulb back in. Make sure the wall switch is flipped to its ON position before you leave the room. The next time you enter, the light will switch on automatically and stay on for at least several minutes. Product reviewers say the motion detection works best when it's at least 2 feet away from the nearest wall and is not blocked by a shade. You can find this type of sensor online or at home improvement stores like Home Depot.

Boost your home's security with smart landscaping. You can't surround your home with a water-filled moat like the castles of the Middle Ages, but you can still make your yard hostile to burglars. Roughly 70 percent of burglars are amateurs who take advantage of easy targets. That means they prefer yards with more places to hide and fewer barriers to a speedy, silent break-in. If your house doesn't fit that description, they may seek easier pickings elsewhere.

Flowers beneath a window are a welcome sight for a thief because he can easily get to the window to break in. But if you plant a hedge of prickly pyracantha beneath that window, climbing over that won't be easy or quick. The thorny hedge may force him to spend more time in plain view of the neighbors while struggling to break in, a problem that may make your home too risky to rob.

So consider growing prickly plants or hedges under your windows, along fences, and around plants or yard features burglars could use for hiding. Good plant choices include spiky hollies, rosa rugosa and other thorny roses, fence climbers like bougainvillea or smilax, palms, cactus, berberis, and pyracantha.

Ask local landscapers about other defensive plants that grow well in your area. Just make sure you plant these yard defenders well away from walking paths and places where they might harm children or pets. Also, be sure to keep them trimmed to 3 feet or less so they make lousy hiding places.

Burglars also like grass and mulches they can cross silently. Surround the prickly plants beneath your windows with an attractive gravel mulch, and you'll hear crunchy, intruder-scaring noises when anyone walks through it.

Smart ways to frustrate pickpockets. The purse you choose or the place you keep your wallet could make the difference between becoming a pickpocket's victim or leaving the crook frustrated. Pickpockets love a purse that is easy to reach into, so foil them by choosing a purse that's tougher to open. Purses with clasps, zippers, or snaps are good choices.

Look for one that also has a strap you can hang diagonally across your body so you can keep your purse in front of you. Men who put their wallets in a back pocket are tempting pickpockets to strike. So experts suggest both women and men should carry money, identification cards, and credit cards in a front pocket or a pocket that buttons or zips. Pickpockets avoid these.

MONEYSAVER

Foil burglars on the cheap

Police say any loud alarm may be enough to make burglars flee. If a home alarm system is too much for your budget, consider stand-alone window alarms that sound off when someone tries to open or break in through a window.

You can find them at home improvement stores, and you may be able to install them yourself. These stand-alone alarms don't attach to a central monitoring system or customer service center, so you won't get any operator assistance. But you also won't pay a monthly monitoring fee.

Stand-alone alarms come both wired and wireless. Wired systems need cables that reach far enough to connect to an outlet. They're also difficult to uninstall when you move and may require professional installation. Wireless systems may be easier to install, but you must remember to change the batteries regularly, and interference may affect the wireless signal.

When shopping for window alarms, be careful to choose one that's compatible with your windows. You may also want a product that comes with a glass-breaking sensor and a decal that warns burglars your windows are connected to a security system.

Home budget

Worry-free ways to take control

Shrink all your bills today. Just one pen and one phone call can save you money all year long on your utility and service bills. Pick one of your most recent bills, grab your red pen or a highlighter, and go over the bill with a fine-toothed comb. Look for charges or fees that fall into one of these categories.

- Out of date. These are for services or products you used in the past but no longer want.

- Mystery. This fee's label is so confusing you can't imagine what it is or why it's there.

- Packaged in. You know what this product or service is, but you didn't know you were paying for it and don't want it.

- Error. You aren't supposed to be paying for this.

Mark these items with your pen or highlighter, even the $1 or $2 charges. These can add up quickly. Also, be sure to check that fine print for any other bill-raising issues that could boost your costs now or in the future. Mark anything you find.

When you have checked all the charges and fine print, call the customer service number on your bill. Ask for an explanation of each charge you don't understand. Ask to cancel any unwanted services or products, and check whether you can waive fees you don't want to pay. Finally, if you need help understanding any items you found in the fine print, ask about those, too. When you hang up the phone, you may be looking at significant savings. Follow this process with all your service and utility bills.

Slash cable costs down to size. Don't just dream about down-sizing your cable bill. Follow this process to make it happen. Save mailers from businesses that compete with your cable company. Read the ones that offer a better deal than the one you have. Also, visit the websites of those firms to determine just how good their offers are, and decide whether you'd be willing to switch to one of them, if needed.

But don't stop there. Keep an eye out for promotions and special offers your own cable company makes to new customers. Check the company website, and monitor print, television, and radio ads for details. Call the company, and ask if you can get that "new customer" deal, too, as a reward for years of customer loyalty. If you are turned down, describe a competitor's offer, and ask if they can match it.

If even that fails, end the call courteously, and decide whether you're willing to switch cable providers rather than keep paying the high price. If switching could be worthwhile, call your cable company again, choose the "cancel service" option, or ask to speak to the customer retention department – not customer service. Describe the competitor's offer, and ask if the company can match that offer. Make sure any offers they make will reduce your costs, but not your services, and be wary of extras you don't need.

If your cable company lowers your bill, it may be a promotional offer that only lasts a few months or a year. So monitor each bill to see if your rate goes up. Keep collecting information about your cable company's promotions, so you'll be ready to ask for a reduc-tion if your rate rises. If your bill increases, and your first try at a reduction doesn't work, try again a few days later with a different customer service representative. On the other hand, if your cable company refuses to lower your bill, you may have to switch after all. Find a competitor offer you like, and check:

- how long the "new customer" deal or rates last.
- whether you get the same level of service.
- what your cancellation penalties would be.

You may be able to take that deal for a while and return to your old cable company when it offers a better deal for new customers.

Watch your favorite programs without cable bills.
"Cutting the cord" is a hot new trend where people save money by replacing cable with something else. You can, too. Investigate options like Smart TVs that can stream shows straight from the Internet or boxes like Roku or Amazon fireTV, and, of course, digital antennas. Check which ones must be combined with video-streaming options like Amazon Prime, Netflix, and Hulu. Be sure to ask:

- how fast your Internet connection must be to use each box or service.

- whether live television shows and sports events will be available.

- which shows or channels are available with each box or service.

- whether you can view the current season of a show.

MONEYSAVER

Bundle up for big savings

Find out if your cable company offers Internet and phone service along with television service. Ask how much the cost of each service can be reduced if you sign up for all three. Keep in mind that bundling them together will make it more difficult to leave your cable company. So run the numbers to make sure their discounts save enough money to be worthwhile.

Stop paying late fees for good. Pay a late fee on a bill just twice in one year, and you may be $56 poorer. But you can prevent that from ever happening. Check with your bank and credit card companies to see if they offer a program that sends alerts to your email or cellphone to remind you when a bill is due. If these services aren't available, you can sign up with a website like Mint.com and set your own reminders. You can also take advantage of calendar or reminder software on your computer, tablet, or smartphone.

If reminders aren't good enough, ask your bank or the company that bills you if they have an automatic payment or deduction service. But don't just set it and forget it. Monitor any automatic payments or deductions you set up to make sure the right amount is charged and paid, and no extra fees creep in.

If you prefer an old-fashioned bill-paying system, set up a basket or box for unpaid bills. Keep them stacked in order of due date with the nearest date on top. When the mail arrives, open each bill, write the due date on the envelope, and return the bill to its envelope. You may also want to mark the bill's due date on a nearby calendar. Place the bill in your unpaid bills basket.

Set aside a time for paying bills each week, and be sure to pay each bill at least one week ahead of its due date. As soon as a bill is paid, record its payment in your check register, remove the bill from your basket, and file it with other paid bills.

5 smart questions to ask before you refinance. Interest rates have dropped, and you're ready to plunge into the murky waters of refinancing. Before you do, make sure this action will genuinely save you money. Start by asking these questions.

- Can I qualify? Check your credit score. If it is below 640, you may not qualify for a refinancing loan. Also calculate your debt-to-income (DTI) ratio by dividing your total debt by your gross income. Thanks to new rule changes, lenders won't lend to anyone whose DTI is 43 percent or higher.

- How long will I be in the house? If your loan has closing costs, you need to own the house long enough for your savings to make up those costs plus the costs of an appraisal and inspection. Visit the refinance calculators at *www.bankrate.com* or *www.hsh.com* to help estimate how long that will take. Hint — if your loan doesn't have closing costs, you'll still pay them in some other form such as extra origination points or a higher interest rate.

- What will my total interest savings be? Figure the total amount of interest you'll pay on your current loan between now and its end, and compare that to the total amount you'd pay on your refinance. If you've been paying a 30-year mortgage for some years and refinance into another 30-year loan, you may end up paying more total interest – or less – depending on the numbers.

- What is my home's value? Some people may still be unlucky enough to own a home that's worth less than the amount of the mortgage needed to refinance. Since that could prevent you from refinancing, you may want to check local prices of similar houses online, or contact a realtor to help determine the value of your home.

- What is my LTV? This is your loan-to-value ratio. To calculate it, divide your loan amount by your home's value. If your LTV is 0.8 (80 percent) or higher, you're required to pay property mortgage insurance (PMI). If you must pay PMI with a refinance, but don't pay it in your current loan, include that in your calculations to help determine whether a refinance loan saves money.

WARNING

Why small loans are a big problem

Think twice before trying for a refinance loan of $50,000 or less. Most lenders won't offer a loan that small. Even if you can find a lender who offers this kind of refinance, the high costs of the loan will probably prevent you from saving money.

No-nonsense way to manage your money. Managing money can be like trying to herd grasshoppers. Just when you get your utility bills under control, your food expenses mysteriously go up.

That's where a budget can help. Budgeting can help track down where your money went. What's more, a budget can also make sure your money doesn't wander off again. To regain control of your money by setting up a budget, follow these steps.

- Write down your total monthly take-home income.

- Make a list of all your vital monthly expenses, including housing, groceries, utilities, car payment, and medications. Don't forget to list expenses you pay once or twice a year, like taxes or insurance premiums.

- Add categories for optional expenses such as hobbies and entertainment. Include entries for birthday presents, Christmas expenses, repairs, maintenance, and other expenses that may not occur every month.

- Estimate how much you spend in each budget category per month – with help from your credit card statements, bank records, and receipts. If you prefer exact numbers, track your spending for one month, and use those numbers instead of monthly estimates. To save toward annual expenses, divide the annual amount by 12 to get the monthly amount you must save to meet that expense.

- Total your expenses and subtract them from your income. If your income is higher than expenses, siphon the extra into an emergency fund that can cover unexpected expenses, like medical bills.

- Set goals for each expense category. If your expenses were higher than your income, cut back on optional expenses first, like entertainment and eating out. Then review critical expenses you can safely reduce, like groceries and electricity. Set new goals for these, and make a plan to achieve them.

- Continue tracking your spending to see how well you meet your goals.

Fun way to save that really works

Cutting back to meet your budget goals doesn't have to be painful — and here's proof. Recently, 14 credit unions asked their members to use a website that turns saving money and paying down debt into a game, complete with prizes. After six months, more than half of the credit union members who participated reported that the game had led them to save more, pay off more debt, or do both. But you don't have to be a member of a credit union to try this, just visit *www.saveup.com* to learn more.

If you don't have Web access, create your own game. Start a friendly competition between family members or between you and a friend. See who can save the most or do the best job of sticking to a budget — and don't forget to include prizes.

5 creative budgeting ideas. Contrary to popular belief, budgeting is not about shoehorning yourself into a rigid system and enduring the misery. In fact, you may be more likely to succeed if you choose the budgeting method that seems to fit you best. See if one of the following methods could be right for you.

- The 50/20/30 budget. Recommended by many experts, this budget doesn't require lots of categories. You merely set a goal to spend 50 percent of your after-tax income on mandatory expenses, like housing and utilities. You are still free to spend 30 percent on optional expenses, like entertainment, but the remaining 20 percent must go toward savings or debt repayment. You can adjust these percentages up or down by as much as 10 percent to fit your needs. But track your spending to determine whether you are meeting these goals. Keep hunting for ways to cut expenses until every goal is met.

- Zero-based budgeting. Many people set goals for each category by basing the amount on what they already spend. But zero-based budgeting starts all categories at zero. That means you must make a solid case for why each expense should be added to the budget, or the expense may never be included. And, of course, total expenses must never exceed your income, so some expenses probably won't qualify to be in the budget.

- The 80/20 budget. Use automatic deductions to put the first 20 percent of your paycheck into savings. Live off the remaining 80 percent of your after-tax income.

- The 80/20 Plus budget. Skim off at least 15 percent of your paycheck straight into savings just as with the 80/20 plan, but then pay all your fixed costs such as housing, utilities, and other must-pay expenses. Whatever is left over can go to optional expenses, but keep in mind that money will have to last for a month.

- The 25 percent budget. This might work best if you are desperate to get out of debt quickly. Mitchell Weiss of Credit.com suggests dividing your pretax income into roughly four equal parts — taxes, debt payment, housing, and living expenses. But be aware that reducing your mortgage or rent payment to 25 percent and living on 25 percent of your pretax salary may require some drastic adjustments to your lifestyle. You can make minor adjustments to the percentages as long as they still add up to 100 percent.

Manage money on a variable income. Planning a budget is particularly tough when your income fluctuates every month. How can you set goals when you don't know how much you'll have to spend? Figure the least amount you are likely to make in a month. If that amount is not zero, set your budget based on that income. Also, be sure to set up a buffer fund that can help you through zero-income months or the months where your income is too low to cover basic living expenses. Contribute to this buffer fund as often as possible.

Of course, you will make more than your lowest income during some months, so create a prioritized list that determines where each extra dollar will go. For example, the first $100 might be used to pay down debts, add to your buffer fund, or cover extra expenses. The second $100 could be used for a splurge or to save for a vacation. The number of goals and amount of money for each is up to you. Just be sure to cover savings, debts, and required expenses before you get to the more optional costs.

GREAT IDEA

3 ways to prevent debit card overdrafts

Avoiding overdrafts can be tricky when you use a debit card. Transactions don't always show up right away, and they may not post in order. This means you can't rely on the balance on your ATM or deposit slips to be completely accurate every time.

Instead, you must balance your checkbook frequently, and find a convenient way to closely track expenses. The expense-tracking methods below are recommended by people who have successfully kept up with their debit cards and account balances.

- Record transactions immediately in a check register, smartphone app, or notebook.
- Save receipts to record later in a spreadsheet, finance software program, Mint.com, or checkbook.
- Subscribe to bank-provided alerts that notify you of each ATM or debit card transaction above a set amount.

Canceling or opting out of fee-based overdraft protection is another option. This prevents overdrafts by causing your debit card to stop working when your balance reaches zero. Before you try it, confirm this will work for your account and card.

Budgeting mistakes even smart people make. You may be sabotaging your own budget and not even know it. Watch out for easy-to-make budgeting mistakes like these.

- Not tracking spending. Without this, you can't tell when your expenses are too high or your budget goals need adjusting. If you can't track every expense, at least track the ones that are a problem for you.

- Forgetting spending categories. This can include very small expenses, like a daily trip to the vending machine, or less-frequent expenses, such as new tires, life insurance, or annual memberships or subscriptions.

- Not planning for temptation or mistakes. Sooner or later, you'll be tempted to go to a concert with friends or splurge on new clothes. Have a plan for what to do when that happens. Make a second plan for how you'll recover when you undermine your budget.

- Having no emergency fund. Siphon a little money for emergencies into a savings account every month, so you won't have to go into debt to pay for unexpected expenses, like major car repairs.

- Not planning for ATMs or cash back. It's all too easy to pick up an extra $20 from the ATM, or use a retailer's cash back button to get money when you use your debit card or some credit cards. To prevent spending creep, plan ahead to limit money from these sources.

- Eliminating fun money. Allow yourself a small amount of splurge dollars or fun money each month. Otherwise, you may feel so deprived that you make purchases you'll regret.

- Spouse-free budgeting. Your budget can't succeed unless your spouse agrees to budget and helps set the budgetary categories and amounts.

- Failing to make budget adjustments. As long as your total expenses don't exceed your income, you can adjust your budget goals for each category to more closely match your lifestyle or adapt to recent changes.

Home improvement

Get show-stopping style for less

10 low-cost ways to spruce up your home. You want to make your home look its best, but can't afford an interior decorator or home stager. Here are 10 ways to boost the look of your home for next to nothing.

- Make small, adjacent rooms appear larger and seamless by painting them the same color.

- Create a comfortable, relaxing bedroom by removing extra furniture and decorating with neutral colors.

- Replace burned out light bulbs in lamps and light fixtures both indoors and outside.

- Opt for translucent window treatments instead of dark ones. Or consider removing curtains altogether, and leaving your windows bare.

- Add table lamps and floor lamps to dark rooms to make them feel warm and cozy.

- Give each room a single purpose. A guest bedroom that also serves as an office is an instant turnoff.

- Mount curtain rods closer to the ceiling and hang longer curtains. This will make your ceiling look higher, and your room look more spacious.

- Display neutral-colored items in groupings on built-in shelves. Neutral colors will draw attention to the bookshelves.

- Paint your outdated appliances with stainless steel paint. If you plan on painting your stove, use a high-temperature product. And for your dishwasher, cover the front panel with a stainless steel stick-on.

- Hang a white shower curtain and white towels in your bathroom. Accessorize with neutral colors, and paint or replace gold and brass hardware with silver.

Boost your home's value for less. Thinking about selling your home? Or just want to increase what it's worth? You don't need to break the bank with a complete remodel. Here are a few quick ways to add value on a budget.

- Flip through current design books and magazines for do-it-yourself inspiration. Or ask a realtor to spend an hour walking through your home. An agent can provide free counsel on current home improvement trends.

- Transform an empty basement into living space like a home office or media room. More living space equals greater value.

- Upgrade the master bathroom with a window over the tub. Use acrylic block windows to let light in without sacrificing privacy.

- Research ways to cut energy costs. An energy-efficient home is more attractive to a potential buyer. This may mean replacing old windows with new ones.

- Rid your home's exterior of mildew. Kill it with a mildewcide spray, and prevent it from coming back with mildew-proof paint.

- Spruce up your garage by getting as much off the floor as possible. Install extra lights and shelves throughout your garage, and clean or polish the floor.

Maximize the space in your home. Revamp your rooms with minimum effort. Simply rearrange your furniture to prime locations throughout your house.

In the living room, move your sofa a few inches away from walls. A bit of breathing room will make the area seem larger. Plus, warm up the ambiance by placing lamps around the room, and divvying up the lighting equally. Split a long, rectangular family room into two squares. Make one square a conversational area with a sofa facing a couple of comfy chairs. Turn the other square into a space for casual eating or playing games with four chairs around a square or round table.

Make beds the focal point of each bedroom. Choose a light headboard for small rooms, and a heavy headboard for large rooms with tall ceilings. Give yourself a path of at least 2 feet all the way around your bed. For a room with plenty of floor space, place a bench at the end of your bed or a chair in a corner for extra seating.

Dining room tables should be centered beneath a light fixture. If possible, place your table a minimum of 3 feet from walls. Chairs should be placed at least 6 inches apart. A round or square table works best in a square room, while an oval or rectangular table fits the bill in a rectangular room.

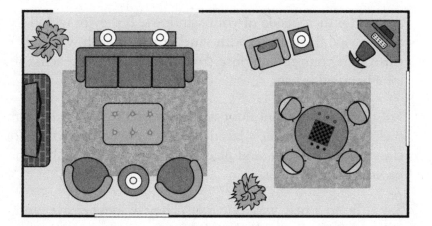

For fun and variety, move furniture pieces from one room to another until you find an ideal spot. You never know — a lone dining room chair may find the perfect home in a guest bedroom.

Create more storage space in your closet. You can make the most of your closet by looking at the space in a new way. Here's how.

- Dedicate two-thirds of your closet for hanging clothes. Get rid of the long closet rod that's in your closet now and install two rods. Mount one rod high for dresses and coats. Mount another about 3 feet off the floor for tops and folded pants.

- Store folded clothes like T-shirts and sweaters on shelves. Adjustable, wire shelving is inexpensive and easy to install. Separate socks, scarves, belts, purses, and undergarments into their own baskets. Hang the baskets on a wall.

- Put a small dresser in your closet for additional storage if you have extra space.

Curb appeal on a dime. You want to make a great first impression to a potential home buyer, but don't know where to start. Go with easy and economical fixes first.

- Spruce up the outside of your windows. If they're within reach, wipe them down with vinegar mixed with water, then rinse with your garden hose. For windows out of reach, use a long-handled brush.

- Freshen up your front door with paint. Pick a color that contrasts with your home's facade. Hang a decorative wreath or a classic door knocker, and place attractive house numbers on, or next to, your door.

- Say hello to a new welcome mat. They're inexpensive, and will make your entry look well-kept.

- Affix a sleek kick plate to save your front door from wear and tear along the bottom edge. For as low as $25, you can find them in brass, satin nickel, and oil-rubbed bronze.

- Create symmetry by placing potted plants, Grecian urns, or sculptures on each side of your front door.

- Blast dirt and debris off the walkway and driveway with a garden hose turned to its strongest setting.

- Replace outdated light fixtures. Or better yet, spray paint them and save a bundle.

- Tidy up your yard by trimming trees and bushes, and weeding flower beds.

Show off your home's true colors. With so many paint colors to choose from, how do you know which ones are right for your walls and decor? Check out a color wheel. It will help you combine colors that look best together. Twelve hues reside on the basic color wheel – the three primary colors of red, blue, and yellow, and their nine derivatives.

For a room that begs for high energy, primary colors will make the biggest splash. But use them sparingly to make them easier on the eyes. Analogous colors reside next to each other like yellow green, green, blue green, and blue. Used side-by-side on a piece of furniture or to decorate an entire room, analogous colors provide a soothing, harmonious feel. Complementary colors fall directly across from one another such as violet and yellow, or blue green and red orange. Put complementary colors together for pops of color on furniture and art projects.

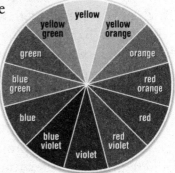

A color wheel can also be divided into warm and cool categories with six colors in each. Combine red violet with yellow for a sense of warmth, or yellow green with violet for a cool, relaxing feel. For more information about the color wheel, search online or talk to a pro in the paint department of your favorite home improvement center.

Flawless picture placement with a sticky note

Don't put pencil marks on your wall to hang a picture. Use a sticky note to show you where to place the hook. It's a cinch to peel off when you're done, and it will keep your wall clean.

Painting tips for a variety of surfaces. You can't paint brick the way you would plastic or drywall. Each surface needs individual attention. Use these guidelines to optimize your next painting project.

Drywall – Clean drywall with either a trisodium phosphate cleanser (TSP) or a mixture of one cup white vinegar per gallon of water. For drywall with greasy buildup, use a cup of ammonia per gallon of water. Prime the wall to cover water and mildew stains and to keep old color from bleeding through. Apply a coat of paint and allow it to dry completely before applying a second coat.

Brick – Wash brick with a scrub brush and mild detergent mixed with water. To remove tougher grime buildup, try a tablespoon of boric acid mixed with a gallon of warm water. Wipe your bricks with a wet rag, and allow them to dry completely. Brush on a masonry sealer. Apply paint with a long-nap roller, and use a brush to fill cracks and crevices.

Plastic – Most plastic projects require light sanding to help paint adhere properly. After roughing up the surface, wipe it with a clean cloth or TSP to remove excess particles. Coat with a primer and spray paint made specifically for plastic.

Laminate — Use water and mild dish detergent to wash laminate surfaces such as kitchen cabinets. Make the surface gritty with fine sandpaper, and wipe it with tack cloth. To keep your paint from scratching or peeling off, use a primer and allow it to dry completely. Paint your surface then seal it with a protective finish.

Pick the perfect roller for your paint job. No need to hire an expert. You can roll on paint like a pro by following a few easy steps.

- Pick the perfect roller for your paint job by following these guidelines.

Type of surface	Roller nap in inches
smooth	3/16 — 1/4
semi-smooth/ light to medium texture	3/8 — 1/2
semi-rough to rough	3/4 — 1
extra rough	1 1/4 — 1 1/2

- Use a lint roller, vacuum, or the sticky side of painter's tape to remove excess lint from a new roller.

- Paint the edge along the ceiling, shoe molding, and around switch plates and outlet covers with a brush before rolling. You may need a couple of coats to avoid brush strokes.

- Run your roller in a paint tray until it's covered with paint without being over saturated.

- Roll paint on the wall in a "W" pattern, overlapping strokes and covering sections about 3 feet wide.

- Pull the roller away lightly from the wall as you finish each section to prevent painting a noticeable line.

- Rewet your roller, and continue filling in your "W" pattern while starting a new one adjacent to it.

Raise your art to the ideal height. Ever wonder how high to hang your works of art or family photos? Use this quick, step-by-step guide to do what design experts do.

Mark your wall 57 inches up from the floor. Measure the height of your picture and divide it in two. For instance, if your frame is 30 inches tall, the midpoint is 15 inches. Then measure the top of the frame to the wire or mounting hardware. Subtract this number from the midpoint measurement. If the wire is 3 inches below the top of the frame, subtract 3 inches from 15 inches. You end up with 12 inches. Mark the wall 12 inches above your 57-inch point or at 69 inches. Hang your hook at 69 inches. The center of your picture will settle at 57 inches.

These guidelines also work for groups of photos or art work. Decide which picture will serve as the focal point, and follow the above guidelines. Surround your centerpiece with the rest of your photos.

Hang a picture with ease. You need to hang a lightweight item on a wall, but can't quite figure out how to mark the spot. Try making this handy tool. A nail and a thin, rectangular piece of wood — like a ruler or paint stick — are all you need. Drive the nail into one end of the piece of wood, but don't drive it all the way through. You want the sharp end of your nail to just poke through. Hang your picture from the flat end of your nail. Decide where you want to place

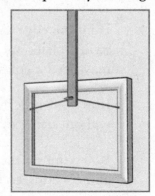

it on your wall. Gently press against the picture, leaving a small nail mark on the wall. Remove your picture, and put down your new tool. Find the mark on the wall, hammer a new nail into it, and hang your picture.

Spice up a wall with scraps. Don't throw wallpaper scraps on the scrap heap. Create an attractive accent wall in a patchwork design, using bright and bold colors or soft and gentle neutrals. Just redoing one wall can revamp an entire room. Consider one of these ideas.

- Cut wallpaper into like-size squares such as 8 inches by 8 inches or 12 by 12. Place the squares next to one another for a checker-board look. But use an assortment of prints to add variety.

- Cut your scraps into several square and rectangular sizes. Adhere your bigger pieces first, then hang smaller pieces around them. Your scraps can be side by side or slightly lay-ered along the edges. Or play up your wall's paint color by exposing sections of it between your scraps.

GREAT IDEA

Find wallpaper scraps for next to nothing

You want to cover a furniture piece or wall with wallpaper scraps, but don't know where to find any. Go to your local home improvement store and ask about old sample books. Many stores will give them away or sell them for cheap. Also try friends and yard sales.

Hang wallpaper scraps as works of art. Don't know what to do with leftover wallpaper scraps? Here's a quick solution — frame them. From a small piece to a large roll, framed wallpaper can look like a pricey painting. Or hang it directly on your wall, and use crown molding as a border. For an even more dramatic display, pick up inexpensive 4-foot by 8-foot wall panels at a hardware store. Cover your panels in wallpaper, and hang them horizontally or vertically.

Whip up a picture perfect wall treatment. Skip the costly wain-scoting and create a winsome wall treatment with picture frames. Paint them white, and hang them below a chair rail. For variety, use frames of assorted shapes and sizes. For a uni-form look, use identical frames.

Window treatment know-how. You'll never wonder about win-dow treatments with these simple tips and tricks. Start by picking the right fabric for the room. A formal dining room begs for silk or velvet, while a cheerful kitchen calls for cotton and cotton blends. Sheer fabrics and linen will infuse a room with brightness, while heavy textiles like tweed and tapestry will block light and keep a room warm.

Do you want your curtain color to blend in or make a splash? That will depend on the mood you want to create. To blend, choose a color that's a few shades darker than your walls. But to make a splash, pick a bold shade from your furniture, dishes, or decor.

To decide if you need solid-colored or patterned curtains, look to your furniture or bedding. Solid color sofas and bedspreads go well with printed curtains. Conversely, furniture with print fabric needs solid color curtains or a subtle print.

If you're wondering how high to hang your curtains, take some advice from design experts. Basically, the higher you hang them, the taller your room will feel. Long panels should slightly graze the floor for a classic look. But it's okay to let curtains pool a few inches on the floor. It's stylish and forgiving for uneven floors.

For the best bang for your buck, skip custom-made curtains. Off-the-shelf window treatments come in a vast array of colors, prints, sizes, and fabrics, and cost much less than custom-made.

Creative, low-cost ways to hang curtains. PVC pipes aren't just for plumbing. A paint job and decorative end caps will turn these pipes into window dressing for a fraction of the cost of curtain rods. Look for spray paint that's formulated for plastics. Or use a latex primer and latex or acrylic paint. Either way, you'll want to rough up your PVC pipes with sandpaper to help the paint adhere better. Allow the paint to air dry and cure completely. Gently run your curtains through your pipes and hang. Use hot glue to attach finials to the ends for a finishing touch. If you want to add a sheer panel to your window treatment, use a bungee cord. Simply string the cord through your curtains. Then strap the cord on to the wall brackets behind your curtains.

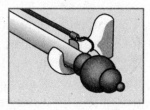

Two cool ways to tie back your curtains. Dress up your draperies with a couple of neckties. Pick up a matching set at a discount store or look for similar styles at a thrift shop. To add pizzazz to your solid-colored curtains, pick ties with a pattern. For panels with a print, choose ties in solid colors. To keep your tie from slipping to the floor, attach Velcro to the back of the necktie loop and on to the wall. For a vintage tieback, shop for old doorknobs at a salvage store. Install doorknobs directly on to the wall. Or affix doorknobs on to vintage back plates with copper pipes. Mount the back plates on to the wall.

Cover your window with a curtain of ribbons. Make an easy, breezy curtain with two items — a curtain rod and yards of ribbon. Simply cut the ribbons a few inches longer than the sill, and tie them side by side across a curtain rod. For fun, use multiple colors and patterns. Or, instead of ribbon, use cotton, linen, or burlap strips depending on the look you want. Go with cotton prints for shabby chic; linen for a clean, airy feel; and burlap for rustic decor. If you don't want to cover an entire window, consider creating a valance. Cut your ribbon or strips the same length, or vary the lengths to make a scallop design.

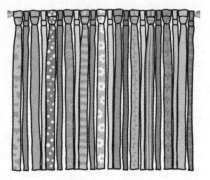

Bright ideas for home lighting. Designers divide interior lighting into three categories — task, accent, and ambient. A perfectly lit room combines all three.

Task-oriented light helps define work areas in a room. In a kitchen, for instance, you can hang pendants and install under-cabinet lighting to illuminate work spaces. Pendants should hang about 30 inches above the work surface, and should be fitted with shades or globes that direct light downward. Floor and table lamps with adjustable arms also provide task lighting. Use them to brighten your favorite reading spot in your bedroom or family room. If you're not sure about the size of a table lamp, design pros suggest bigger is better. You can also achieve task lighting by installing recessed ceiling lights and pointing them toward a work space. In bathrooms, shoot for lights that keep shadows and glare away from mirrors.

Draw attention to a focal point in a room with accent lights. A recessed ceiling light aimed at a work of art or family portrait is an example of an accent light. This type of lighting can also shine on architectural features such as interior columns illuminated with candle sconces. The key is to direct light toward an attractive element in a room, and away from unappealing places.

Ambient light fixtures provide mood and general lighting. Torchères or floor lamps with shades that direct light toward the ceiling and then diffuse it throughout a room deliver ambient light. So do recessed lights and dining room chandeliers controlled by a dimmer switch. To pick out a new chandelier for a dining room, go with a classic that won't date your space. Hang about 30 inches above your dining room table.

GREAT IDEA

Extend the life of your carpet

Your new carpet can last for years or deteriorate quickly depending on the pad you place underneath it. Consider three factors — density, thickness, and material — when shopping for padding. For a combination of cushion and durability, choose a pad with 6 to 8 pounds of density. Make sure your pad meets your carpet manufacturer's specs for thickness. If you don't, you may void your carpet's warranty. Consider going with a rebonded material — it's recycled and reasonably priced.

3 things you need to know about buying carpet. Picking carpet is like shopping for cereal – with so many choices, it's hard to know which one is right for you. If you're in the market for new carpet, the three things to consider are traffic flow, desired feel, and price tag.

For high-traffic areas like hallways and living rooms, go with nylon. It's durable, versatile, and moderately priced. A space with lots of sunlight needs the fade resistance of polyester. This fiber also repels stains easily. Plus, it's easy on your pocketbook. Olefin is a cheap fiber that is easy to clean and fends off the sun's rays. It also gets dirtier faster than the other fibers. Keep it out of high-traffic zones, but it works well in a sunny room. For a soft feel with the durability of nylon and the fade resistance of polyester, go with triexta. Made with corn sugars, a renewable resource, it's also a "greener" option.

In addition to picking the right fiber, consider the carpet type or pile. A twist or cut pile is soft to the touch, looks casual, and works best in a low-traffic room like a bedroom. Loop pile, also known as Berber, offers loads of durability without the softness of cut pile. It's the perfect pile for an active family room or basement. A patterned carpet, which combines cut and loop piles, packs a visual punch and is best served in a formal dining or living room.

Turn a concrete floor into a work of art. Painting a concrete floor may seem like an over-the-top undertaking, but the payoff is priceless. Experiment with a small section of floor first. Tape off a smaller square or rectangle. With additional tape, create a grid pattern and paint it black and white or two other contrasting colors. Your design will look like tile. If your square is in an open area without furniture, turn it into a large checkerboard or chess board with oversize playing pieces. For the more adventurous, use a stencil with an intricate pattern or paint thick, bold stripes.

Never use regular latex wall paint. It's not formulated to hold up to foot traffic. Instead, pick up paint specially made for concrete floors. Or you can try Chalk Paint — it adheres to most surfaces, and makes a beautiful base for a stenciling project.

Fix a nick in a jiff. When you want to cover a nick in your wood floor, turn to a box of crayons. Hold one that best matches the floor color over the nick. Using a butane lighter, melt the end of the crayon, and let it drip into the nick until it's full. If you need to, melt a crayon of another color until you achieve the desired shade. Wait until the wax dries, then remove any excess with a plastic scraper. You can try this idea on wood furniture, too.

Trim tile with ease. You're installing vinyl floor tiles, but can't cut the tiles with a utility knife. Try using your rotary fabric cutter. It's easy on the hands, and works like a charm.

Make a splash with an unconventional backsplash. Tin tiles look terrific, but they're expensive. Metal skirting — the sheets used to cover the exposed, lower part of mobile homes — can deliver a comparable look that packs a punch. Pick them up for a fraction of the cost of tin tile from your local home improvement store — then cut and glue in place. The dimpled, block design creates an attractive texture, and metal skirting is durable and easy to clean. For a slick look, affix galvanized metal sheets. They're cheap, sleek-looking, and also easy to install. Don't like the thought of silver metal hanging from your kitchen walls? Prime and paint the metal skirting or sheets to match your kitchen colors.

Old kitchen cabinets get a new look. Spruce up your kitchen cabinets by removing their doors. The open shelves work with any interior design from contemporary to country. Display a collection of china, heirloom glassware, or modern bowls, pitchers, and vases. To spice up the look even more, paint or wallpaper the insides of your cabinets. Keep the doors on a few cabinets to hide stacks of unsightly pots and pans or tacky coffee mugs. The contrast between open and closed cabinets will give your kitchen the update it needs.

Add privacy to glass cabinet doors. You know what's behind your glass cabinet doors. The problem is, so does every-body else. What can you do to keep people from peeking into your kitchen cabinets? Cover them up with paint, paper, or cloth. Purchase a can of acrylic or resin paint. An acrylic will give your glass more coverage, while a resin will be transparent. Or pick up spray paint made especially for glass from a hobby store. Paint the glass from the inside of the cabinets. You can forego painting altogether, and cover the glass with fabric or decorative paper. Use staples to secure from the inside.

Spruce up tile countertops with paint. You can breathe new life into old tile countertops by painting them. It's easier than you think, and won't cost a pretty penny.

To prep your tile, remove grime with an abrasive tile cleaner, and bleach areas covered in mold. Repair any cracks or chips with caulk or epoxy. Then finish prepping your surface with an epoxy-based primer. Choose an epoxy paint for durability, and carefully apply several thin coats. Allow each coat to dry completely before applying another layer. Once you're satisfied with the coverage, allow two to three days for the paint to cure. Finish your project by protecting it from moisture and scratches with a clear, water-based top coat.

For around $40, you can try a product made specifically for sprucing up old sinks and tile called Homax Tough Tile, Tub & Sink Refinishing Kit. It comes with a cleaning solution, paintbrush, and epoxy paint, and can be used on fiberglass, porcelain, glazed ceramic tile, and countertop laminate.

GREAT IDEA

Imaginative way to corral your tableware

You're throwing a party, but don't know where to put your tableware. Use terra-cotta pots. Stencil each pot with a utensil design — one with a fork, one with a spoon, and one with a knife. Tie a colorful ribbon around the upper lip of each pot for added flair. Fill them with your favorite silverware or plastic cutlery. Terra-cotta pots will work with any theme, especially a cookout or garden party.

Give your dishwasher a facelift. Your dishwasher works fine on the inside but looks ugly on the outside. Give your old dishwasher a fresh look with bead board. A panel will run about $12. Use double-sided tape and construction adhesive to secure your board onto the dishwasher door. Allow the adhesive to dry completely, and then apply caulk across the top of your board. Your dishwasher will look like new.

Clever ways to save on granite countertops. You're ready to redo your countertops, but want to save money in the process. No problem. Start by choosing a common color like an earth tone over a rare one like blue. Pick a square edge over a beveled or curved. Order granite for your countertops only. Choose another option for your backsplash. Shop the remnant section if you need granite for a small area, like a bathroom vanity. Granite remnants are leftovers from bigger jobs, and sell for a fraction of the cost. If these ideas still put you out of your price range, consider granite tile. It costs less than a single slab, and it's cheaper to install.

Transform a bathroom for a bargain. You can add a lot of style to your bathroom with little effort and expense.

- Switch out an old medicine cabinet for a new mirror. Or frame your existing mirror with glass tiles or fluted door casings.

- Install matching towel bars, hooks, cabinet hardware, outlet covers, and toilet paper holder.

- Add sconces on either side of a mirror or window. Place battery-powered candles on them for a soft glow without the risk of a real flame.

- Brighten grout lines with a grout cleaner that removes ground-in dirt.

- Paint soothing colors on your walls and cabinets doors. Go with neutral colors or two harmonious hues. Add splashes of color with towels and accessories.

- Go with white sinks, toilet, and bathtub. They cost less and offer squeaky clean appeal.

- Coordinate light fixtures with the rest of the bathroom's hardware. For instance, install polished nickel light fixtures to match polished nickel towel bars and cabinet pulls.

- Toss out an old window treatment, and hang a Roman shade or install louvered shutters.

- Replace a standard shower head with a multipurpose one. Or pick out a handheld sprayer to ease rinsing off, hair washing, and tub cleaning.

GREAT IDEA

Give your shower a facelift

Replacing a shower door is a value-packed way to freshen up a bathroom without breaking the bank. "Most older shower doors have soap buildup that is difficult to scrub away," says Scott Cole, a bathroom remodeling contractor. "People also say they can't seem to clean shower doors because of hard water stains. But the glass doors have actually been etched with chemicals and minerals from the water, so they can't be cleaned." Scott recommends a clear glass door over a frosted one for an updated look. "Clear glass will also make a bathroom look larger," says Scott. He also steers clients away from gold and antique brass trim. Says Scott, "Brushed nickel, oil rubbed bronze, or chrome are the way to go."

Add a splash of color to a plain shower curtain. It's easy to paint and personalize a shower curtain. All you need are a solid-colored curtain made of fabric, your favorite stencil, repositionable mounting adhesive, sponge brushes, and fabric paints. Start by spraying the mounting adhesive on the back of a stencil. You can pick up a can of adhesive for around $10 at an office supply or hardware store. Stick the stencil to your curtain. Fill the stencil with fabric paint using a sponge brush. Allow it to dry completely. For quick results, use a fan or hair dryer. Repeat until you've created the design you want – a border along the top and bottom of your curtain, a diagonal pattern, or complete coverage. Follow the instructions for setting the paint completely before hanging.

Turn a boring bathroom wall into a mural. A collection of antique, handheld mirrors will add vintage charm to a bathroom wall. Hang them up with 5-inch plate hangers. Or tie lace around the handles, and hang them from pegs or hooks. For a more eclectic statement, hang several framed wall mirrors in a variety of shapes and sizes. Paint the frames the same color for a cohesive collage.

Old barrel becomes a unique mirror. You can fashion a mirror that is both bold and rustic from an old barrel. Look for one in the gardening department of your local home improvement store. The inside, bottom of your barrel will serve as the base for your mirror. Saw your barrel to just above the second metal ring. This will keep your staves in place and your barrel from falling apart. Take your barrel to a glass and mirror expert, and ask him to cut a mirror to fit the bottom of your barrel. Using a super strong adhesive, put glue on the back of the mirror and gently press into place. Allow the bond to dry completely according to the manufacturer's guidelines. Hang your mirror with strong mounting hardware and wall anchors.

Pennies make great tile spacers

Don't spend money on the plastic tile spacers you find at home improvement centers. Use pennies instead. You can stand them up between each tile. Pennies are easy to work with, and they will help you achieve a uniform look.

Build an entertainment center and save big. You can spend a fortune on an entertainment center. But you don't have to. Give your TV and stereo a place to call home with stock kitchen cabinets. "We did this in our family room," says Kari Cedric. "The bottom 'built-in' cabinets on either side of the fireplace are simply stock upper kitchen cabinets. We topped them with one piece of wood, and then added a few shelves. Big savings!" Stock cabinets are less expensive than custom-made, but you'll need to assemble them. Measure your space and TV first so you'll buy the right size cabinets. Rearrange them and add shelves above to suit your needs. Finish your custom-built unit with crown molding and filler strips. You can also remove a couple of cabinet doors or replace them with glass-front doors. This idea also works as attractive storage and library space.

Never lose track of time at home. There's no time like the present to create a super-size statement in your home – a colossal wall clock. For this project, you'll need a battery-operated clock kit with self-contained housing and long hands – the longer the hands, the bigger the clock. Pick up one at a hobby store or order online. Plus, you'll need 12 objects to represent your numbers. You can use anything, like postcards or framed photos.

Or try theme items such as colorful dice for a game room or teacups in a kitchen. If you opt for numbers, choose a font and color that match your room's decor.

Charming ways to decorate a nonfunctional fireplace.
Make your nonworking fireplace the centerpiece of any room with these fun, firebox fillers.

- Stack books vertically and horizontally for an eclectic look. Or cover your books with solid-colored paper for a sleek, clean feel.

- Create cozy ambiance by filling your fireplace with logs or a collection of twigs and branches tied with burlap.

- Cover the back of your firebox with wallpaper, and add shelves in a coordinating color. Place photos, magazines, and decorative items such as baskets or seashells on your shelves.

- Go ahead and light a fire with a collection of candles. Use a variety of sizes and stagger them by height.

- Fill your fireplace with a chalkboard. Use it to write messages. Better yet – draw a roaring fire.

Trendsetting headboard ideas. You can use salvaged doors to create a beautiful backdrop behind your bed. An old barn door evokes a rustic feel. A newer door with a glossy coat of paint becomes a custom headboard with a contemporary feel. A large vintage sign will add down-home country charm to a space. Use it as the focal point in your bedroom, and choose wall colors and accessories to match.

Bring the outdoors indoors with window shutters. Paint them a cool aqua color for a beach decor or antique white for a country feel.

Once they're painted, you have two options. Either hang each shut-ter across the wall behind your bed. Or, to hold the shutters in place, consider attaching a strip of wood across the top and bottom.

If you need a headboard with storage, pull out your drawers – your dresser drawers. Or pick up an old dresser at a garage sale. Measure your headboard space and then fiddle with drawers on the floor. Use plywood scraps to fill empty spots between drawers. Before you do anything else, decide if you want to keep or replace the old pulls. Use screws to turn the drawers and plywood into one large piece. Then paint your new headboard. For a finishing touch, place wallpaper or staple fabric to the insides of each drawer. You now have an attractive and unique piece with shelves for books, photos, and small lamps.

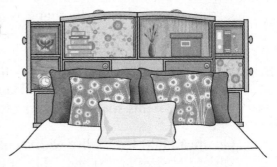

To hang any of these headboards, you'll need a heavy-duty mount like a French cleat.

Create a cleat to hang heavy items. Here's a great idea for hanging cabinets, headboards, and shelves – anything that's heavy. Create a French cleat out of scrap wood flooring or cut lumber. A French cleat is made up of two pieces of wood, each with an angled edge. Secure one piece to the wall on a couple of studs, angle-side

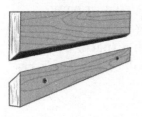

up. Affix the other piece to the object you are hanging, angle-side down. Place the two pieces together to form a snug fit. In addition to giving your heavy object extra support, a French cleat also allows you to slide your item back and forth until it's perfectly placed on your wall.

Create a one-of-a-kind headboard. A giant picture frame can make a dreamy headboard for any bed. Measure the width of your bed, then look for oversized frames at thrift shops, flea markets, or antique stores. Decide what to frame such as leftover fabric or wallpaper. Staple the fabric or adhere the wallpaper to a 1/2-inch piece of plywood.

For a cushioned look, sandwich batting between your fabric and board. Make sure the plywood is the right size to fit snugly into the picture frame. Then attach the board to the frame with nails or brackets. Hang your new headboard with French cleats for super support. Can't find a giant frame? Skip it altogether and hang wallpaper directly on to the wall behind your bed. Frame it with molding for an instant headboard.

GREAT IDEA

Revamp your outdated doorknobs

Brass is out. But you can give old, brass doorknobs new life with spray paint. Pick up a can for $7, and update several doorknobs at once. Paints come in black, gold, silver, and copper metallic colors. Plus, you can use your leftover spray paint to update the hardware on cabinets and furniture. If you think you want to buy a new doorknob, think again. They run around $30.

Perk up a dull ceiling. Complete the look of an elegant room with a ceiling painted metallic gold, silver, or copper. Paint over the entire ceiling or a section of it. Use painter's tape to create a square or rectangle. Cover the area with primer, and let it dry for a few hours. Roll on your first coat of paint. Wait a few hours, and roll on a second coat. Two coats may be all you need. Finish the treatment by framing your painted square or rectangle with crown molding. If metallic paint sounds too bold for you, transform your ceiling with wallpaper. Stick to a subtle pattern for a pretty accent or a sky motif for something fun. Think of your ceiling as a fifth wall — it deserves attention, too.

Buy the perfect ceiling fan. Choosing the best ceiling fan is easier than you think. Start by measuring the length and width of your room to calculate square feet. Next, use this chart to determine the fan diameter you need.

Room size in square feet	Fan diameter in inches
Up to 75	29 to 36
76 to 144	36 to 42
144 to 225	44
225 to 244	50 to 54

Also, consider the height of your ceiling. Go with a flush mount if your ceiling is 8 feet high. Use a downrod mount for taller ceilings.

Ceiling fans can help you save money on your energy bill. In the summer, run the blades counter clockwise to make your room feel 7 to 10 degrees cooler. And during winter, reverse your blade rotation to keep a room warmer. Don't want to stand on a chair to yank your fan's chains? No problem. Some ceiling fans come equipped with wall controls or handheld remotes. Control your fan from the comfort of your living room sofa, and enjoy the breeze.

Update an out-of-date popcorn ceiling. Nothing dates a home more than a popcorn ceiling. But you can easily scrape away this textured relic over a weekend.

Start by removing everything in the room. Next, cover the floor with plastic sheets or drop cloths. For the next few steps, you'll need eye protection, a handheld garden sprayer, a step ladder, and a ceiling scraper, putty knife, or drywall knife. Spray a 3 foot by 3 foot section of ceiling with water. You can also ask your local hardware store about a solution that will soften the texture. Try scraping off the popcorn. If it's too dry, spray it again and wait a few minutes. Keep working one section at a time until you have scraped the entire ceiling. When you're done, apply drywall mud if needed, then sand the ceiling with a sanding pole and screen. Finish your ceiling with primer and paint.

One word of caution before you get started – if your home was built before 1979, ask a pro to test the ceiling for asbestos.

Simple recipe for chalkboard paint. You can make your own chalkboard paint with unsanded grout and flat latex or acrylic paint in any color. The recipe is simple – mix 2 tablespoons of grout for every cup of paint. If you want to paint a larger surface, mix 1 cup of grout with a half gallon of paint. Stir your mixture in a well-ventilated area. Mix it thoroughly to keep it from looking grainy. Then paint away. Allow the surface to dry and cure for two to three days. Rub chalk along the surface and gently wipe it off. Grab a piece of chalk and start writing. Use your custom chalkboard paint for any surface in your home from an entire wall to a kitchen or cabinet door.

GREAT IDEA

Memory trick for painters

The next time you paint or stain a door in your house, jot down the name of the color on top of the door. If you ever need to repaint or re-stain it, you'll be able to find the color in no time at all. And no one will ever see your handwritten note.

Add a finishing touch to wood furniture. Applying stain to a piece of bare or stripped wood furniture will highlight the beauty of its natural grain. To pick the best stain for your project, follow these guidelines.

Oil-based stains buy you time. They allow you to stain large surfaces such as floors, cabinets, and paneling without leaving brush strokes. Use oil-based stains in a well-ventilated area. Water-based stains are ideal for small projects. They dry quickly, don't emit a strong odor, and come in a variety of colors.

Start by sanding your surface in the direction of the grain. Wipe away dust with tack cloth. If you're working with a soft wood, like pine or poplar, brush on a wood conditioner next. Depending on the type of stain you're using, apply it with cloth, a foam or bristle brush, or an aerosol spray. For a deep, rich color, leave the stain on longer or apply a second coat after the first one has dried completely. Wipe away any excess with a clean, dry cloth. After you achieve the desired results, allow the surface to dry overnight. Finish strong by applying a clear sealant to protect your stain and your wood.

Label outlet covers with breaker numbers

Here's a quick tip that will save you time and frustration. With permanent marker, label the back of your outlet covers and switch plates with their corresponding circuit breaker numbers. The next time you need to cut off power to a section of your home, remove a wall plate in that area. You'll know exactly which breaker to turn off.

Design your own dry-erase board. Hanging a boring white board in your kitchen can take away from your decor. A pretty picture frame is an attractive alternative — just choose one with glass. Simply cover a piece of cardboard with burlap, a piece of fabric, or scrapbook paper with colors that complement your kitchen. Pop it into your frame like you would a photo. Write messages on the glass using regular dry-erase markers. They work on glass just like they do on white boards.

Two-sided tape helps position strike plate

If you need to install a new dead bolt, stick a piece of double-sided tape to the end of the dead bolt. Make sure the bolt is retracted. Close your door and turn the bolt as if you're going to lock it. Your tape will stick to the door jamb at the precise place you need for your strike plate.

Jog your memory in style. Making a magnetic memory board is easier and cheaper than you think. Try one of these simple ideas.

Open up your kitchen drawers, and look for an old metal burner cover or pizza pan. If you don't have either of these, you can pick up one at a dollar store. On the lip, drill two small holes several inches apart. Trace your pizza pan on to a piece of scrapbook or contact paper, and cut it out. Then spray paint the edge of your pie plate. When it dries, brush Mod Podge on the inside of your plate and press your paper into it. Wait until it's completely dry then brush another layer of Mod Podge on top of the paper. Seal it with a clear, acrylic spray. Tie ribbon or yarn into the two holes and hang.

You can try the same idea with a cookie sheet. Instead of covering it with fabric, spray paint the entire sheet with a fun color. Sand or prime a nonstick pan before you begin. If you have a pan with greasy buildup, let it soak in 2 tablespoons of baking soda, a squirt of dishwashing detergent, and hot water for 15 minutes. Then scrub with a scouring pad. Drill holes in your cookie sheet and run ribbon through them for hanging.

For lovers of rustic decor, here's one more magnetic idea — use a salvaged piece of metal like an old tailgate as a memory board. Post messages and hang photos using souvenir magnets.

Paint a pretty picture with bleach. Turn a plain throw pillow into a custom creation with a paintbrush and bleach. But before you start, take a few safety precautions — protect your eyes, hands, and clothing from coming into contact with bleach.

Pour the bleach into a glass or ceramic bowl. Take off your pillow cover and place it on a flat surface. Place a piece of cardboard inside your cover. Sketch your design with chalk. This will make it easy for you to "erase" and re-sketch until you're satisfied. Any design will work, from swirls or stripes to a monogram or a poem. Dip a synthetic brush into your bowl of bleach and follow your chalk lines. Re-dip your brush every 2 inches. When you have finished painting, set your pillow cover in the sun for an hour — then rinse, hang to dry, restuff, and display.

For smaller, more intricate patterns or words, use a bleach pen. You can "write" with one just like you would a regular pen.

Create charming candleholders with kitchenware. If you want to warm up a room with candles, try making one of these two captivating candleholders. Start with soup ladles. Even though they are kitchen tools, hanging them as candleholders will work in any room from a cozy bathroom to a lavish living room.

A ladle's bowl provides the perfect home for a tea light, votive, or pillar candle. Collect several ladles, and screw them directly on to a wall or attach them to a shelf or a wood base — painted or stained a coordinating color.

Here's an even easier idea that will light up your dining room table — turn wine glasses upside down.

Place a tea light or votive candle on the base of the stem. Tie white lace, colorful ribbon, or strips of burlap to your stems for a finishing touch.

Decorate a vase with paintbrushes. Add an artistic flair to a vase by surrounding it with paintbrushes. Place two rubber bands around a tall, round vase. Tuck paintbrushes into the rubber bands until the vase is completely surrounded. Your brushes should be taller than your vase. For a clean look, use wood-handled brushes that are the same color. Or for a vase that packs a punch, spray your brushes and vase with a metallic spray paint. If you like the look of your masterpiece, make it a permanent fixture by gluing the paintbrushes to your vase. Fill with flowers and display as a centerpiece.

GREAT IDEA

Boost the life of your bouquets

Lumps of coal aren't just for Christmas stockings. Dump a lump or two into a vase full of freshly cut flowers. Coal will keep the water clean and clear, and lengthen the life of your bouquet. If you don't have any coal, use bleach. A mixture of one tablespoon of bleach per quart of water will keep it clean and get rid of the stench of stagnant water. Here's another tip to keep droopy flowers standing tall — use drinking straws. Thread stems through wide straws and place them in a vase. Your flowers will stand taller and last longer.

Add a pretty tint to mason jars. They're not just for canning peaches and preserves. Turn mason jars into a colorful container collection. To get started, gather food coloring, Mod Podge or Elmer's glue, and a stirrer like a plastic spoon or popsicle stick. Pour glue into your jar followed by a couple of drops of food coloring. Stir until the food coloring is completely blended in with the glue. Tilt and roll the jar in all directions until the inside is completely covered in the glue mixture. Place your jar upside down on a paper plate and allow the excess to trickle out. This may take up to an hour. Flip the jar over and allow it to air dry for 24 to 48 hours. Your jar will come out looking tinted. Use to display dried flowers or hold craft items like buttons or yarn. Don't use to store food or liquid.

Wooden clamps make great book holders.

Tired of standing your books on a table or shelf only to watch them fall over? Put the squeeze on them with wooden clamps. They will keep your books secure and standing tall. Older, rusty clamps will add charm to any home. Pair a couple with classic books for a vintage display.

Let your creativity flow with unique stencils

Creating a stencil to add a pattern to a wall or art project is easy. One way to make a stencil is to use something from around your house like a screen or hardware cloth. You can spray paint over the metal mesh on to a small piece of furniture to achieve a simple crisscross pattern. Lace and paper doilies deliver a delicate design, great for tiles and lampshades.

You can also find plenty of stencil designs online. Your best bet is to print a pattern on to a thin plastic sheet. Find plastic sheets at a craft store, or go to a print shop and pick up overhead projector sheets. You will also need a utility knife to cut out your image, and spray adhesive to stick your stencil on to the surface you want to paint.

Home maintenance

Clever ways to fix it yourself

Can't-miss tips for finding studs. A stud finder is not necessarily the easiest way to find the studs in your wall. A lamp or a strong magnet may yield better results with less hassle.

Begin by holding a flashlight or bare-bulb lamp near the wall as you slowly walk its length. Look for the small, rounded shapes of raised nail heads under the paint or wallpaper. If you see several marching straight up the wall, chances are good you've found a stud. Test by drilling a small pilot hole through the drywall. Poke the end of a hanger into the hole. If you hit something solid behind the drywall, you've found it.

A strong magnet can take away the guesswork. Rare-earth magnets work best, especially on plaster walls, but a sturdy refrigerator magnet will do in most cases. Tape a piece of masking tape to the magnet to use as a handle, and slowly drag it along the wall. When it finds a nail or screw, it will stick. Run it up the wall vertically to check for a line of nails suggesting a stud.

Pick the right size nail for your needs. It matters — too long, and your nail will poke through the other side of the wood. Too short, and it could come loose. The same is true with screws. Get it right with this rule of thumb. Nails and screws are generally used to attach a thin piece of material to a thicker one. Choose a nail around three times longer than the thickness of the thin piece. So if you're nailing a 1/4-inch piece of plywood to a 2x4, use a nail that is three times thicker than the plywood — 3/4-inch. For screws, choose one around two-and-a-half times longer than the thickness of the thin material. That means you'll need a screw 1 1/4 inches long to attach 1/2-inch drywall to a wall stud.

Never drop a screw again. Do small screws keep slipping from your fingers in tight spaces? A screwdriver with a magnetic tip can be very useful. But if you don't have one, or if the screw you're using is brass or aluminum, use a piece of plastic kitchen wrap to keep the screw on the screwdriver.

Tear about 6 inches of plastic wrap off the roll. Push the screw through the wrap and put the screwdriver in the screw head. Pull the wrap around the shaft of the screw-driver, and the screw is secure. When you're done turning the screw into place, just pull off the plastic wrap. Masking tape works, too — push the screw through the sticky side.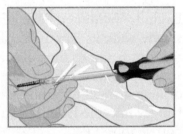

How to remove a stuck screw. Stripped screws are hard to remove but not impossible — if you know which tricks to try. Start with the simplest strategy. For a screw that's only partially stripped, insert the largest screwdriver that will fit, and tap the end of the handle with a hammer. This may seat the tool deeply enough to get traction in what's left of the head.

If that doesn't work, lay a wide rubber band over the screw head. Tap the screwdriver in again with the hammer. With luck, the rub-ber band will grab the inside of the screw enough for you to turn it. Sometimes a flathead screwdriver can turn a screw when a Phillips can't. Use a hacksaw to create or deepen a slot for the flathead to give it more grip.

What if you only get the screw partially out? Don't despair. Unscrew it far enough to slip a pair of locking pliers around the shank, then turn the pliers counterclockwise to remove the stuck screw.

Four quick fixes for loose screws. Everyone has a few loose screws. While these tips won't fix the ones in your head, they're sure to tighten the ones around your house.

For a screw or nail that only wiggles a little, brush clear nail polish along the shaft then put it back in its hole. It should stay put once the polish dries. This won't work when screws are very loose. In that case, try a longer screw. It may be able to bite into fresh wood beyond the too-big hole.

Or fill the hole with more wood. Toothpicks and kabob skewers work well for small holes. Remove the screw, dab wood glue onto the stick, and insert it into the hole. Cut it flush with a utility knife once the glue dries, then simply reinsert the screw.

Some screws, especially the ones in door hinges, need a sturdier remedy. First, enlarge the hole with a drill bit, then find a wood dowel the same diameter as the bit. Brush wood glue onto it, and insert it into the hole. Let it dry, cut it flush, and sink the screw into the dowel.

GREAT IDEA

Drive nails straight as an arrow

Avoid the frustration of bent nails and banged thumbs. Drill a pilot hole slightly smaller than the nail to get it started and help it go in straight. Hold the nail in place with a clothespin or needle-nose pliers to protect your thumb while hammering.

You can also stand it between the teeth of a comb or push it through a piece of cardboard to keep it steady while you hammer.

Handy tricks for drilling holes. Drilling a straight hole sounds simple enough. Professional carpenters do it all the time. But after you've driven a few screws in sideways, you'll remember why you normally hire someone else to do the work.

Carpenters have more than just experience on their side. They also employ some handy tricks. The simplest involves a speed square. These have a built-in right angle and one flat side, or fence. Rest the fence along the top of your drill and press the other side of the square against your work surface to drill a perfectly perpendicular pilot hole.

A reflective surface can also help you line up your drill bit. Don safety glasses and drill a pilot hole through an old CD or DVD. Place it with the shiny side facing out. Line up the bit with its reflection on the disc, and you'll have a straight-on hole in no time.

Or make a drilling guide from a small block of wood. Cut one end of the wood perfectly square and draw a pencil line down the center of that end, perpendicular to the edge. Place the block against your work surface, line up the drill bit with your pencil line, and start drilling.

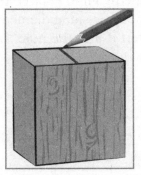

Put an end to annoying squeaks. Stop living with squeaky hinges. You have everything you need to silence them for good right in your pantry. Close the door and remove one of the hinge pins by tapping a nail up through the bottom of the hinge. Rub an ordinary candle all over the pin to coat it in wax, then tap it back into the hinge. Do this with each squeaky pin, one hinge at a time.

A dab of petroleum jelly will do the trick, too. Coat the pin lightly, and put a small dollop of jelly in the top of the hinge for good measure. The petroleum jelly will attract dust and dirt, so candles work best if you have them on hand.

Stubborn pins sometimes refuse to come out. Never fear. You can still fix the squeak. Rub a dry bar of soap along the outside of the hinge, working it into every crevice. Open and close the door a few times to spread the soap throughout the hardware.

Pop the lock on interior doors. Locking yourself out of your bathroom by accident is annoying. But frantically trying to reach a loved one who has fallen inside a locked bathroom is terrifying. Fortunately, it's easy to spring most locks in just a few seconds.

These tricks work on doors that lock by pressing and turning the knob or by pushing a button in the center. Look for a hole in the center of the knob. Simply slide a small, straight item, like a tiny flathead screwdriver, into the hole. Fish around until you feel it catch on a slot, then push it and turn the knob at the same time. This should unlock the door. Don't see a hole in the center? Check the knob's stem or plate. The same instructions apply – insert your homemade lock pick, push, and turn the knob.

Anything small, straight, and sturdy will pop the lock. Hex (Allen) wrenches, hairpins, or even a cotton swab with the cotton removed from one end will get you inside.

What to do when doors stick. Some doors stick only in summer, when they swell from humidity and catch on the frame. If that's the case with yours, simply sand the swollen top or side of the door until it closes. Then seal the edges with paint or varnish to keep them from swelling again. If your door catches even during the dryness of winter, it's probably a loose hinge. Check each hinge for loose screws and tighten any you find.

Fast fixes for a drifting door. If you have a door that drifts closed, either partly or all the way, it's probably not hanging straight. Also, the top may be leaning away from the door jamb.

Before calling for help, here are a few things to try to make the door behave.

- Use a door stop. Keep in mind you'll have to move it in and out of place each time you want to open or close the door.

- Tighten the screws. Make sure the screws holding the hinges in place are secure and haven't loosened – particularly on the top hinge. If they have, simply tightening them may solve the problem. But the screws may not tighten if the holes are too big. You can fix the problem by putting a wooden kitchen match or toothpick in the hole and breaking it off flush. Then when you screw it back in, it will stay tight. If the screw is worn out, replace it with a new one.

- Bend the pin. Another simple fix involves removing the pin from the hinge. Start with the bottom hinge, and make sure the door is closed and latched. Loosen the pin by prying the top away from the hinge with a screwdriver then pulling it out. If that doesn't work, use a screwdriver or other sturdy tool that fits in the bottom of the hinge – a nail or even a chopstick could work – and tap upward with a hammer. Once the pin is removed, lay it on a safe hard surface, hold the pin securely, and use the hammer to give it a whack in the middle. The goal is to bend the pin just slightly, maybe an eighth of an inch. When you put the pin back in the hinge, there should be just enough friction to make the door stay put.

Easy way to mend a broken drawer. Is your kitchen drawer falling apart? Did the back fall out or the sides fall in? Fix it fast with a piece of trim. Cut a small piece of quarter-round molding to the same height as the inside of the drawer. Dab a little glue on the two flat sides of the trim, and nestle it in the broken corner. Let the glue set, then nail or drill a screw through the drawer and into the molding.

Fix a fixture that burns out bulbs quickly. A fixture that blows through bulbs faster than the others in your house may have an easy-to-solve problem. Vibrations, perhaps from a wobbly fan, can pop the lights in a ceiling fan before their time. The solution is simple – buy bulbs made for "rough service" from your local hardware store. These have a sturdier filament, which should help them withstand the shaking.

Bulbs that are too strong for the fixture can also blow early. You might expect that a 75-watt bulb in a 60-watt socket would last longer. In fact, it generates more heat than the fixture can handle, damaging both the bulb and the socket. When you buy bulbs, read labels and choose the right wattage bulb.

Screwing bulbs in too tightly can also shorten their life span. The base of the bulb can flatten the brass tab inside the light socket. Normally, this tab sticks up about one-quarter of an inch so it touches the bulb. If past bulbs were screwed in too tightly, they may have flattened the tab. Turn off the power to the light and remove the bulb. Check the tab. If it's too flat, gently lift it with a flathead screwdriver. If it's properly positioned but dirty, clean it with a cotton swab dipped in rubbing alcohol.

Unscrew hard-to-remove light bulbs.

Unscrewing a bulb in a recessed light fixture can be hard, but arthritis can make it almost impossible. Let duct tape do the work for you. Tear off a strip about 12 inches long. Press the middle of the tape to it, then unscrew it by pulling the two loose ends and twisting them counterclockwise.

Savvy tips for labeling breakers. Take time to label the breakers in your electrical panel once. It's easier than you think, and you'll be glad you did.

First, figure out which outlets go to which circuit breaker. Plug a lamp into every outlet in a room, and turn on every light and fan switch. Have a friend stand in the room while you slowly flip each breaker off. Arm yourselves with cell phones, if you have them, so your friend can call you when a light or fan turns off. Or do it the old-fashioned way and yell to each other.

Testing switches works best with two people, but you can test outlets on your own without any leg work. Plug in a radio, and crank up the volume so you can hear it from the breaker panel. When the radio goes silent, you know you've located the breaker.

Number the breakers directly on the panel, then write the corresponding breaker number on the inside of each switch and outlet plate. Work room by room, and remember to test outside lights and outlets, too.

Camera captures what's hidden in walls

Spread the word — the next time someone you know is about to start a major remodeling job, tell them to snap photos of the open walls before the drywall goes up. Stretch a tape measure along the bottom of the wall or tack a yard stick to one of the studs for reference. Then, if a question comes up later about locating studs, electrical wires, or pipes, the picture will provide all the answers.

Clear clogs with a coat hanger. Stubborn clogs may need snaking. Improvise your own auger by untwisting a coat hanger. Leave the hook on the end, straighten the middle portion, and bend the other end into a handle, so you don't drop it down the drain. For bathroom sinks, you'll need to remove the rod under the sink that raises and lowers the stopper.

Start by removing the stopper. Then reach under the sink and unscrew the thumbscrew that attaches to the rod. Pull the rod back and out of the drain. Now slide the hooked end of your coat hanger down the drain, twisting and jiggling it up and down as you go. Gently pull it out. With any luck, the gunk causing the clog will come out with it.

Quick tricks to fix a stuck sink. Believe it or not, you can free most clogged drains yourself without spending money on plumbers or chemical decloggers. First, make your soda-drinking habit pay off by recycling a 2-liter bottle into a makeshift plunger. Remove the sink stopper and plug the overflow drain with a wet rag. For double sinks, plug the second drain. Next, fill the empty bottle with water. In one fast motion, shove the mouth of the bottle into the drain and squeeze it hard. Water will blast down the drain, blowing apart any clogs in its way.

If you have an old-fashioned, wide-mouth plunger, you can clear a clogged sink as easily as a clogged toilet. Take out the stopper, fill the sink with several inches of water, and stuff wet rags in the over-flow or second drain. Wipe a thick layer of petroleum jelly around the rim of the plunger to create a stronger seal. Plunge vigorously for about 30 seconds. Yank the plunger out of the water hard on the final upstroke.

If the sink doesn't begin draining freely, plunge again. Once you clear the clog, run hot water to flush any particles still stuck in the pipes.

You can prevent many clogs in the first place with a monthly flush of the drains you use most often. Pour half a cup of baking soda down sink, kitchen, and tub drains, followed by half a cup of vine-gar. Let the mix fizz for half an hour, then chase it down with a kettle of boiling water.

Suck out tough clogs fast. Some toilets may be strong enough to flush a bucket of golf balls, as in TV commercials, but it's prob-ably a bad idea to try it at home. Most of the time, when hard objects fall down a drain or toilet it's by mistake and not on purpose. While plungers may work wonders on soft clogs, they usually fail at freeing hard trapped items, like toothbrushes or toys. Try a wet/dry shop vac instead. Suck out the water first, then dry the surface of the toilet bowl, sink, or bathtub. Stick the hose down the drain, and seal the space between the hose and drain with tape to create the tightest seal possible. Tape the overflow hole closed, too. Then turn on the vac. With luck, whatever is stuck will come right up.

Solve plumbing problems with a straw. Put an end to running toilets, and install a new one with ease. All thanks to a simple straw. Toilets often run because the chain on the flapper inside the tank gets kinked. Keep that from happening in the future. Unhook the chain, slide a straw over it, and reattach it. If the straw is too long, just cut it to size.

Straws can also make replacing a toilet much simpler. The hardest part – lining up the holes in the base of the bowl with the bolts in the floor. Do it wrong, and you mess up the wax ring. Get it right the first time by sliding straws over the bolts, then use them as guides when you lower the bowl. Slide the bowl holes over the straws for a perfect fit.

Silence the sound of dripping water. The drip, drip, drip of rain in your downspout is enough to drive you batty. Put an end to sleepless nights. Tie a nylon rope to the gutter hanger just above the downspout. Then drop the rope down the spout, and wait for the next storm to roll through. Water will run down the rope rather than striking the aluminum. Don't try this if your gutters tend to overflow or get clogged with leaves and debris, though. A rope could worsen these problems.

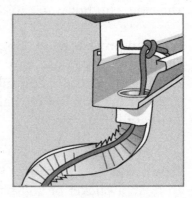

The same idea also quiets a dripping faucet. Tie a piece of string around the faucet head, and let it trail into the sink bowl. Water will wick down the string silently until a plumber can get out to fix the drip for good.

How to tell if old paint is any good. Paint stored in a tightly sealed container can last a long time. Latex paint generally has a 10-year shelf life, while oil-based paint can last 15 years. That said, test it before putting it on your walls. Crack open the can and sniff. Good paint will have a chemical odor, while bad paint will smell rancid. Remove any skin that has formed on top and stir. See if you can blend the liquid that has separated back into the paint. Next, brush the paint onto newspaper or cardboard and look for lumps. Lumpy paint is bad paint. If yours passes all of these tests, then congratulations — it's still good.

MONEYSAVER

Turn old paint into free primer

Is your basement full of paint you'll never use again? Colors you bought and hated or have outgrown? Don't throw them away. Mix together leftover paint and use it as primer on future projects. Combine similar tones, such as light with light or dark with dark, and types of paint — latex with latex and oil with oil. Sheen doesn't matter. Put a coat of the light mix under light-colored paints and the dark concoction under dark colors in place of expensive, store-bought primer.

Give new life to gummed up paint. Old paint needs extra TLC before it's fit to put on a wall. Start by skimming off any skin that has formed on top and mixing the paint thoroughly. An old whisk and a little elbow grease will do the job fine. For even less work, slide the beater from an old handheld mixer into your drill, and run it until the paint is blended. To cut down on spatter, place the can in a paper grocery bag first or lower the beater into the paint before turning on the drill. Avoid mixing on high speed. You'll work air bubbles into it, which will end up on your wall.

Finish prepping your old paint by straining it. This removes any dried bits or lumps that formed while it sat on the shelf. Cut off the leg of an old pair of pantyhose and stretch it over the mouth of a clean container, something large enough to hold all the paint. Secure the stocking with masking tape or a rubber band. Cover the floor with newspaper, and don a pair of rubber gloves. Then slowly pour the paint into the stocking.

Paint is thick, so straining it takes time. Be patient, and you'll end up with perfectly usable paint that you otherwise would have trashed. When you finish, gather up the gunky stocking, squeeze it to release the remaining paint, and toss. Seal your new container tightly to keep the contents fresh.

Revive old brushes before buying new. Bring dried, crusty nylon brushes back to life with a hot vinegar bath. Heat a saucepan of distilled white vinegar to a simmer. Use a funnel to pour it into a mason jar or other sturdy container. Soak the brush for 30 minutes, then wash it in warm, soapy water. Use your fingers to loosen the bristles and free trapped paint. For extra help, run a brush comb through the bristles or brush them downward with a nylon fingernail brush.

Cut brush-cleaning time in half. Make paint cleanup fast and painless by soaking your brush in fabric softener. Start by scraping excess paint out of the bristles with a brush comb or old fork. Mix half a cup of fabric softener with one gallon of warm water, or place a couple of used dryer sheets in a bucket of warm water. Let your brush soak in the mixture for several minutes, then swirl it vigorously until it's free of paint. No need to rinse with water afterward. This trick only works for latex, not oil-based, paints.

Prep the brush before painting, and cleanup will be even easier. For latex paints, dip the brush in water all the way up to the base of the bristles. For oil-based paints, dip it in mineral spirits. Blot with a paper towel until the brush is only slightly damp, and get painting.

Help keep the angle on a sash brush sharp by laying it on a glossy magazine page after cleaning. Shake out the extra water, then fold the page around the brush, following the angle of the tip. Tape it closed and hang the brush by the handle to dry until the next time you need it.

Clever trick protects brushes

Have an old three-ring binder hanging around? Use it to make a drying rack for your freshly washed paintbrushes. Remove the metal portion in the middle of the binder and screw it to the wall. Snap open the rings, slide the hole in the brush handle onto one, and snap closed. They'll dry in an out-of-the way place and avoid the risk of bent bristles.

Add heat to help tape stick. Painter's and masking tape both lose their stickiness after sitting on the shelf for a while. Before you throw out an expensive roll, try popping it in the microwave for 10 seconds. Heat softens the glue, giving your roll new life. Don't try this trick on duct tape or other plastic tapes, however. They might melt. Warm painter's tape creates a better seal against paint when masking trim, floors, and fixtures. Run a putty knife along the taped section to further prevent bleeding. Heat also helps remove stubborn tape. Aim a hairdryer at the tape as you slowly peel it off.

The secret to perfectly smooth painted trim. The pros know all the tricks, but who has the money to hire a professional painter? Never fear. With a little wrist work and a good angled brush you can achieve professional-looking results for a fraction of the cost.

Pick up a bottle of paint conditioner at your local hardware store, and add a few ounces to each gallon of paint. It helps the paint flow better and dry slower, giving you more time to spread it on and smooth out brush strokes.

Dip an angled brush about 1 inch deep in paint. Wipe off the excess to prevent drips, then swipe your brush along the trim in several back-and-forth motions. This technique is called "laying on" the paint. Once the paint is off the brush and on the trim, it's time to smooth out your strokes with a finishing pass. Drag the tips of the bristles lightly over the wet paint in one long stroke, lifting the brush off the trim at the end of the pass. Start your stroke on a dry or unpainted area and brush toward the wet paint.

Reload your brush with paint, and lay it on the next stretch of trim. Again, begin the stroke on an unpainted area and brush toward the wet paint. Otherwise, you'll mar the smooth finish you worked so hard to create.

WARNING

Seal vents during dusty remodel

Hanging plastic over doorways can keep dust from drifting when you are sanding walls or undergoing a major remodel. But don't forget your central heating and air system. Cover return vents with plastic and seal the edges with tape, so dust doesn't get sucked in. You run the risk of clogging the filter and shaving years off the life of your HVAC. Turn it off completely, if possible, to keep it from circulating any dust it does pull in throughout the house.

Get perfect caulk lines every time. Caulk is sticky and messy, but laying a smooth bead is essential if you want your work to look its best. Perfect your skills with a few tips from the pros.

- Lay strips of blue painter's tape or masking tape along either side of the line you plan to caulk. Press the tape edges firmly to get a good seal.

- Cut the tip of the tube very close to the end if caulking trim and other woodwork, leaving a 1/16-inch opening. For caulking tubs, showers, or sinks, create a bigger opening, about 1/8 inch.

- Always cut the opening at a 45-degree angle, then smooth any rough edges with sandpaper.

- Squeeze the tube or caulk gun trigger with gentle but steady pressure as you move down the line.

- Smooth caulk with your fingertip for a perfect line. For latex caulk, wipe your finger on a damp rag or dip it in water before touching the caulk. A wet finger makes a smoother bead and keeps the caulk from sticking to you. Wipe your finger off occasionally on a damp rag. To smooth silicone caulk, dip your finger in dish soap rather than water.

If arthritis or tremors make it hard to smooth the caulk by hand, try using an old spoon. Simply run the backside of the spoon's tip along the bead.

Put peeling wallpaper in its place. Bring the old glue back to life by holding a warm, damp rag over the peeling area for a couple of minutes. Gently pull back the loose paper, and brush some glue onto the backing with an artist's paintbrush. Even ordinary, all-purpose, white glue will do. For seams that won't pull open far enough to slide a brush beneath, squeeze the glue onto a sheet of paper, slide this behind the wallpaper, and wipe the glue onto the backing. Press the wallpaper against the wall, and roll the seam flat with a rolling pin. Wipe off extra glue with your damp rag.

Blend wallpaper patch seamlessly

Saving your leftover wallpaper is a no-brainer, because one day you may need it for a patch job. But if you keep the extra rolled up and tucked in a closet, the patch may look newer than the surrounding paper. That's because wallpaper ages over time, fading or yellowing from sunlight, cigarette smoke, and the years. Plan ahead. After hanging new paper, tack a leftover strip to an attic or closet wall so it can age at the same rate.

Erase ugly ceiling stains. You may not need to paint your ceiling to block out a water stain. Try spraying it with bleach water first. Cover the floor beneath the stain with plastic, and don gloves and goggles. Spray light stains with a solution of one part bleach and nine parts water. Let it dry, then mist again if the stain hasn't completely faded. Dab straight bleach on old or dark stains, or spritz with a store-bought mildew remover that contains bleach.

Repair, don't replace, your linoleum floor. Burn marks, gouges, cuts, and peeling seams don't have to mean installing all new linoleum. You can repair these and other vinyl floor disasters with a hair dryer, Super Glue, and nail polish.

To fix edges that are peeling off the subfloor, start by holding a hair dryer 1 or 2 inches away from the linoleum. This softens the flooring and makes it more flexible. Pull the floor back slightly, and vacuum any grains of dirt underneath it. Pick up a glue made for bonding acrylic at the hardware store. Basic Super Glue will work in a pinch.

Squirt it onto a flexible putty knife, and wipe it onto the underside of the flooring and onto the subfloor beneath. Reheat the linoleum first, if needed, to make it flexible again. Weigh the flooring flat with several heavy books until the glue dries.

For burn marks and gouges, try this trick. Clean the area, then sand a small, spare piece of linoleum until you have a tiny pile of powder the same color as the damaged area. Mix this with a little clear nail polish, and paint it directly on the burn or gouge. If you don't have an extra piece of linoleum, try painting the area with a nail polish as close to the floor's color as possible.

6 surprising uses for felt pads. Felt pads can save your flooring from furniture scratches, but experts suggest replacing them every three to six months. Grains of dirt get embedded in the pads over time and can actually scratch floors instead of protecting them. Don't stop there. Check out these six other uses for felt pads.

- Cover the rubber feet on the bottoms of small appliances like coffee makers or microwaves. The machines will slide more easily when you need to move them.

- Place them on the backs of cutting boards to add stability while you chop and slice.

- Stick them on the bottoms of jars and canisters to keep them from scratching the countertop.

- Slap them on the front and side bumpers of your vacuum to prevent it from scuffing your baseboards.

- Put them on the backs of hanging pictures and wall clocks to protect wall paint.

- Protect the wall from doors that swing open on their own. Stick a felt pad or two on the wall where the knob usually strikes.

Protect the wall when pulling off trim. Prying off trim isn't hard, but doing it without damaging the wood or the wall is. Or so you thought. Cut along the top of the trim where it meets the wall with a sharp utility knife. This cuts through any caulk and paint so that when you pull off the trim it doesn't take the drywall paper with it.

Slide a wide putty knife behind one end of the trim to protect the wall, and gently pull it forward. Once you have enough space, slide a pry bar between the trim and putty knife. Carefully pull the trim away from the wall. Move along the wall and repeat until the whole piece has come free. If the molding begins to crack, slip a stiff putty knife between the pry bar and the trim before each pull.

Pull stuck nails with ease. You would think that something as basic as pulling a nail out of wood would be simple. It's usually not, unless you have this cheat sheet. Follow this guide to get the nails out.

- Remove a nail that has lost its head by locking a pair of locking pliers tightly where the head should be. Hook a pry bar or hammer at the base of the pliers and pull back to lift out the nail. Slide a wood block beneath the hammer to protect the wood and gain leverage.

- For wood you don't mind denting, hook the claw of your hammer at the base of the nail. Instead of rocking the hammer backward, pull it sideways. The nail will bend but also rise out of the wood. Pull the hammer from side to side to gradually work the nail out. Protect the wood from dings by sliding a 1/4-inch plywood scrap beneath the hammer.

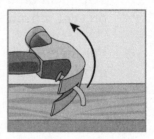

- Get nails out of trim and other finished wood without doing any damage by pulling them through the back. Rest the trim face-down on a carpet scrap to protect the finish. Grab the nail shank with a pair of nippers and rock it from side to side until it pulls through. No nippers on hand? No problem. Use your locking pliers as you would for the headless nail, and pry it out with a pry bar or hammer.

WARNING

A hint before you tint your windows

Reflective window tint can be a valuable, energy-saving addition to your home. Usually, window film is applied to the inside of single-pane windows. But if your windows have two or more layers of glass, the film should be installed only on the outside.

Putting it on the inside of a multi-pane window can cause damaging heat buildup between the panes, and will void the warranty of most manufacturers. Get the right product for the job — film specifically designed for multi-pane windows — and check your warranty before you apply film to any window.

5-minute fix for holes in siding. Patch up holes in your vinyl siding with a squirt of caulk. The key to making a nearly invisible repair is to match the caulk color to the siding. Home improvement stores sometimes carry caulk in a variety of colors. If yours doesn't, head to a siding supply store or shop online. Take a spare piece of siding with you, if you have one, to match the color as closely as possible.

Once home, wipe the area around the hole clean so the caulk can seal properly. Squirt it into the hole, filling the space behind the hole, between the siding and the house. Pull the caulk tube back as the hole fills, and leave a small blob sticking out beyond the siding. Let it dry for several days, then shave off the excess with a razor blade or utility knife, leaving the caulk flush with the siding.

First aid for ice dams. Ice dams are like the aches that accompany the flu – they're a symptom, not the cause of the problem. Ice dams form when warm air rises from the house into the attic and heats the roof unevenly. Too little insulation and ventilation in your attic are often the real culprits.

Warm air from the house can warm the attic, too, melting snow on parts of the roof. Meanwhile, the roof's edge stays cold. When water from melting snow hits the edge, it refreezes into an ice dam, blocking the gutters. Melting water then builds up behind the ice. Over time it can find its way under your shingles and into your attic, ceiling, and walls.

The long-term fix is to add insulation, increase the ventilation, and seal the places where warm air in the house leaks into the attic. All three will keep the roof colder in winter, which will prevent snow from melting on the roof and refreezing along the edges.

Until then, treat the symptoms. If you spot leaks in the attic or along exterior walls, act fast. Set a box fan in the attic, and tilt it so it blows air directly at the leak. This will freeze the water fast, stopping the leak until you can clear the ice and snow off the roof. Use a roof rake with wheels to remove snow on one-story homes.

Cut a path through the dam so melting snow has a way to drain. On a warm day, aim a garden hose at the roof to carve out a channel in the ice. Can't catch a warm day? Cut the leg off a nylon stocking, and fill it with calcium chloride ice melt. Tie it closed and lay it atop the ice dam, perpendicular to the roof's edge and crossing the gutter. Use a long-handled hoe to push it into position if needed.

Eventually it will melt through the blockage. Keep in mind that calcium chloride may harm plants near the gutter and downspout.

Which last longer — light or dark shingles?

Experts don't necessarily agree. Dark shingles get hotter in summer, and heat can shorten the life of many materials. But the sun's ultraviolet (UV) rays may have a bigger impact on roof life than heat does. Still, some experts say light-colored roofs tend to last longer.

One thing is certain — light shingles stay cooler and keep the temperature in your attic and house lower than dark-colored shingles. A dark roof can reach 180 degrees on a sunny, windless day. A roof with premium white shingles may stay 30 degrees cooler.

Consider light-colored shingles or roofing the next time yours needs replacing if you live in warm climates. People in cold climates, on the other hand, may do better with dark roofing to keep their homes warmer in winter.

Check your chimney for deadly creosote. A wood-burning fireplace can keep you warm and cozy on a cold night. It can also burn your house down. Burning wood produces soot, creosote, and glaze, all of which gradually build up on the inside of your chimney. And all of which are combustible. That's why the National Fire Protection Association suggests having your chimney inspected at least once a year and getting it cleaned when needed. You may not be able to clean it yourself – that's a job for the professionals – but you can inspect it for dangerous buildup in a few minutes' time.

Hang a length of toilet paper over the mouth of the fireplace, and watch which way it blows. If a downdraft blows it into the room, then open a door or window to reverse the airflow up into the chimney.

Don goggles, a dust mask, and a hat, and stick your head inside the fireplace. Hold a flashlight in one hand and a poker in the other. Scratch a line in the black stuff coating the inside of the chimney, just above the damper.

Call in a chimney sweep if the black stuff is flaky or bubbly and 1/4-inch thick; or if it's shiny, tar-like, and more than 1/8-inch thick. Both are forms of creosote buildup. At levels that high, a chimney fire could break out the next time you use it.

Lengthen the life of your air conditioner. Preparing your air conditioner (AC) for winter is a cinch. All you need is a small piece of plywood and a few bricks. Brush away leaves that have collected around the condenser unit outside. Then lay a piece of plywood just large enough to cover the top. Weight that down with four bricks, one on each corner. That's it.

Ignore the advice of anyone who says you should wrap the unit with a tarp. Inevitably, water will find a way under it and become trapped, where it will have all winter to rust your condenser. Tarps also create an inviting home for rodents, that will chew away at the wiring.

Leaving the unit covered but unwrapped protects it from snow and ice, while allowing water to evaporate and discouraging critters. Be sure to remove the plywood before you turn on the AC next spring. If you are worried you'll forget, simply unplug the AC from its power source or flip the circuit breaker that controls it before putting it to bed for winter.

Thaw frozen pipes in a flash. It's a fact of life during winter — pipes sometimes freeze. You should do everything you can to prevent that — drip your faucets during cold spells and insulate exposed pipes, for instance. But if all your efforts fail, you can still thaw them yourself. Just be prepared with a mop, bucket, and dry towels in case the ice has lead to burst pipes.

First, try to locate the frozen section. Look for pipes coated in frost. Those in unheated basements, crawl spaces, attics, garages, and inside kitchen or bathroom cabinets are likely culprits. So are pipes that run up exterior walls. Don't see any frost? Use the process of elimination to figure out which line is frozen. Turn on every faucet in the house, both the hot and cold water, and flush each toilet. A fixture that has very low or no water pressure may be frozen. Shut off water to the area that's iced, or turn it off where the main supply line enters the house.

Chances are, you have everything you need to thaw the pipes yourself. Open the taps nearest the frozen section of pipe. Water moving through it will help the ice melt faster. Wrap a heating pad around the frozen section, rub the area with a hot towel, or aim a hair dryer at it. A space heater nearby can also help defrost the ice blockage. Whatever you do, don't try to melt the ice with a lighter, blow torch, or other open flame. You could damage the pipe or start a fire.

GREAT IDEA

Get a better hold on tool handles

Arthritis can put a crimp in your fix-it plans, making hammers, screwdrivers, and yard tools hard to hold tightly. Get a better grip by wrapping the handles in insulation. Cut a piece of foam pipe insulation to the right size, and duct-tape it around the handle. Or wrap a length of self-adhesive foam weatherstrip around and around the handle, sticky side down.

Organize hand tools with homemade solutions. Need more storage but can't afford a fancy tool chest? Take a super-simple approach, and nail a belt or tie rack to the wall. Use it to hang tools with a hole in one end, like wrenches and paintbrushes.

You can also make "pockets" to hold tools that don't have a hole in their handles for hanging. Cut a leaky garden hose into short pieces and tack the back of each one to the wall. Slip screwdrivers, pliers, and other items in them.

Have some old mason jars? Group like items together in each one. Just stretch a piece of hardware cloth over the top, and screw on the metal lid. Slide screwdrivers or paintbrush handles through the metal grid for standup storage.

Free storage for small tools. Create a place to store pencils, drill bits, and other small tools from scraps of wood and Styrofoam. It's a convenient way to store small items, no pegboard needed.

Drill holes at a 45-degree angle part way through a block of wood. Size the holes based on what you plan to store in them – pencils, drill bits, awls, Allen wrenches, and more. Mount the block on the wall or side of your tool bench.

Save yourself all the trouble of drilling by using Styrofoam, instead. Glue a piece of foam on plywood, and screw that plywood to the wall or the side of your workbench. Then poke a hole at a 45-degree angle in the Styrofoam for each tool. Make your "pilot" holes with an awl or small bit, and enlarge them to the perfect size by pushing each tool into its hole.

GREAT IDEA

Keep small parts handy with packing tape

Keep screws, washers, and other small parts from getting lost. Tear off a piece of clear packing tape and lay it sticky side-up. Drop each small piece on one end of the tape. Fold the tape over on itself, sealing the items inside. Label your makeshift pouch with a permanent marker and set aside until you're ready to use them.

Free and cheap tool storage. You don't need to spend a fortune on fancy tool chests or storage systems. You already have handy storage hiding all over your house. You're just not using it to store tools.

- Use seedling trays or muffin tins to organize screws, nuts, and washers. Place them in shallow drawers, or stack them on top of each other on open shelves.

- Keep longer nails, bolts, and screws in plastic food storage containers, like Glad or Rubbermaid. They're affordable, nearly indestructible, and clear, so you can see what's in them at a glance. Look for stackable ones that lock into each other if you plan to stack them on shelves.

- Slip an old silverware organizer into a drawer to corral wrenches, awls, screwdrivers, and other small hand tools.

- Protect metal parts and hardware from rust by storing them in old ammunition boxes. They're rugged and waterproof. Buy them used at military surplus stores.

- Repurpose old metal file cabinets to hold your power tools. Attach casters to the bottom, or set the cabinets on scraps of carpet so they don't stain the garage floor if the bottoms rust.

Make sure your level is level. The next time you hang a picture, stop and check your level's accuracy. That little bubble is carefully calibrated. A good hard drop can knock it off kilter for good.

Set your level along the edge of a flat surface, like a table or countertop. The surface itself does not need to be perfectly level. Line up one end of the level with the table corner. Make a mental note of where the bubble is.

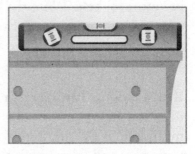

Turn the level 180 degrees, and line up the other end with the same corner. Finally, roll the level over so that the vial is upside down. The bubble should appear in the exact same spot each time. If it's farther to the left or right, then your level is no longer accurate.

Do the same against a wall to check for plumb. Line the tool up with the outside corner of a wall and take note of the measuring plumb.

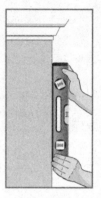

Now roll the level on to its other side. The bubble should be in the same place. Don't just check your home level. Use these tricks to test one in-store before you buy it.

Secret to reassembling things with ease.
Taking something apart is usually easier than putting it back together. You always think you'll remember which piece goes where and in what order, but that rarely happens. The fix is an easy one. Take photos. Each time you remove another part, snap a picture with your camera or cellphone. When the time comes to put things back together, you'll have your own illustrated instructions on hand.

Never forget another measurement. Remembering a measurement long enough to get to your saw isn't easy. Get it wrong, and you'll be heading to the store to buy more wood. Writing it on your hand can help, but there's a better solution. Paint the sides of your tape measure with black chalk paint, and carry a piece of chalk in your tool belt. Write the measurements on the tape itself and erase when you're done. Even simpler, stick masking tape on the side of the measuring tape, write on it, and remove it when finished.

Store scrap lumber for a rainy day. You know you'll find a need for that extra wood as soon as you throw it out, but in the meantime, it's cluttering up your workshop. Satisfy your need to be both neat and frugal with these free and cheap storage solutions.

Stand tall lumber upright between wall studs. Screw eye hooks into the studs and hook a bungee cord across the front of your lumber "rack" to keep the wood from falling over. Try not to stand the wood directly on a concrete floor. Moisture from the floor can wreak real havoc on lumber. The solution – place some scrap plywood or 2x4 beneath the pieces.

Standing boards vertically sometimes causes them to bow in the middle. Fight this tendency by stacking the pieces straight up, not leaning, and tightly against each other. Leave as little wiggle room as possible. Flipping the boards every few months may also minimize warping.

Skip these problems completely by storing your lumber horizontally. An old step ladder or step stool makes a perfect lumber rack. Screw scrap pieces of wood onto the back of the ladder at the same height as the rungs on the front, if needed.

Lay plywood on top of the rungs, running from front to back, if you want a sturdy platform for your wood. Move the ladder against a wall and slide your lumber atop the rungs.

Extend the life of dull saw blades. That dull saw blade may not need replacing – it may just need a good cleaning. Wood pitch, glue, and other gunk build up on a blade's cutting teeth over time. Even if the blade is sharp, it will cut as though it's dull. Getting the gunk off could restore its bite and save big on replacement blades.

Amazingly, ordinary oven cleaner works best, and it won't harm carbide-tipped teeth. Buy generic oven or grill cleaner and follow the instructions. Be sure to wear gloves, eye protection, and an apron. Cleaners like this may damage Teflon- and plastic-coated blades, though, so apply them at your own risk.

Smart way to store saw blades. Miter and circular saw blades are sharp and brittle, but storing them safely is simple. Repurpose a holiday cookie tin that's collecting dust in the closet. Gently stack the blades on their sides inside the tin. You can also hang your blades vertically by inserting a heavy-duty hook into your pegboard, or hammering a nail directly into the wall. Slide the hole in the center of the blades over the hook or nail.

Whichever method you choose, add spacers between the blades to keep them from rubbing against each other and chipping a tooth. Old CDs work well, or raid the Tupperware drawer and put all those extra lids to use. Drill a hole in their centers to hang over the hook or nail. Place a CD or lid between each blade.

Tidy up your tool shed. Straighten up even the worst mess in your garage or gardening shed. Best of all, you can do it for free using scrap materials.

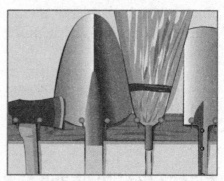

Screw a piece of 1x4 lumber to the wall horizontally, being sure to attach it to studs. Hammer pairs of long nails into the board, but leave them sticking out an inch or two. Space the nails about 2 inches apart so they will cradle the head or handle of the tool.

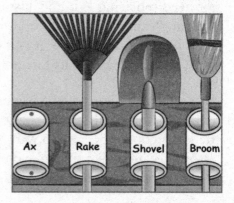

For a fancier look, make holders out of spare PVC pipe. Saw the pieces into 6-inch lengths, cutting both ends at an angle away from the center. Sand off any plastic burrs. Drill pilot holes through the backs of the pieces on each end, and attach them to a horizontal 1x4 or directly to the studs.

Once you finish, slide your tools handle-first through the mounted pipes. Write the name of each tool on its pipe in permanent marker to up your chances of staying organized.

Tote yard tools with ease. Turn a plastic out-door garbage can into standup storage for rakes, hoes, and any tool with a long handle.

Fill the inside of the can with a bag of sand to keep it from tipping over. Then drill large holes through the lid with a spade bit, making them big enough to slide tool handles through. Roll your tool caddy around the yard by strapping it to a hand truck.

Erase unsightly oil stains. Oil and grease seep into concrete fast, so clean them up as soon as they happen. Stop the oil from spreading by pouring a circle of sand, dirt, sawdust, or cat litter around it. Then pour plenty of cat litter onto the spill itself. Level it with a push broom, and let sit for at least an hour. Sweep it up once it has absorbed all of the oil.

Reach for baking soda to clean up any unsightly stain that's left. Spray a little water over the stain and pour baking soda over it. Let it sit for as long as it takes you to boil a large pot of water. Pour the hot water over the stain and scrub with a stiff nylon brush.

Old oil stains may need special treatment to remove them. Make a paste out of ordinary baby or talcum powder. Mix an ounce of TSP (trisodium phosphate) or TSP substitute with one cup of water and a cup of powder. Smear the paste onto the stain up to half an inch thick with a putty knife. Let it dry for a full 24 hours, then scrape it off with your putty knife and throw it away. Scrub what's left with a nylon brush, and rinse with clean water. Repeat the process if needed.

GREAT IDEA

First aid for cement burns

Take extra care when working with concrete, cement, mortar, plaster, grout, or stucco. Wear gloves and keep a big bottle of vinegar on hand. All of these mixtures contain portland cement, which will suck the water right out of your skin if it gets on you. But worse than drying out your hands, they can all cause serious chemical burns because they are highly alkaline.

If these mixes touch your skin, rinse the area immediately with plain water for several minutes. Don't wait until you finish a job. Alkaline begins killing tissue as soon as it penetrates your skin. You may not feel any pain until hours later, and by then it will be too late to prevent the burns. Follow up by soaking the area with white vinegar to neutralize the alkalinity.

Experts suggest wearing long-sleeve shirts and pants, eye protection, and either butyl or nitrile gloves, not rubber gloves, when working with these products. If they get on your clothes, take off that piece of clothing immediately, and rinse your skin with water and vinegar.

Housekeeping

Amazing answers to everyday problems

15-minute trick keeps clutter under control. This is the one cleaning tip you can't live without. Set aside 30 minutes a week, and you'll always have a clean, clutter-free house.

Do a quick, de-cluttering sweep twice a week. Set an egg timer for 15 minutes, grab a laundry basket, and go. Move through each room, putting items in the basket that don't belong in that room and taking out items that do. When the timer goes off, stop. You may not make it through the whole house in 15 minutes, but with twice-a-week sessions everything will eventually return to its rightful place.

Give your back a break by using a wheeled wagon or cart instead of carrying a basket. For two-story homes, place small baskets at the top and bottom of the stairs. Drop items that belong up- or downstairs in the appropriate basket, and always take an item with you when you make a trip.

7 ways to clean your house quicker. Stop spending all of your spare time cleaning. The key is to work smarter, not harder. These seven tricks will slash the time it takes to tidy up your home. Get started and use the extra time to do anything you want.

- Remove kitchen grease without scrubbing. Soak a towel with hot water and lay it over the stuck-on gunk for 10 minutes. Then use the same towel to wipe off the softened mess.

- Run your shower on the hottest water possible for several minutes before you clean it or the tub. The steam will loosen the dirt, so you can do less work.

- Wash tough-to-clean items in the dishwasher — glass globes from light fixtures, the grille from the exhaust fan, soap trays, plastic hairbrushes, scrub brushes, dish drainers, and more. Turn off the heated dry, so nothing melts accidentally, and place delicate items like glass light globes in the top rack. Wash household items separately from your dishes.

- Clean rooms by moving in one direction, either clockwise or counterclockwise. You'll use fewer steps and be less likely to get sidetracked.

- Wear a tool belt or apron with pockets while house cleaning. Stash a dusting cloth, sponge, scrub brush, cleaners, and other tools in them. You'll have everything on hand as you work through a room and make fewer trips to fetch supplies.

- Dust last, after you have vacuumed and finished your normal cleaning routine. Cleaning, especially vacuuming, stirs up dust. Let it settle for a few minutes then wipe down surfaces.

- Wipe hard-to-dust places like the baseboards with a dryer sheet. The sheets will grab existing dust and repel it in the future, so you won't need to dust as often.

Leave dust at the door. Your shoes are the source of most of the dust and dirt in your home. An incredible 80 percent of the dirt in your house travels in on your shoes. Cut down on dirt and clean less with a few simple steps.

First, institute a no-shoes rule in the house. Have everyone remove their shoes as soon as they come in. If that's not an option, then designate one or two pairs as indoor-only shoes. Take off your outside shoes as soon as you walk in the door and slip into your inside shoes to avoid tracking in dirt.

Second, invest in a commercial-quality walk-off mat, the kind of doormat you see at the entrances to grocery stores and office buildings. These are specially made to trap dirt and water. Look for them at janitorial supply stores. If that's not in the budget, at least buy a good carpet runner for indoors, and place a doormat outside each entrance to your home.

Beware of hidden hazards in household cleaners.
Household cleaners are responsible for thousands of calls to poison control centers every year. Although two-thirds of those calls involved young children, accidents and mistakes with cleaners harm adults, too. For example, a simple cleaner like bleach can create toxic gases if it's mixed with other cleaners, including ammonia and vinegar. Many cleaners contain ingredients that can irritate your eyes and lungs. What's more, some cleaners put volatile organic compounds (VOCs) into the air. VOCs are chemical gases that can cause headaches, dizziness, fatigue, nausea, and throat, eye, or nose irritation. And they can remain in the air for a while after you finish cleaning.

To help avoid serious problems, take these precautions.

- Read household cleaner labels carefully. Pay close attention to the instructions and information about hazards.

- Do not mix bleach with other cleaners.

- Open a window or door and turn on the vent fan when cleaning your bathrooms.

- Keep people out of recently cleaned bathrooms and kitchens for 30 minutes.

Don't fall for fake 'green' cleaners

Sometimes baking soda and vinegar don't cut it, and you need the power of store-bought household cleaners. But which ones are safe for both your health and the earth's?

Read labels carefully. Words like "nontoxic," "natural," "plant-based," "organic," and "biodegradable" sound friendly, but in reality they don't mean a thing. The government does not regulate the use of these words on cleaning products, and the words have no standard meaning in the industry. A product can claim it is plant-based or organic and still contain toxic, irritating, or cancer-causing ingredients.

Look instead for specific seals of approval, including the EcoLogo, Green Seal, and Design for the Environment seal. Each means the cleaner meets certain health and safety standards.

Show countertop germs no mercy. Your kitchen counter is like an airport for germs. Every time food, mail, keys, purses, lunch boxes, or cellphones come in for a landing on your counter, a load of germs hop off. But this doesn't mean you need expensive, name brand cleaners to get rid of them. You can disinfect your counters on the cheap with common household products if you know the right tricks.

For best results, wipe or scrub your counter with hot, soapy water before you disinfect. This helps remove bacteria. Rinse with fresh water, and wipe dry with a clean paper towel. Then sanitize with one of these.

- White distilled vinegar or hydrogen peroxide. Vinegar has antibacterial powers, and hydrogen peroxide is famous for its disinfecting ability — both will kill bacteria. To disinfect your counters the fastest way, you need a cooking thermometer and a heat-tolerant spray bottle. Heat vinegar or hydrogen peroxide to 150 degrees in a saucepan, pour it into your heat-tolerant spray bottle, and spray your counter right away. Let sit for one minute, and wipe dry with a clean paper towel. If you don't heat the vinegar or hydrogen peroxide, you must wait at least 10 minutes after spraying your counter before you wipe it dry. Avoid using vinegar if your counters are marble, limestone, soapstone, or unsealed granite.

- Household bleach. This is the best disinfectant for a counter that has been exposed to meats or their juices. Mix one table-spoon of bleach in two cups of water. Spray your countertop well, and wipe with paper towels.

Ditch nasty garbage smells. You took out the garbage, but your kitchen trash can still smells. No problem. Here's what to do.

Take your trash can outside and give it a thorough rinsing. Wipe it dry. If you have a cleaner designed to clean up after pets, you have a good cleaner for your garbage can. If not, put on rubber gloves, and mix two-thirds cup of washing soda into three cups of water. Keep your rubber gloves on, and use your cleaner to scrub both the inside and the outside of the can. Rinse thoroughly and let dry.

To help absorb odors and prevent a smelly can in the future, line the bottom with newspaper, and pour in some baking soda or an inch or two of cat litter.

Scent your house with homemade air fresheners.
Store-bought air fresheners are loaded with chemicals and artificial fragrances. They're also expensive. Why spend money on costly air polluters when you can make natural air fresheners at home?

Gel fresheners are as easy to make as jello. Boil a half cup of water, and slowly stir in two packets of unflavored gelatin. Once mixed, add one teaspoon of salt and a half cup of water. Mix thoroughly and remove from heat. Stir in 10 to 15 drops of your favorite essential oil, then pour the gelatin into a mason jar. Once it cools, place it in a room that could use a boost of fresh air.

Here's an even simpler recipe. Pour a half cup of baking soda into a mason jar, add 10 drops of essential oil, and mix well. Cover the mouth of the jar with fabric to match the room, and tie it on with a ribbon. Or punch holes in the metal lid with a hammer, and nail in a decorative pattern. Give the jar a shake every week or so to boost the scent.

For fresh scent on demand, make your own room spray. Mix together one part vodka, three parts distilled water, and 10 drops of essential oil. Pour into a pretty spray bottle and shake, then spritz. Add more oil for a stronger fragrance. Remember to shake the bottle well before spraying as the oil and water will separate between uses.

Mask the sharp smell of vinegar

Cleaning with vinegar can be an unpleasant chore only because of the odor. Breathe easier and leave a room smelling great by adding a few drops of your favorite essential oil to your vinegar cleaning solutions. Oils such as rosemary, lavender, eucalyptus, and grapefruit may even give your cleaner a germ-killing boost.

Tidy your bathroom in 7 minutes. Surprise! Company is coming, and they'll be here in 10 minutes. You don't have time to deep clean your bathroom, but you can spot clean it in seven minutes with these clever ideas.

- Contain clutter. Hide counter and floor clutter in your bathroom cabinets, or stash it all in a garbage bag and hide it behind your shower curtain.

- Sanitize sinks, faucets, and counters. Wipe away spatters and stains with a disinfectant wipe or two.

- Tame the toilet. Speed clean your toilet using a toilet brush with a disposable cleaning head. If you don't have one of those brushes, pour three-fourths cup of bleach in the bowl, quickly clean off the visible stains with a standard brush, and flush. Wipe the toilet seat with a disinfectant wipe.

- Make over your mirror. Mix equal parts vinegar and water in a cup. Dip a lint-free cloth in the cup, and wipe away mirror splashes and smudges.

- Finalize with finishing touches. Close your shower curtain, and either fluff your bath mat or replace it. If you have time left, sweep the floor, or spot clean with a damp paper towel.

Clean toilets and tubs without scrubbing. Why scrub and scrub your toilet and tub when you can just spray and walk away? Discover just how much easier cleaning can be with these clever tricks and tips.

White vinegar alone can be enough to remove those irritating waterline marks on your toilet. Just pour one cup into a spray bottle, spray around the inside of your toilet bowl, and leave overnight. If you have hard water, pour in an extra cup of vinegar. The next morning, simply flush the toilet to rinse the marks away.

For an even stronger cleaner, drop two denture cleaning tablets into your toilet bowl, and let them spend all night attacking the stains. The next morning, you shouldn't need to scrub. Just run your toilet brush over the stains, and flush them away.

If your toilet requires major cleaning power, flush the toilet, and sprinkle one cup of borax all around the bowl before pouring one cup of vinegar around the bowl. Let sit overnight. If you have particularly heavy stains, a little scrubbing may be necessary the first time you do this. But you probably won't need to scrub again if you use this powerful cleaner regularly.

To clean your tub, mix one part warm vinegar with one part dish-washing liquid, and pour in a heat-tolerant spray bottle. Spray on the tub, and walk away. After one hour, return to wipe away any grime and rinse off the tub. Some Internet bloggers claim you won't get the best results unless you use the original, blue Dawn dish-washing liquid.

For a no-scrub shower cleaner, pour 8 ounces of rubbing alcohol into a 32-ounce spray bottle and top it off with water. Spray the walls and door right after a shower. You don't even have to rinse. Do this daily, and you may never need to scrub.

Solve the plunger drip problem

Don't spend your hard-earned money on an overpriced specialty plunger holder. Much cheaper options are available. For example, if you have an extra flower pot drip saucer, it's practically tailor-made to catch plunger drips and keep them off your floor. You can even line the saucer with plastic wrap or aluminum foil to make cleaning easier. If you prefer a holder that makes the plunger less noticeable, use a plastic garbage can. You can leave it bare or line it with a plastic bag.

Make ring-around-the-tub disappear for good. Just because you can't use abrasive, scouring cleaners on fiberglass and acrylic tubs doesn't mean you are stuck with a bathtub ring. Try one of these super ideas to make that annoying ring disappear forever.

- Wipe the ring with a fabric softener sheet. Some people have even reported success with used sheets.

- Apply a paste of baking soda and warm water to the ring, and rub with a soft cloth.

- Apply shampoo to the ring immediately after a hot bath, and use a soft nylon net sponge or bath pouf to scrub. This works well because a bathtub ring is mostly a combination of body oil and soap residue. Since shampoo is designed to remove oils and clean away styling product residue, it can also do a good job on tub rings.

GREAT IDEA

Zap powdery residue with vinegar

Baking soda makes a great soft scrub cleaner for your bathroom and kitchen, but it sometimes leaves a faint white film or dusty residue behind. If rinsing with warm water doesn't work well enough, rinse with equal parts vinegar and water, and wipe with a wet cloth.

Erase soap scum from shower doors. Say sayonara to soap scum on your shower doors and tracks. You won't even need commercial cleaners to do it.

First, heat vinegar and pour it into a heat-tolerant spray bottle. Spray it on your shower doors, and wipe clean with a microfiber cloth. If you have stubborn spots, dip paper towels in very warm vinegar, and spread each one across a trouble spot. Leave for 10 minutes, so the vinegar can do its job thoroughly. After that, simply remove the paper towels, rinse, and wipe dry. To scuttle soap scum in the shower door tracks, pour heated vinegar in the tracks, and leave it for an hour. Scrub with a brush, rinse away the gunk, and wipe dry.

Once you've banished that unsightly soap scum, prevent it from building up again. Either spray the shower door with vinegar after each use, or give it a quick wipe down with a squeegee as soon as you finish showering.

Add a grime resistant coating to shower walls. The car wax that protects your car can also shield your shower against soap scum, hard water deposits, and mildew. Car wax makes moisture bead up and slide away so soap scum and other grime can't build up.

To get this protection for your tile or fiberglass shower, clean your shower walls and doors thoroughly, and make sure you remove all soap and water residue. Apply a light coating of cheap liquid or paste car wax to your shower walls and door. Be careful not to get any wax on the shower floor, and never apply it to a bathtub. The car wax would make a shower or tub floor slicker than an ice-covered sidewalk – and just as dangerous.

The wax coating should help prevent soap scum, hard water deposits, and mildew for at least six months. Reapply the car wax once or twice a year.

Safeguard hands and clothes while cleaning

Rubber gloves go a long way in protecting your hands while you clean, but pulling them off can be tricky. A dash of baby powder, baking soda, or flour can help. Dust your hands before slipping on the gloves, and they'll slip off just as easily. Protect your clothes, too, with a homemade sleeve garter. Cut the elastic band off an old sock or knee-high stocking. Push up your sleeves and slip a band over each one to hold it in place and away from your hands.

Banish rust rings from your bathroom. Put an end to rust rings and rust stains on your porcelain sinks and tubs. To get started, pick up some cream of tartar from your supermarket spice aisle. For a quick cleaning, make a paste of cream of tartar and hydrogen peroxide. Cover the ring or stain with this paste, and scrub with an old toothbrush. Rinse thoroughly.

For more stubborn rust rings, mix the cream of tartar with lemon juice, apply to the stain, and let sit for up to two hours. Rinse with warm water, and the stain should be gone.

To prevent future rust rings on your counters, sinks, and tubs, save low-rimmed plastic lids from your kitchen. Place all your rust-forming containers on top of lids from now on. Just as coasters help protect your coffee table, these lids help prevent rust rings on your counter, sink, and tub surfaces. Problem solved.

Prevent nasty toilet tank problems. Even if your toilet bowl is always spotless, it's easy to forget the power behind the throne — your toilet tank. But over time, mold, germs, mineral deposits, and even sediment can build up in your tank, leading to mechanical problems or even health concerns. That's why it pays to clean your tank every once in a while. Here's how.

- Remove the toilet lid. Don't panic if you see a small amount of dirt or sand in the tank. It will be gone soon.

- Turn off the water supply control to the toilet using the valve at the back of the toilet near the floor.

- Flush once or twice to empty the toilet tank. If you saw sediment in the tank, this should help clear it out.

- Make sure the bathroom is well-ventilated, and then spray chlorine bleach on the inside walls and floor of the tank. Let sit for 30 minutes.

- Pour in two gallons of water or enough to nearly fill the tank. Flush to remove the bleach. Keep adding water and flushing it away until the bleach is gone.

- Pour a few cups of vinegar in the tank, and let sit for a few hours. Keep in mind the bleach must be completely gone before you add vinegar. Bleach and vinegar can produce a toxic gas.

- Scrub the inside walls of the tank with your toilet brush. Be careful to avoid dislodging any tubes, chains, or connectors.

- Flush once or twice to remove the vinegar.

- Turn the toilet's water supply back on, and flush to rinse the toilet tank.

Make your bathroom mirror shine. Don't fret if you're out of glass cleaner. Just look for your bottle of rubbing alcohol, or brew some tea.

To clean foggy hairspray deposits off your mirror, dampen a lint-free cloth with rubbing alcohol and wipe. If your bathroom is well-ventilated, you can spray the rubbing alcohol on your mirror and wipe it with a coffee filter.

For an all-purpose mirror cleaner, brew regular black tea, and chill it in your refrigerator. Pour some of the tea in a spray bottle. Spray a small section of your mirror, and wipe away stains, spots, and smudges with a coffee filter or lint-free cloth. Keep spraying and wiping until your entire mirror is clean. You'll give your mirror a sparkling shine that might just put chrome to shame. Be sure to wipe any tea residue off counters and fixtures below the mirror. Use any leftover tea to clean other glass surfaces.

Simple solution for grimy grout. Clean your bathroom floor grout without smelly, toxic cleaners. Mix seven cups of water with one-half cup of baking soda, one-third cup of lemon juice, and a quarter cup of vinegar. Pour into a bowl, and apply directly to grout with an old toothbrush. For dirtier grout, pour the mixture into a spray bottle, spray your floor grout, and let sit for up to 10 minutes before scrubbing. Although you will love the citrus smell, be sure to rinse thoroughly, and wipe up any residue.

To get rid of mildew stains on tub or shower grout, make a paste of hydrogen peroxide and baking soda, apply to the grout, and let sit for 30 to 45 minutes before scrubbing.

3 smart ways to fight mildew. Turn your bathroom into hostile territory for mildew. You can even make the room look and smell better while you do it.

- Save and clean several berry baskets and their lids, and spray paint them with a color that matches your bathroom decor. Line the lower half of the basket with aluminum foil and drop in a piece of charcoal. Distribute these baskets around your bathroom to absorb the moisture mildew loves. You'll find the charcoal will absorb odors, too. Change the charcoal regularly, and you'll help keep your bathroom moisture-free.

- If you already have mildew, make a mildew-fighting spray by adding one drop of tea tree oil to one cup of water. Spray directly on mildew to kill it.

- Put a timer switch on your bath fan to remove moisture from the air after you shower. It will shut off automatically when the moisture is gone. You can even find switches that turn on automatically when humidity is high.

Kill the germs on mops and sponges. Cleaning your cleaning tools is just as important as cleaning your house. After all, they spend their lives picking up dirt and germs. Don't spread bacteria and viruses around your home with a dirty mop or sponge. Disinfect them regularly, and do it the right way.

Sponges have a special "ick" factor — they're both dirty and germy. Start by washing off as much grime as possible, then sanitize them in the dishwasher. Secure them to the top rack with a large binder clip, so they don't fall into the heating element below. Then run the dishwasher on the longest, hottest setting possible, and use the heated dry cycle. The U.S. Department of Agriculture found that this method kills 99.9 percent of bacteria in sponges.

Don't have a dishwasher? Wet the sponge thoroughly, and pop it in the microwave for one minute on "high." Handle the hot sponge with tongs or let it sit until cool. Never microwave a dry sponge or one that contains metal. They may start a fire.

Sanitize sponge mops with removable heads the same way as sponges – in the dishwasher. Mop heads made of string or strips of cloth, on the other hand, can go in the washing machine with bleach and hot water.

Clean mops with stationary heads in a bucket with one gallon of hot water and one cup of hydrogen peroxide. Let soak for 10 minutes then wring out and air dry. Bleach will also do the trick. Soak the mop for one minute in one cup of bleach mixed with one gallon of warm water. Then rinse, wring out, and air dry.

Bathe your broom for a cleaner sweep

Even your broom needs occasional cleaning. Shake off excess dirt outdoors, and pick off tangled hair or dust bunnies by hand or with a vacuum attachment. Fill a bucket with warm water and dish soap. Swish the broom head around to release trapped dirt, then gently wash the ends of the bristles. Rinse it thoroughly. Stand it with the bristles up to dry, or hang it by its handle on the wall.

Banish the smell of smoke. Your chain-smoking house guests just left, and now your whole home reeks of cigarette smoke. Reclaim your domain. Chase away the stinky smell with vinegar. Soak a hand towel in equal parts white vinegar and water. Wring it out slightly then whirl it around over your head in each room, as if imitating a helicopter. Redip your towel as needed.

At night, set a bowl of white vinegar in the worst rooms. By morning the smoky smell will have vanished. These tricks also work for the odors of burned food and chimney smoke. So the next time your burned toast sets off the fire alarm, whirl a vinegar-dampened towel beneath the smoke detector. It should turn off almost immediately.

No-scrub solution for stuck-on food

Don't get bested by burned food in pots, pans, and casserole dishes. Whip up a paste of baking soda and water. Smear it on the stubborn spots, let sit for one hour, then wipe away. The stuck food should go with it.

Shine up silver without polishing. Don't spend your precious time polishing your silver. Get silver jewelry and serving pieces gleaming again, no polishing necessary. Pour one tablespoon each of salt and baking soda into an aluminum pie pan, or line a bowl with aluminum foil. Cover with hot water, and stir until the mixture dissolves. Drop your silver into the solution, and leave until the tarnish has disappeared, usually just a few minutes. Heavily tarnished pieces may not come completely clean. For these, you may need to follow up with a little polishing.

Of course, it's even easier to prevent tarnish in the first place with a sneaky household trick that costs just pennies. Buy a box of white blackboard chalk. Break the chalk into pieces, and slip them into your jewelry box and wherever you store silver. They will absorb the substances that cause tarnish. Replace with fresh chalk every two months.

Wipe out rust and tarnish. Rub out the rust spots on plated silverware with this all-natural remover. Make a paste of three parts salt to one part lemon or lime juice. Rub it on rusty areas with a dry cloth, then rinse with warm water and buff dry.

Polishing copper and unlaquered brass is even easier. Cut a lemon in half, and press the cut side onto a plate of salt. Rub it over the tarnished spots, rinse well, and wipe dry. A paste will handle stubborn stains on uncoated brass and copper. Dissolve one teaspoon of salt in a cup of vinegar, and mix in enough flour to form a paste. Apply this and let it work for 15 minutes, then rinse it off with warm water and buff the items dry.

Clever trick cleans cast iron skillets. Scour away food in your cast iron cookware with a cup of coarse Kosher salt. Pour the salt into your skillet while it's still warm, then rub it in with a hand towel or paper towel until the food loosens. Rinse the pan briefly under hot water, and heat it over medium-low heat to dry it thoroughly. Prevent it from rusting by placing a clean coffee filter in the pan when you store it.

Soften up hard deposits on faucets. Stubborn lime and hard-water deposits on your kitchen faucets can require more elbow grease than most people have, so don't try to go it alone. Instead, dip paper towels in white vinegar, and wrap them around the faucet base or any other sink surface where mineral deposits have lodged. For the tightest spaces, you may need to cut paper towels in half or in strips to make them fit snugly.

Let the vinegar-soaked paper towels eat away at the deposits for an hour – or a little longer if you have very hard water. Then remove the paper towels, and scrub the softened deposits away.

And here's a bonus tip. Vinegar-soaked paper towels can also help remove cloudy hard-water deposits from glassware. Even better, you only need to leave the paper towels in place for minutes to get results.

Tidy up kitchen clutter problems. Cluttered counters, drawers, refrigerator shelves, and pantry can make kitchen work difficult. Use these ideas to reduce clutter and make cleaning – and everything else – easier in the kitchen.

- Your longest utensils don't have to sit in a container on your counter. They can fit in a drawer if you store them diagonally. Just make sure their ends are at opposite corners of the drawer. Position everything else in the drawer diagonally, too. If this leaves you with two empty drawer corners, place a shallow bowl or container in each of the two corners, and fill it with corncob holders, measuring spoons, and other small items.

- Free up drawer space and add extra storage by hanging your dry measuring cups along the inside of a cabinet door. If you are not an experienced do-it-yourselfer, hang the cups from temporary adhesive hooks. If you are good at handyman work, follow these instructions. Cut a wood strip, ruler, or paint stirrer to fit across your cabinet door, and sand the cut edges smooth. Mount the strip inside the cabinet door, attach cup hooks to it, and hang your measuring cups on the hooks. Regardless of whether you use removable hooks or something more permanent, position the hooks so you can shut the cabinet door after the cups are hung. And remember, your cups may clatter when you open or close the door.

- Create extra space in your pantry or refrigerator by grouping items in baskets and bins. You can even corral some things with shallow food crates that previously held produce from your supermarket. Some people also label their baskets, bins, and crates to help organize their items by type or to assemble ingredients for a dish or meal.

3 easy ways to organize with tension rods. Uncover extra space in your cabinets, and make better use of kitchen drawers with tension curtain rods.

- Create more room for cleaners in your under-the-sink cabinet. Install a tension rod in the empty space above the cleaners. Hang spray bottles by hooking their trigger levers over the rod the same way you hook a clothes hanger over a closet rail. The weight of spray bottles may pull down standard rods, so be sure to choose a heavy-duty tension rod, and tighten it securely.

- Stop struggling to find the lids for the plastic containers in a large kitchen drawer. Remove all containers from the drawer. "Fence in" the front section of the drawer by placing a tension rod 2 or 3 inches from the drawer front and halfway between the top and bottom of the drawer. Stand lids on their ends in this new "lid corral," and fill the rest of the drawer with the plastic containers that belong to the lids.

- Some of the most notorious kitchen cabinet space hogs include baking sheets, cutting boards, serving platters, racks, and trays. Make them take up less of the usable space in your cabinets by storing them on their edges. To do this, set up tension curtain rods in your cabinets so they resemble rows of Greek columns. Using two or three rods, create a row of rods as shown in the picture. Slide baking sheets, cutting boards, and other long, flat items between the rods and the cabinet wall. For even more storage, add more rows of rods, and set your large, flat space hogs between the rows.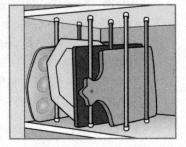

Kiss carpet stains goodbye. Skip expensive, chemical-laden carpet cleaners in favor of old fashioned vinegar for treating fresh stains. Blot up as much of the mess as possible with a clean, damp cloth. Then spray the stain with a mixture of one part white vinegar and two parts cool water. Cover the area with paper or cloth towels, and lay a plastic bag over them. Put your old encyclopedias to use by stacking heavy books atop the plastic and towels. Leave them overnight. The weight will help the towels absorb the last traces of stain and water.

Put an end to pet hair. Fluffy's fur sticks to everything, which is why manufacturers hawk vacuums made especially for pet hair. Save your money and try these tips instead.

- Mix one part liquid fabric softener and three parts water in a spray bottle. Spritz your rug or carpet and wait for the solution to dry, then vacuum. The fabric softener squashes static electricity, making pet hair easier to pick up.

- Lightly mist the dust bunnies hiding in corners with the same solution, then sweep. They won't be able to blow away and escape your broom.

- Drag a dry sponge or the rubber edge of a squeegee over upholstery to pull pet hair off sofas and chairs.

Tricks to keep Fido off furniture. You love your sofa. So do Fido and Whiskers. And as much as you love your pets, you don't want them getting comfy on the couch. Prevent your pooch from lounging on your furniture with these pain-free remedies.

Make comfortable furniture uncomfortable, and your pet will find someplace else to nap. Block access to sofas and love seats by placing barriers such as cases of soda, boxes loaded with stones, laundry baskets filled with water bottles, or dining room chairs turned upside down. You've just made your divan not so divine.

Carpet runners – the plastic sheets used by professional carpet cleaners to protect paths between rooms – make excellent deterrents. These runners have tiny spikes on the bottom. Cover couches with runners, spike side up, and Fido will go back to sleeping on his own bed.

For cats, you can also try these two cheap tricks – aluminum foil and double-sided tape. Felines can't stand the crackle of foil, and they doubly hate the stickiness of tape.

GREAT IDEA

Keep curtains out of the way

Stop sucking your curtains into your vacuum cleaner. Slip the end of each panel over a hanger, and hang this over the curtain rod until you finish cleaning.

Discover the best cleaner for your floors. Soap and water may not be the best way to clean your floors. Many types of flooring are better off being mopped with plain water or water and vinegar.

- Mix half a cup of white vinegar in one gallon of hot water to damp-mop hardwood floors that have been finished with a sealer such as polyurethane. Don't use vinegar on waxed hardwood floors, though, as the acid in vinegar could strip the wax.

- Vinyl and linoleum floors may need the added power of mild soap to lift off dirt. If that's true for yours, add a drop of liquid dish soap to your vinegar-and-water solution.

- Mop ceramic tile with plain warm water, no soap needed. Use a microfiber mop pad rather than a sponge mop, which tends to spread grime into the grout lines.

When damp mopping, spritz your cleaner on the floor with a spray bottle, then go over it with your mop. Don't dip the mop head in a bucket of water. This leaves behind too much water, which can damage wood floors.

Bring a high shine to sealed hardwood and glazed ceramic tile floors by buffing them with a dry terry cloth after mopping.

Brew up polish on the cheap. Dust your wood furniture to a stunning shine without using an expensive brand-name polish. Just brew several cups of strong unsweetened black tea, let it cool, and pour it into a small bowl. Dip a cloth in the tea, wring it out, and use it to dust your wood furniture. Not only will the wood look beautiful when you're done, but the tannins in the tea may help fend off dust mites.

You can also use brewed, black tea to clean dark hardwood floors, but you'll need one or two quarts of unsweetened tea to get the job done. To start, dampen one microfiber cloth with tea, wipe a section of floor, and immediately wipe dry with a dry, microfiber cloth. Keep cleaning sections until the entire floor is gleaming clean.

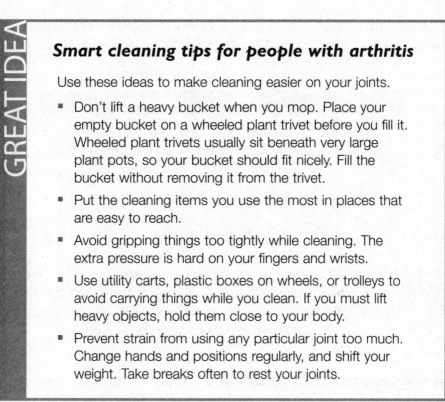

GREAT IDEA

Smart cleaning tips for people with arthritis

Use these ideas to make cleaning easier on your joints.

- Don't lift a heavy bucket when you mop. Place your empty bucket on a wheeled plant trivet before you fill it. Wheeled plant trivets usually sit beneath very large plant pots, so your bucket should fit nicely. Fill the bucket without removing it from the trivet.

- Put the cleaning items you use the most in places that are easy to reach.

- Avoid gripping things too tightly while cleaning. The extra pressure is hard on your fingers and wrists.

- Use utility carts, plastic boxes on wheels, or trolleys to avoid carrying things while you clean. If you must lift heavy objects, hold them close to your body.

- Prevent strain from using any particular joint too much. Change hands and positions regularly, and shift your weight. Take breaks often to rest your joints.

Remove ceiling lint and dust the easy way. Dust your ceiling without having to stand on a ladder or strain your back. To easily remove lint, simply break out the hard floor attachment on your vacuum, and lightly vacuum the lint off the ceiling.

For a more thorough dusting of both your ceiling and ceiling lights, slide a pillowcase over the head of a broom so it fits snugly over the bristles. Secure it in place with twine. Just before dusting, spritz the top end of the pillowcase with water or furniture polish so the dust stays on the pillowcase instead of raining down on you. Then simply raise your broom head to the ceiling, and clear the dust bunnies away.

Clean couches for keeps. Spills happen. So when one happens on your sofa, you need to act quickly. Blot the stain — don't rub — with a clean, white cloth. Then look for the manufacturer's tag with cleaning instructions, often hidden under the couch. The tag will include one of four codes. Use the table below to interpret the codes and follow their instructions.

Codes	Cleaning instructions
W	Use water and a water-based detergent.
S	Use a solvent. No water.
SW	Use either a solvent or water-based detergent.
X	Must be professionally cleaned.

To keep your sofa looking spiffy longer, vacuum your couch weekly and rotate cushions periodically. Mend loose threads and buttons. Consider spraying your sofa with a soil retardant, but always read the manufacturer's label first to make sure this is safe.

Knock out furniture nicks and rings. Chances are your furniture has taken a beating over the years. But before you cart off your dining room table, try these simple ways to fix — or at least cover up — nicks, scratches and water rings.

For scratches on oiled, waxed, or unfinished pieces, a fresh coat of oil or wax should do the trick. Furniture coated with shellac, varnish, or polyurethane needs a bit more TLC. Apply one part shellac and one part denatured alcohol with a watercolor brush. Allow to dry.

Hide minor nicks by rubbing them with a shelled pecan, walnut, or Brazil nut. The nut's natural oils disguise blemishes. Or steep tea to the same color as your wood and apply to scratches.

Consider an option from your medicine chest — petroleum jelly. Coat your small scratches and allow to sit for a day. Then rub the jelly into the wood and wipe off any excess. Polish like you normally would.

To tackle white water rings, allow the stain to dry, then cover with a lubricant like paste wax or petroleum jelly. Or rub in nongel toothpaste.

Take care of your wood for good. Your home is filled with wood furnishings. With proper care and maintenance, your wood-made goods can last a lifetime. Use this handy table to know how to preserve these five popular woods.

Type of wood	Characteristics	How to care for
Cherry	Strong, durable, resistant to shock and wear and tear	Wipe with warm water and nonabrasive soap. Rinse, then wipe dry. Use lemon oil occasionally and a thin coat of paste wax annually. Avoid exposure to direct sunlight.
Mahogany	Heavy weight, even texture	Apply a solution of warm water and vinegar with damp cloth. Avoid abrasive cleaners and exposure to direct sunlight.
Maple	Dense, resistant to shock	Dust daily and wipe smudges with a damp cloth. Polish weekly. Oil annually.
Oak	Durable, resistant to wear and tear	Avoid direct sunlight. Maintain a room humidity level between 25-35 percent. Dust often. Use coasters and place mats to protect.
Pine	Lightweight, great for paint and varnishes	Avoid direct sunlight. Maintain even room temperature. Use coasters and place mats to protect. Wipe with a damp cloth. Apply wax periodically.

Smooth out scratches with baking soda

Before ordering a new piece of glass to replace a scratched-up table top, try this easy solution. Mix about a teaspoon of baking soda with nongel toothpaste, and rub it on the table with a clean, damp cloth. Wipe dry and check the scratch. If it's smoother, keep working on it. It may take a few attempts to buff it out completely.

Whip up your own furniture polish. It sounds more like salad dressing, but it's not. It's a homemade recipe for furniture polish. By mixing 3/4 cup olive oil, 1/4 cup white vinegar, and a tablespoon lemon juice, you can freshen up furniture with a polish you can make in a jiffy. Spray your solution on a soft cloth, and rub it into the wood, wiping along the grain. For a piece with intricate details, use a soft-bristle brush to work the solution into the grooves. Store solution in a labeled glass or plastic container in your refrigerator.

Photos help keep rooms clean. It's sweet when your family helps you clean house, but they probably don't do it exactly the way you do. They forget to dust or fail to arrange the pillows the way you like. Don't drive yourself crazy. Simply snap a photo of each room after you have cleaned it, showing everything arranged the way you want. Print your photos, and on the back of each one write the list of chores to be done in that room every time it gets cleaned. Put all the photographs together in an album for helpers to flip through as needed.

Make your bed while lying in it. Sounds crazy, but it's easier to make your bed from the middle while under the covers than it is standing to the side of the bed. Before you get up in the morning, center yourself in your bed, and bring up the covers neatly around you. Fold back one side to slip gently out of bed, then fold it back. At most, all you have left to do is a little smoothing or tucking.

If you suffer from arthritis, you may find tucking sheets uncomfortable. Keep a spatula or wooden spoon by your bed and give that a try. You can have a neat and tidy bed despite your discomfort.

But if you want an excuse not to make your bed, blame it on dust mites. According to researchers in London, dust mites thrive in a humid environment, and airing your sheets will make your bed less humid and, therefore, less hospitable to the tiny bugs.

Simple way to fold a fitted sheet. Don't let the elastic in your fitted sheets frustrate your neater nature. Here's how to deal with them for a tidy fold.

- Lay the sheet on your bed, opening up.

- Fold it in half, inserting corners inside-out. Square off corners to make them neat.

- Fold in thirds horizontally, like a letter — bottom part up, top part down.

- Fold in half or thirds vertically, depending on the space in which the sheet will be stored.

No more rolling them up into a ball — now they'll sit neatly on a shelf or in a drawer.

Where to put your extra blankets. You want them handy when you need them, but you don't want them lying around all the time. Here are five ideas to keep your room looking tidy.

- Keep extra blankets in shams — no need to put a pillow back in every morning.

- Put them in zippered pillow covers and use them as throw pillows.

- Lay them between the mattress and the box spring.

- Hang them on a sturdy hanger or a curtain rod fastened to the back of the bedroom door.

- Roll them and put them in a basket or a big planter.

Spend less for softer clothes

Don't waste money on chemical-filled dryer sheets. A little white vinegar will do the trick instead. For the softest, fluffiest laundry ever, add up to one cup of vinegar to the fabric softener dispenser or your rinse cycle. It costs just pennies per load.

Or try dryer balls. But don't buy them — make your own. Take a tennis ball and wrap it in three or four good-sized sheets of aluminum foil. Use two or three balls, and they'll make laundry softer, cut drying time, and stop static electricity.

Keep closets smelling fresh. Keeping closet doors closed may lower your heating and air conditioning bill, but it can also lead to musty closets. If you notice an unpleasant smell in a closet, leave the door wide open to let it air out for a few days. To prevent future odor problems, try one of these deodorizers. Don't forget to replace them regularly.

- Grab a few unused tea bags, or tie up loose tea in a coffee filter, and place in your closet. You may be surprised at how well the tea absorbs odors.

- Save a large metal coffee can, and poke at least 15 holes in the plastic lid. Fill the can with charcoal briquettes or clay kitty litter, put the lid on, and place it in the closet.

- Tuck an open box of baking soda in a shoe box or large, clean can. Hide it away on a closet shelf.

Make laundry sorting simpler. Take the chore out of separating clothes for the wash — do it each night before you go to bed. Keep two baskets or bags in your bedroom for sorting. You can label them — dark/light, colors/whites, cold/warm — depending on your personal style for doing laundry. Before you get into bed, put the clothes you wore during the day into the right basket. When laundry day arrives, your clothes are ready to go. Save space in the bedroom by using baskets that slide under the bed or fit in a closet.

Keep table linens looking great. Here are some clever ways to keep your tablecloths and napkins looking like new even if you don't use them every day.

- Use a pants hanger to hang tablecloths and napkins to keep them uncreased.

- To remove candle wax, first let it harden — putting it in the freezer works really well. Then use a dull knife to scrape off the wax. For any left over, put paper towels both above and below the area, then press with an iron on low heat with no steam. The gentle warmth will draw the remaining wax into the paper towel. Repeat with fresh towels until it's all gone.

- For a troublesome gravy stain, remove any excess, then cover the spot with flour or cornstarch to absorb the grease. Soak in warm water with a bit of dishwashing liquid for about half an hour, then launder as usual.

- For red wine, blot up as much as possible; soak the stain with club soda, white wine, or white vinegar to neutralize it; then blot again with an absorbent cloth or paper towel to remove it. Repeat as necessary.

- To remove coffee and tea stains, dab cold water on the area, add a few drops of dishwashing liquid, rub, and rinse. Mix one part white vinegar with three parts water, and pour on the stain. Rinse again, then wash the cloth as usual.

Get the bug, not the stain.

Stop — if you squish that bug, it will leave a nasty stain on your wall, carpet, or curtain. Instead, roll up a piece of packing tape or regular tape around your fingers, and press it on the bug. The bug sticks to it and can be disposed of — without the leftover mess.

Follow 4 steps to prevent pesky pests. Bugs and rodents are always looking for food and shelter. Make your home a no-pest zone by following these helpful guidelines.

Step one — clean. Don't give pests a meal of leftovers or a comfy spot to nestle.

- Sweep and vacuum your floors regularly.

- Keep bathroom and kitchen areas dry.

- Take out garbage daily and keep garbage cans clean.

- Clear out stacks of newspapers, magazines, packing material — all good hiding places for pests.

- Wipe up spills immediately.

- Keep ripe fruit in the fridge.

- Don't leave dirty dishes in the sink.

- Make sure all food and drink containers outside the fridge or freezer are tightly sealed.

Step two – deny access. Keep pests out by making a barrier they can't get past.

- Interior. Cockroaches and mice often enter homes through holes around the plumbing under the kitchen or bathroom sinks. Plug these tightly with rags or steel wool to stop them in their tracks.

- Exterior. Mice, rats, squirrels, and bugs can all get in the house through holes and gaps. Stop them with copper mesh, expanding foam, or caulk in the gap – whatever best fills it. Keep vegetation, firewood, and other debris away from the exterior of your house so pests can't climb up and in. Put screens on the front of vents, or repair holes in any already there.

Step three – repel. Try these natural methods to keep those creepy creatures away.

- Eucalyptus and pennyroyal oils – a teaspoon of each in a spray bottle of water is a good, all-purpose repellant.

- Mint – ants and flies both dislike the smell. Grow a plant or leave sachets out.

- Cucumber peel – ants hate cucumber. Leave peels out to send them running.

- Basil – keep a plant growing in your kitchen. Flies hate the smell and will stay away.

- Peppermint essential oil – put a few drops in a spray bottle of water. Spray to keep mice and spiders away.

- Build a moat. Put the pet bowl into a pan of soapy water to stop ants going after pet food. And don't leave pet food out during the night.

Step four – exterminate, but avoid highly toxic, harmful chemicals.

- Use your vacuum cleaner for individual bugs – they'll usually suffocate in the bag.

- A mixture of baking soda and salt will kill ants.

- You can also put small piles of cornmeal where you see ants. They can't digest it so they die after eating it. Be patient as it can take about a week to be effective. Cream of Wheat and Minute Rice also work the same way.

- Borax mixed with powdered sugar will lure ants and roaches and poison them. But don't use it if you have children or pets.

Spray disease away

Be careful when handling mouse droppings. They can transmit disease. Before you sweep them up and throw them away, always spray them with a disinfectant.

Natural health

Safe & simple remedies for common complaints

Boost your immune system with yogurt. You want a strong immune system – one that can battle cold and flu viruses before they bring you down. Look to probiotics – friendly bacteria that live in your digestive tract, keeping it healthy. Since two-thirds of your immune system lies in your gut, these good "bugs" perform an essential service, and probiotics help them flourish.

Yogurt is loaded with probiotics. Studies show that two probiotics in particular – *bifido-bacterium* and *lactobacillus* – can reduce the number of colds you catch. Just make sure your yogurt has the "Live & Active Cultures" seal to ensure a favorable amount of living bacteria.

Kefir, a drinkable yogurt, typically packs in even more beneficial bacteria than yogurt. Try mixing this tart beverage with low-fat milk or adding it to a smoothie. Look for kefir in the dairy aisle of your favorite supermarket.

Another way to promote gut health is to consume prebiotics. Prebiotics are nutrients, not bacteria, that stimulate the growth and activity of probiotics. Think of them as probiotic food. To add prebiotics to your diet, graze on oatmeal and other whole grains, leeks, onions, garlic, legumes, raisins, bananas, and asparagus.

2 fabulous foods that can keep you healthy. Nourishing a strong immune system prepares you for cold and flu season like a soldier readies for battle. Take a bite out of these foods to keep viruses at bay.

- Goat milk. Not all milk is created equal. Goat milk, for instance, is brimming with immune-boosting nutrients and anti-inflammatory agents not found in cow's milk. It also prompts your body's cells to attack intruders. If you can't give up your daily glass of moo juice, try goat cheese or goat milk yogurt.

- Lima beans. What do lima beans, pears, and Brussels sprouts have in common? The obvious answer — they're all green. The not-so-obvious answer — they're all great sources of soluble fiber, a potent immune-system supporter. Foods high in soluble fiber act like brooms, sweeping your digestive tract of unwelcome visitors, like germs. Not wild about lima beans? Besides pears and Brussels sprouts, graze on apples, oranges, and legumes like black beans and kidney beans.

Plan of attack for cold and flu season. You can take charge of your health during cold and flu season. Here's how.

- Wash your hands often to rinse away cold and flu viruses. Use soap and water or hand sanitizer. Remember to dry your hands completely. Germs thrive in moist environments.

- Make getting a good night's sleep a priority. Not sleeping enough weakens your immune system. A study at Carnegie Mellon University found that people who slept more than eight hours were less likely to catch a cold than those who slept less than seven hours.

- Check with your doctor about getting a flu shot. According to the Centers for Disease Control (CDC), about 90 percent of flu-related deaths occur in people 65 years and older during a regular flu season. The CDC states that an annual flu vaccine is the best way to prevent the flu.

GREAT IDEA

Tasty ways to calm a cough

Don't reach for cough syrup the next time you suffer a miserable cough. Try one of these home remedies instead.

- Pineapple juice. For a treat reminiscent of a tropical paradise, drink pineapple juice. Combine 8 ounces of warm juice and 2 teaspoons of honey.

- Hot lemonade. This soothing drink combines the juice from three lemons, 3 cups of water, 1/2 cup of honey, and 1 1/2 teaspoons of grated lemon peel. For a little spice, add cinnamon sticks. Warm the mixture over medium heat in a saucepan. Pour into your favorite mug. Sip and relax.

- Chicken soup. Undoubtedly, you've heard that chicken soup may help fight a cold. But did you know it can help banish a cough, too? The hot liquid will moisturize the back of your throat, while pungent herbs, like garlic, can clear up congestion.

Sip sage tea to soothe a sore throat. Your throat is under attack, but drinking sage tea may help you fight back. Sage inhibits the growth of bacteria and decreases mucous secretions. In fact, the U.S. Department of Agriculture says white sage will treat nearly all sore throats. To make a cup of sage tea, boil water and add either 1 teaspoon of dried sage leaves or 1 tablespoon of fresh sage. Allow it to steep for three to five minutes. Now you have two choices — either sip the tea or gargle with it first, then drink it.

Clear a stuffy nose in seconds. No need to take a decongestant. Your tongue and finger will do just fine, according to a professor at Michigan State University's College of Osteopathic Medicine. Push your tongue flat against the roof of your mouth. At the same time, press a finger between your eyebrows. Hold for about 20 seconds. The pressure will stimulate a bone that runs through your nasal passages to your mouth, causing your sinuses to drain.

Warning for neti pot users. Rinsing your nasal passages using a neti pot and saline solution provides rapid relief for people suffering from congestion due to colds and seasonal allergies. But the Food and Drug Administration has issued a warning after linking two deaths in Louisiana to neti pot use. A rare amoeba found in tap water was to blame. The amoeba causes an infection that destroys brain tissue and is almost always fatal.

While rare, you can take a few simple steps to avoid the infection. Use distilled or filtered water, or boil tap water and let it cool. The Centers for Disease Control and Prevention recommends mixing 1/8 teaspoon of unscented liquid household chlorine bleach per gallon of water, or two drops of bleach per quart. Stir the solution, and let it stand for 30 minutes or longer before using. Store the disinfected water in a sanitized container with a tight cover.

Relaxation technique for better sleep. Do you have trouble falling asleep? Or do you wake up in the middle of the night, unable to drift back to sleep? Progressive muscle relaxation may be just what you need. This technique works by taking the focus off your worries and on to your muscles.

Lying in bed, breathe slowly through your nose. Tense your toes for five to 10 seconds – then relax them. Next, squeeze and relax your feet, then your calves. Work your way up to your face, tightening and relaxing your muscles as you go.

You could start with your head and neck, and work your way down to your toes, too. Either way, this relaxation technique should help calm your mind and ease your body into a peaceful slumber.

Work out the kinks with tennis balls. Tame tense back muscles with a canister of tennis balls and an old tube sock. If you don't have an old tube sock, substitute one leg from a pair of tights or support pantyhose. Empty the tennis balls into the sock, and tie it off with a rubber band at each end. Make sure the tennis balls sit snugly side by side and you can firmly grasp each end of the sock. Stretch this massager around your back, and move it around to unwind tight muscles.

Or lie down on the carpet, place the massager underneath your lower back, and use your back to gently roll the tennis balls up and down or side to side. These techniques can help you melt away the stress of the day.

Make music to conquer anxiety and depression

Whether you tickle those ivories, strum a guitar, or blow your horn, you have a great way to fend off stress. Researchers say playing an instrument is not only powerful enough to fight stress, but it may even lessen anxiety and depression. So pull out your old harmonica, xylophone, or any other instrument, and start playing. Lose yourself in the music, and let your stress slip away.

Appealing way to defeat stress. When life hands you lemons, don't just make lemonade. Simmer a lemony stress buster on your stovetop. Scientists say lemons can help fight stress because they contain a powerful compound called linalool. In fact, simply inhaling linalool can reduce the wear and tear of stress.

To put this science to work for you, save the peels whenever you use lemons. When you're ready for some stress relief, throw the peels in a small pot on your stove and cover them with water. Allow the mixture to simmer for several hours on the lowest setting. Add water as needed. Over time, the lemon scent will spread throughout your kitchen and beyond. When you breathe in that fresh scent, you reap the benefits of stress-fighting linalool. Try this same trick with basil, lavender, or marjoram. They contain linalool, too. Use fresh cuttings from your garden or wilting sprigs from the super-market. You'll love the relaxing results.

Breathe your way to relaxation. Glossy magazines may recommend a trip to the spa to melt stress away, but you need something you can do right now. Try this five-minute breathing exercise, and see if you don't feel better.

- Close your eyes, and breathe slowly and evenly. Inhale so your belly expands, counting to four as you breathe in. Count to four again as you breathe out, deliberately pulling your stomach back in to push out all the air. Breathe this way five times.

- Breathe in, filling your ribcage with air so your ribs move up and out. Slowly exhale allowing your ribs to relax. Do this for five breaths.

- Inhale so you draw air into your upper chest and your collar-bone rises. Breathe out, letting your chest relax again. Do this five times.

- Now combine them all. Breathe in filling your stomach first, then your ribcage, and finally your upper chest. When you exhale, release air from your upper chest, then your ribcage, and finally your stomach. Do this at least five times.

If you've been sitting or reclining while doing this exercise, open your eyes, and look around for a few moments. Rise slowly and carefully, and return to your regular activities.

Wash away achy joints with wintergreen oil. Nothing feels better than a hot bath to soothe the aches and pains of arthritis. For additional relief, try mixing in one to two drops of the essential oil wintergreen. The wintergreen herb packs a powerful, pain-relieving punch. It contains a chemical similar to aspirin that may help reduce pain and swelling. If you take aspirin regularly or are allergic to salicylates, consult your doctor before using wintergreen oil.

GREAT IDEA

Wacky way to end back pain

You may want to put away your tighty-whities — or cotton briefs — if you suffer from lower back pain. A recent study found that wearing wool underwear decreased pain and improved flexibility in people with chronic lower back problems. To find a pair of wool underwear, check your local camping store or search online.

Put the brakes on arthritis with broccoli. You know eating your greens is good for you. But eating a specific green – broccoli – may help prevent or slow the progression of osteoarthritis. A recent study shows that sulforaphane, a compound found in broccoli, slows the destruction of joint cartilage. It actually blocks the enzyme that causes joints to deteriorate. Sulforaphane is released when you chow down on cruciferous veggies such as Brussels sprouts, cabbage – but most importantly, broccoli.

For a sulforaphane boost, shop for "super broccoli," a specially grown crop with two to three times the amount of glucoraphanin, a compound needed to produce sulforaphane. Look for super broccoli – sold under the name Beneforté – in regional supermarkets such as Ingles, ShopRite, Whole Foods, and Harris Teeter.

Battle arthritis with your toothbrush. A link between gum disease and rheumatoid arthritis (RA) suggests that brushing your teeth could help prevent the early onset of RA. What's more, maintaining healthy gums may also decrease the condition's progression and severity. Researchers at the University of Louisville discovered that the bacterium responsible for gum disease produces an enzyme that reacts with proteins in your body. The body then wages an attack on these proteins, and the results are catastrophic – chronic inflammation responsible for the destruction of bone and cartilage within your joints. It's no surprise that gum disease is more prevalent in people with RA, according to previous studies. Scientists believe the link between healthy gums and the prevention of RA deserves more investigation. In the meantime, keep brushing, flossing, and visiting your dentist.

Ease legs cramps in a pinch

The next time you wake up with cramps in your legs or feet, pinch your upper lip just below your nose. Hold for 20 to 30 seconds. This "acupinch" technique, used widely in sports medicine, may reduce the pain and duration of muscle cramps.

Unexpected way to ease muscle cramps. Take a cue from the athletic community – reach for a jar of pickles the next time you suffer a muscle cramp. In a small Brigham Young University study, researchers tested a group of male volunteers. Those who drank 2.5 ounces of pickle juice from a jar of Vlasic dills felt relief from cramps 37 percent faster than those who drank water, and 45 percent faster than those who drank nothing. Athletic trainers have been serving pickle juice to jocks for years. They don't really know why it works – it just does.

Summer treat soothes sore muscles. Five thousand years ago, ancient Egyptians placed watermelons in their kings' burial tombs to nourish them in their afterlives. Thankfully, you can reap the benefits of watermelon today. A study published in the *Journal of Agricultural and Food Chemistry* found that watermelon juice calms sore muscles after exercise. Watermelon is rich in L-citrulline, an amino acid that ultimately relaxes blood vessels and improves circulation. While experts agree that more research is needed, you can do your own experiment at home. If you exercise regularly or plan on doing strenuous work around the house over several days, try this — drink a glass of watermelon juice before your workout one day. Go without it the next day, and compare the results. If the juice makes your muscles feel better, keep chugging it before each workout.

Sweet way to heal a wound. In baseball, the "sweet spot" refers to the location on the bat that produces the maximum batted ball speed. But in England and Africa, the sweet spot may take on a whole new meaning.

In a recent British study, people treated topically with sugar for bed sores, leg ulcers, and deep wounds recovered faster than people being treated with antibiotics — and without any negative side effects. Sugar draws moisture away from wounds. This speeds up healing because bacteria need moisture to grow. In Zimbabwe, this folk remedy has been practiced for years to heal cuts and reduce pain.

The next time you suffer a small nick or cut, make a beeline for your kitchen. Wash the area with soap and water. Then cover it with white or brown sugar and a bandage. Replace with fresh sugar and bandages several times over the next 24 to 48 hours. Your sweet spot should heal in no time.

GREAT IDEA

Take the sting out of bug bites

Bees and skeeters can't help it. They love to bite and sting human prey. Often, despite your best efforts, you can't keep them away. To alleviate the pain and swelling from a bite, dab on a little toothpaste. Toothpaste contains glycerin, which dries out the venom in the affected area. Or apply a gauze pad soaked in witch hazel. It will relieve the sting and swelling of any bite.

Sweet relief for a burned tongue. You sip on a cappuccino when – Ouch! – you burn your tongue. Don't you hate that? Thankfully, relief is within spitting distance. Reach for a packet of sugar, and sprinkle it on your tongue. The sugar crystals will quickly dissolve, drawing heat from your tongue and numbing the pain.

New way to treat a burn. If you think running cold water on a burn is the best way to heal it, think again. A study published in the *Journal of Plastic, Reconstructive & Aesthetic Surgery* suggests otherwise. Experts found that warm water improved circulation and decreased tissue damage. While cold water may zap the initial pain, warm water restores skin in the long run. Consider following one researcher's remedy. Apply cold water first for about a minute. Then, to restore blood flow, use warm water.

Heal blisters with witch hazel

Don't pop a blister. Dry it out with witch hazel. The mild astringent helps fight bacteria and reduce swelling. Simply soak a gauze pad with witch hazel, place it on the blister, and wrap it with a bandage.

Simple recipes for younger-looking skin. Start your day with an energizing facial scrub packed with vitamin C – a potent antioxidant used in skin care products to treat the signs of aging. Combine a tablespoon of dried citrus peel – lime, lemon, orange, or grapefruit – with a 1/2 cup plain yogurt and 1 teaspoon raw honey. Blend the ingredients until smooth.

Or try this sugar scrub for a fresh, youthful glow. Combine 1/2 cup dark brown sugar and 3 tablespoons olive oil or raw honey. Add a yummy scent with 1/2 teaspoon nutmeg, cinnamon, or pumpkin pie spices. Mix the ingredients until they form a paste.

Dampen your face, apply your favorite scrub — massaging gently for one to two minutes, rinse with warm water, and pat dry. Place any leftover scrub in your refrigerator for up to a week.

Help move things along with rye bread. If your internal plumbing clogs up from time to time, eat rye bread. University of Finland researchers found that whole grain rye bread beat laxatives — thanks to a unique fiber — for gently moving food through your intestines. Rye even beat wheat for constipation relief. So the next time you feel the need to go but can't, reach for some whole grain rye bread.

Simple rehydration drink could save your life. If you're working outdoors on a hot, humid day, and you start to feel weak and dizzy, you're probably dehydrated. Dehydration occurs when your body loses more fluids than it takes in. Your ability to sweat and urinate decrease, and your body feels out of sorts. To rehydrate, you can make a simple solution by mixing 1/2 teaspoon baking soda, 3/8 to 1/2 teaspoon table salt, 1/4 teaspoon potassium-based salt substitute, and 2 tablespoons sugar with 1 quart of water. Drink, rest, and stay out of the sun. If your symptoms worsen, seek medical attention right away. Severe dehydration can be fatal.

GREAT IDEA

Quell queasiness without drugs

Motion sickness is miserable. But a little acupressure may go a long way toward relieving it. Find a spot on the inside of your forearm, about 2 inches from the crease of your wrist. You should feel two tendons. Press firmly between the two tendons for five to 30 seconds. Repeat until the nausea subsides.

Latest twist on the BRAT diet. You've heard doctors recommend the BRAT diet — bananas, rice, applesauce, and toast — for a troubled tummy. The BRAT diet is starchy, bland, and low in fiber, which most people can easily digest when experiencing diarrhea.

Then two variations came along — the BRATY and BRATT diets. The BRATY diet added yogurt, which provided protein, fat, and calcium. And the BRATT diet included tea.

But some experts believe the BRAT diet and its two modified versions don't offer enough balanced nutrition. Many doctors now say to limit the diet to three days, which should give the bowels plenty of time to rest and recover. Then switch to a healthy, well-balanced diet, which includes a variety of foods. Just keep these tips in mind.

- Drink plenty of fluids to avoid dehydration.

- Gradually add milk, eggs, crackers, baked fish, cereal, cooked vegetables, and skinless chicken.

- Don't eat greasy foods, raw fruits and vegetables, or foods high in simple sugars such as gelatin-based desserts.

- Pass on drinking caffeinated drinks, alcohol, and concentrated or undiluted juice.

- Limit fiber intake.

- Avoid foods that are too hot or cold.

Call your doctor if you don't see any improvement after several days.

Give hiccups the heave-ho. Hiccups happen — nerves become irritated, triggering the involuntary spasms that produce a funny, croaky sound. As a kid, you probably found hiccups amusing. But as an adult, not so much. Your kitchen contains everything you need to get rid of hiccups. But here's fair warning — these home remedies burst with sour power. Pucker up at your own risk.

- Douse a lemon wedge with Worcestershire sauce. Suck on the lemon wedge. Just be sure to rinse your mouth with water after to protect your tooth enamel.

- Squeeze fresh lemon juice into a glass of lukewarm water. Add a pinch of salt and a teaspoon of raw honey. Drink it like you would any beverage.

- Sip on a teaspoon of vinegar or pickle juice every 10 seconds.

The remedies work by soothing, or overwhelming, your irritated nerves – no one really knows for sure. Still, they're worth a shot.

Squelch garlic breath with milk. You love the taste of garlic, but hate the bad breath it leaves behind. No problem. Wash away the smell with a glass of milk. In a study published in the *Journal of Food Science*, researchers found that drinking a glass of milk before and during a garlicky meal keeps stinky breath at bay. You can thank the proteins in milk – they mask garlic's unpleasant odor. So go ahead, enjoy your favorite garlic-laced dish, but do so with a glass of milk on the side.

GREAT IDEA

Slay dragon breath with vinegar

Here's a quick and easy recipe for fresh breath. Dilute 1 to 2 tablespoons of apple cider vinegar in a cup of warm water. Swish the solution between your teeth and gargle with it. Spit it out and rinse. No more dragon breath.

Cool a fever blister with aloe. There's nothing cool about fever blisters. They're painful, unsightly, and highly contagious. Caused by the herpes simplex virus, the fluid-filled lesions – also known as cold sores – usually erupt outside of the mouth on your lips, chin, and cheeks. Blisters tend to merge then burst, leaving an open sore that crusts over. While there's no cure for the virus, there's no need to suffer the agony of an outbreak.

Keep aloe vera gel in your refrigerator for instant relief. With a cotton swab, dab the gel on to the cold sore several times a day. The coolness will provide comfort, and the aloe's polysaccharides will speed up healing.

Dynamic duo calms a canker sore. Canker sores – those pesky little craters that crop up on your tongue or the inside of your cheeks – can cause incredible pain and discomfort. Stress, rough tooth brushing, and acidic foods like oranges or tomatoes are often to blame.

Usually, a canker sore will go away on its own within five to 10 days. But in the meantime, here's a cocktail to help you handle the soreness. Mix a liquid antacid, like Milk of Magnesia, with a liquid antihistamine, like Benadryl. Swirl the solution in your mouth and spit it out. These super heroes will neutralize the acid and numb your pain.

You could also try a rinse with water and baking soda or salt. The salt may sting a little, but it will speed up the healing process. As for over-the-counter mouthwashes, steer clear of them. The chemicals may further irritate a sore.

Personal care

Simple steps to look your best

Look younger with sunscreen. Sunscreen does more than guard against sunburn – it prevents wrinkles, too. Rubbing on a little every day, even if you don't think you will need it, can help stop your skin from aging. In an Australian study, people were assigned to wear sunscreen either every day or only when they thought they needed it. After four and a half years, those who wore it every day showed no signs of sun-related aging.

"Protecting yourself from skin cancer by using sunscreen regularly has the added bonus of keeping you looking younger," explains the study's lead researcher Adele Green. "This is one of those beauty tips you often hear quoted, but for the first time we can back it with science."

People in this study wore sunscreen with an SPF of 15 or higher on their faces, arms, and hands daily. Look for products labeled "broad spectrum" for the best protection against sunburn, skin aging, and skin cancer.

TLC for tough wintry skin. Soften dry knees and elbows in winter with a homemade almond paste. Grind a handful of almonds into a fine powder, then mix with enough coconut oil to form a paste. Rub gently into rough skin, then rinse with water. Soothe dry hands by soaking them in warm whole milk for at least five minutes. For whole-body healing, try a hydrating skin bath. Pour a can of unsweetened coconut milk into a warm bath and settle in for a 10-minute soak. Resist the urge to wash your whole body with soap every day in winter. It will dry out your skin faster. Lather up the important parts daily, including your hands, feet, face, underarms, and private areas. Your arms, legs, and the trunk of your body will settle for a good rinse.

WARNING

Beware hidden danger of sunscreen

Sunscreen is supposed to protect you from burns, but in a freak accident, it could actually cause them. Many sunscreens contain flammable ingredients such as alcohol, so applying them near an open flame is an obvious no-no. What you might not guess is that they could catch fire even after they have dried on your skin.

That's exactly what happened in five frightening cases documented by the Food and Drug Administration. One person's sunscreen-covered skin caught fire when they lit a cigarette. Another's while standing too close to a citronella candle. A third person's while walking toward a barbecue grill.

Spray-on sunscreens aren't the only flammable products to watch out for. Some bug sprays and sunscreen lotions could also catch fire. Read labels carefully. Don't use any product labeled "flammable" if you plan to smoke, grill, or otherwise be near open flames or sparks.

The secret to making lipstick last longer. Dry lips don't hold lipstick well. Exfoliate and moisturize your kisser for color that lasts. Start with a gentle homemade scrub. Mix half a teaspoon of sugar with a few drops of olive oil. Gently massage it into your lips with a circular motion. Rinse it off and pat your mouth dry. Beware of lip balms made with salicylic acid. This ingredient actually damages chapped lips. Camphor and menthol are no-nos, too, as they can dry your lips. Apply a thin layer of petroleum jelly on your lips before bed, instead, for added moisture.

Play it safe and limit "touching up" your lips. Constantly touching up your lipstick could have dangerous consequences. An eye-opening new study discovered dangerous levels of metals like cadmium, chromium, aluminum, and manganese in common lipsticks and glosses. "Just finding these metals isn't the issue; it's the levels that matter," says researcher S. Katharine Hammond, professor of environmental health sciences at the University of California, Berkeley. "Some of the toxic metals are occurring at levels that could possibly have an effect in the long term."

Lip products pose a special problem – they end up in your mouth when you eat something, drink something, or simply lick your lips. Researchers in this study estimated how much metal women wound up "eating" each day from store-bought lipsticks and glosses. For 10 out of 32 products, reapplying them two or three times a day could expose you to dangerous amounts of aluminum, cadmium, chromium, and manganese. Chromium in particular has been linked to stomach tumors, while manganese can be toxic to your nervous system.

You don't have to trash your favorite lipsticks. Simply be judicious in how often you wear and reapply them. Most importantly, keep them away from children. Three-quarters of these products contained lead, which can be dangerous to kids in any amount.

GREAT IDEA

Take years off your appearance instantly

Darken your eyebrows and wear red lipstick if you want to look younger. The greater the contrast between your skin color and facial features, the younger you'll look, says new research. The difference between the color of facial features, such as eyebrows and lips, and your skin tone is greatest when you're young and shrinks as you age. Makeup can heighten that contrast again, making you look more youthful. Adding color will also make you look healthier and less sallow.

Best way to beautify your face. Is your bathroom full of skin care products that don't work? Maybe you're applying them in the wrong order. Wrinkle creams, under-eye serums, and basic cosmetics need to go on in a particular order to be effective, say dermatologists.

Wash your face to make sure all of your beauty products get absorbed by your skin. Then apply treatments such as anti-aging creams, serums, or medicated ointments. Begin with the lightest-weight one and finish with the heaviest. Apply eye creams with your ring finger. It's the weakest finger, so it pulls your skin the least. Wait two or three minutes between each product to give it time to soak into your skin. Next, put on your moisturizer or sunscreen, and finish things off with makeup. For oily skin, brush a very thin layer of cornstarch over your face to set your makeup and help it last longer.

Don't slather on too many products in your quest for beautiful skin. "Using several products at the same time may not only negate the benefits of each product but also irritate the skin," says dermatologist Susan Taylor. "Using too many products," especially anti-aging treatments, "may cause redness, stinging, and dryness." Side effects like these could actually make you look older.

Banish the bruised look of tired eyes. For a fast fix, place a cold, used tea bag over each eye for several minutes. The combination of caffeine and cold constricts the blood vessels below your eyes, making your dark circles look lighter. For a longer-lasting solution, try castor oil. Gently pat a drop over the dark areas until it gets absorbed, once in the morning before donning makeup and again at night before bed. The oil moisturizes your skin and plumps it up, making the bluish blood vessels behind the circles less visible. Pat it along laugh lines and crow's feet, too. It acts as an anti-wrinkle serum, adding nutrients to your skin and preventing wrinkle-causing oxidative damage.

Squeeze the most out of each tube. Beauty products can put a big dent in your wallet, so make the most of every ounce.

- Stretch the last of your lipstick by scraping it out of its nearly empty tube into a small jar. Clean, empty, eye cream containers are perfect. Add a small scoop of petroleum jelly and mix together with the lipstick for a tinted lip gloss.

- Persuade your remaining mascara to be swept out by standing the tube in a glass of warm water. The same trick works for toothpaste. Use hot water this time, and submerge the tube for a full minute. The last little bit will squeeze out with ease.

Guard against cellphone rash

That pesky rash on the side of your face and ear could be caused by your cellphone. Many of these gadgets contain nickel, cobalt, and chromium, metals that cause skin allergies for some people. Flip-style cellphones are the biggest culprits. In one study, nine out of 10 contained nickel and half contained cobalt. The phone's keypad, buttons, back, and the frame around the screen are the most likely sources. You could stop using your cellphone if you notice a rash, but that's not the only solution. Experts suggest buying a case for your phone; putting clear, plastic film over the keys and screen; and carrying it in a belt pouch rather than your pocket.

Do-it-yourself dandruff treatments. An overgrowth of yeast-like fungus on your scalp could be the culprit behind your dandruff. The fungus feeds on natural oils in your scalp, drying it out and causing the skin to flake away. You could spend top dollar on medicated shampoos to treat it, but homemade remedies will work just as well.

Crush two aspirin into a fine powder and mix them with one capful of your favorite shampoo. Work the concoction into your scalp during your shower, let it sit for two minutes, then rinse your hair thoroughly. Aspirin contains salicylic acid, the active ingredient in some dandruff shampoos.

Allergic to aspirin? Try baking soda. Wet your hair and work a handful into your scalp. It gently scrubs away flakes and eliminates the extra oil that the fungus feeds on, discouraging it from living there. Rinse your hair thoroughly with water, no shampoo necessary.

Whichever method you choose, finish off with an apple cider vinegar rinse. This kitchen staple tamps down flakes. It changes the pH balance of your scalp just enough to make it an inhospitable home for fungus. Mix one part vinegar with one part water, pour it in a spray bottle, and spritz on your scalp and hair. Let it sit for at least 15 minutes, then rinse. As a bonus, this vinegar rinse will blast away residue left by styling products, plus leave your hair soft and shiny.

Beat split ends. Brushing your hair 100 strokes each night won't make it shine. In fact, the opposite is true. That much brushing can damage your hair and cause split ends. Keep brushing to a minimum for healthier hair, and don't brush or comb it while wet. Wet hair generally breaks more easily. Let your hair partially air dry first, then style it as usual. The exception – tightly curled or textured hair. This type breaks more easily when dry, so comb it while it's still wet.

WARNING

Scary side effect of hair-straighteners

Brazilian treatments and keratin smoothing are great at straightening hard-to-tame curly tresses, but they may have an unintended consequence. Many are chock-full of the cancer-causing chemical formaldehyde. Twenty-eight out of 31 salon straighteners contained unsafe levels of formaldehyde in recent tests.

You can't believe safety claims made by the manufacturer, either. Another study found that, although 16 products contained dangerous levels of formaldehyde, only one listed it as an ingredient. Your best bet — learn to love the hair you were born with. If you can't stand to give up your straightening sessions, then at least have them done in a salon with excellent ventilation.

Divvy up shampoo and save. Save your shampoo and conditioner bottles once they're empty. The next time you need more, go big and buy the jumbo sizes. Rinse out your empties, then divide the giant bottles amongst them. Put a bottle of shampoo and conditioner in each bathroom. Make your shampoo last longer by using only a dollop the size of one or two quarters to lather up. Too much shampoo can strip your hair of its natural oils. Focus on your scalp rather than the ends of your hair. People with curly or dry hair can get by with fewer washes.

Brighten or darken hair naturally. A homemade rinse can pump up your hair's highlights and low lights. Steep a tea bag in hot water for several minutes and let cool. Wash your hair as usual, then slowly pour the tea over your head, working it through your hair. Put on a shower cap and let the rinse sit while you finish bathing, then rinse your hair. Brunettes should opt for black tea, blondes for chamomile, and redheads for berry teas. Coffee works on brunettes, too, with an added bonus — its natural acids dissolve hairspray buildup, leaving tresses soft and shiny.

Top tips for stronger nails. It may seem odd, but if you want tougher nails, steer clear of polishes that contain nail-strengthening ingredients. They make your nails stiffer, but that can cause them to break more easily. Other nail-weakening culprits include gel manicures and acetone polish removers. Experts also warn there's another good reason to avoid gel manicures. The UV lights used to dry and harden the polish can cause long-term damage to your hands and increase your risk of skin cancer. For healthy nails, limit harsh chemicals and procedures. Opt instead for a home remedy — a 10-minute soak in warm olive oil. It nourishes and moisturizes your nails and cuticles naturally.

Say goodbye to new-shoe blisters. Keep a stick of gel deodorant on hand. The next time you break in new shoes or step out in your barely worn heels, dab a little gel on the areas of your feet where the shoes tend to rub. The lubrication will help the shoe slide smoothly against your foot. Aerosol antiperspirant works, too. Just spray it on blister-prone areas before donning your shoes. It blocks sweat that makes the rubbing worse.

When you shouldn't shave your legs. So you have a pedicure appointment today and you haven't shaved in a week. Leave your legs hairy until after your feet are finished. Shaving right before a pedicure is an invitation for infection. Bacteria from foot baths and nail tools can enter your body through a razor nick on your leg. Shave at least 24 hours before your pedicure, or wait until afterward. Consider buying your own tools if you frequently have your nails done and ask the salon to use those, instead, to further reduce your risk of infection. Prefer to do your own manicures and pedicures at home? Moisturize your nails afterward. "Nails need to be moisturized, especially after removing nail polish," says Phoebe Rich, assistant professor of dermatology at Oregon Health Science University. "Be sure to apply a cream regularly."

Eat these foods for naturally whiter teeth. Cheese and wine make a perfect pair. Aside from tasting good together, cheese is rich in calcium, perfect for keeping teeth white while you sip staining beverages like red wine. It's also loaded with lactic acid, which helps prevent tooth decay. Hard cheeses even help scrub particles off your pearly whites. Other foods act like natural whiteners, too. Munch on a few celery sticks to stop soy sauce from staining your teeth after your next order of Chinese food. Crisp fruits and vegetables, like apples, celery, carrots, and cauliflower, work like natural toothbrushes, scrubbing teeth while you chew. Want to polish your teeth? Snack on strawberries or oranges for a natural shine.

Refreshing way to defeat gum disease. Swish with a mouthwash designed to kills germs if you want to beat back plaque and gum disease. Rinsing with a germ-killing mouthwash twice a day, in addition to brushing and flossing, reduced plaque and gum disease in a recent study. Christine Charles, director of Scientific and Professional Affairs at Johnson & Johnson, says that regular brushing and flossing still tend to leave bacteria in your mouth. "It's simple – mouthrinses can reach nearly 100 percent of the mouth's surfaces, while brushing focuses on the teeth, which make up only 25 percent of the mouth."

But make sure your mouthwash kills germs and contains fluoride. If it doesn't have fluoride, wait half an hour after brushing before you swish. Rinsing with a nonfluoride mouthwash too soon after brushing cancels out the cavity-fighting power of toothpaste.

Travel

Sensational tips for carefree trips

Call ahead of time or get declined. You don't need to worry about your credit cards getting declined on your travels. Simply contact your bank and credit card company in advance to give them a heads up. Otherwise, your credit cards may get turned down when they pop up for purchases away from home. Companies refuse transactions to protect your account. Still, being declined can be inconvenient and embarrassing.

Call or email ahead of time, and have your itinerary handy with dates, locations, and accommodation details. This will give them a chance to place travel alerts on your cards. And remember to take your debit card with you – you can use it to withdraw cash as needed. Plus, jot down your credit card numbers, expiration dates, and toll-free numbers. Then leave this information with a friend. If your cards are lost or stolen while you're on vacation, you will be able to access all the numbers you need quickly and easily.

Dodge a dispute with a snapshot. Rental cars and condos come with their fair share of risks. Rental companies rake in cash from unsuspecting consumers by blaming them for preexisting damage. Even if you jot down the details of any damage on your paperwork, a rental company can still come after you. To protect yourself, photograph or video record the exterior of your rental car. Look for nicks, dings, and scratches. Also check the wheel rims and windows. And don't forget the vehicle's interior. Look for stains and tears on seats and floor mats. Use your camera with a date stamp or your cellphone's video recorder.

This tip works for vacation rentals, too, from beach condos to mountain cabins. Look for stains on carpeting, cracked mirrors, and broken door handles. If the owner slaps you with a claim, you can easily prove the damage was already there.

Snap your way back to your hotel. You don't want to waste time getting lost on your vacation. But you don't want to keep up with little bits of paper either. Instead, use your cellphone's camera to snap a shot of your hotel room door. If you forget your room number, you can check your phone. You can do this with your cabin number on a cruise, too. And before hailing a cab, take a photo of your hotel's street address. Then pull out your phone when you're ready to head back. This idea also works for airport parking. Take a picture of the location signs near your parking spot, and never get lost in an airport lot again.

TIMESAVER

Fly your valuables past the gate agent

Don't pack essential items in your carry-on and expect to board your plane without incident. Due to space limitations, a gate agent may ask you to check your bags as you board the plane. You risk never seeing your valuables again if you hand them over. Instead, pack the things you can't live without — jewelry, prescriptions, even souvenirs — into a separate, smaller bag. Then place the smaller bag in your carry-on. If you are asked to check your hand luggage, you can easily remove the smaller bag. Enjoy your flight knowing your valuables are safe and sound.

Protect your possessions with a picture. Before you leave for the airport, take a picture of the items in your suitcase and create a detailed list. Upon arrival at your destination, go through your luggage and make sure nothing is missing. If you can't find an item, you can easily search for it in your photo and on your list. If it's missing, file a claim with the airline and your insurance company immediately. You will have picture proof.

Sort and pack with repurposed zippered bags. You know those clear, plastic bags your sheets, curtains, and pillowcases come in? Don't throw them out. They come in handy when it's time to pack your suitcase. You can pack shorts and T-shirts in larger bags – and undergarments, hairbrushes, and accessories in smaller ones. The clear plastic allows you to find what you need easily and quickly when you open your suitcase. Plus, you can use one to "zip up" odors from dirty laundry, and keep the rest of your clothes smelling fresh. If you don't have any stashed away, ask a friend or check with your local thrift stores.

Turn your cooler into a carry-on. If you need a cooler on your next vacation, use one as your carry-on bag. Pick a soft-sided cooler with straps for easy handling. Fill it with your travel-size toiletries and valuables. When you reach your destination, empty it and use it to pack drinks and snacks each day. You won't have to buy a disposable foam cooler while on your trip.

Pack your polish perfectly. Eyeglass cases make the perfect manicure kits. Just toss a nail file, clippers, and a small bottle of polish into a hinged case, and you're good to go. You could even throw in a couple of cotton balls, cotton swabs, and a tiny bottle of nail polisher remover. An eyeglass case will protect your clothes from spills. Plus, you can fit one into any little nook in your suitcase. If you don't wear glasses, ask a friend who does for an extra case.

Don't plan an escape without duct tape. It can fix just about anything – at least temporarily – from the hem of your favorite pair of pants to the broken handle on a suitcase. Even astronauts take it on space missions. So why not take a roll with you on your next vacation? Measuring 2 inches by 100 inches, travel-size duct tape is small enough to toss into a suitcase or carry-on. You can pick up a two-pack for around $4 online or at your local hardware store. Or you can make your own travel roll from duct tape you already have. Just wrap the tape around an old credit card or piece of cardboard. You'll end up with a flat roll that's easy to pack.

Spray foam keeps valuables safe. Foam spray may be, first and foremost, a sealant for air leaks around window jambs. But did you know you could use it to pack valuables, too? Just follow these simple steps. First, make sure to wear safety goggles and rubber gloves. Then, spray the foam into a plastic bag and seal the opening. Next, press the fragile item on top of the bag, and allow the foam to expand and surround it. It will form a protective mold around your treasure. Lastly, pack it in your suitcase. You can pick up a can of foam spray at any home improvement store for less than $5. Just remember to always follow the safety instructions.

GREAT IDEA

Recycle magnets to remember dates

On your next cruise, spend less time sorting through piles of paperwork. Pack several magnets — like the ones you peel off your Yellow Pages. They will stick to your cabin walls with ease. Use them to post daily activity schedules and invitations to special events, like the Captain's Welcome Aboard party.

"Pinning up papers with magnets helps me stay organized onboard," says Charlotte, an avid cruiser. "I want to make sure I don't miss out on a fun activity or a special offer. Instead of going through stacks of invitations, I just put them on my walls. They're so much easier to find this way."

Carry on, contact wearers. You can pack large bottles of contact lens solution and eye drops, and not worry about a TSA officer confiscating them. The TSA considers them over-the-counter medications and does not limit them to the usual 3.4 ounces or less. Just be sure to show them to the screener. And remember the basic 3-1-1 guidelines to get through airport security hassle-free — no liquids in bottles over 3.4 ounces; 1 quart-size clear, zip-top bag to store your liquids; and 1 carry-on bag per passenger placed in a screening bin.

Pack a week's worth of jewelry with ease. Your pill organizer isn't just for pills. You can use one to organize your jewelry for a week's vacation. Each compartment will keep jewelry tangle-free. Also, a pill box can be tossed into a suitcase without taking up space. Need more than a week's worth of jewelry? Try a pill organizer with morning and evening compartments. Need less? Try a contact lens case instead.

Veil your valuables in a vest. No need to lug a handbag or a backpack on your next vacation. Try a photo vest instead. With about 20 pockets, you can easily stash away small items from passports to prescriptions. Plus, you can tuck away money and credit cards in hidden pockets. And you don't have to worry about a thief running off with your purse. Just remember to reserve one pocket for one of your most prized possessions — your camera.

Pack backward before you move forward. Before driving off on a road trip, think about how you'll pack your car. Start by cleaning it out. Throw away trash, and put away anything you won't need on your trip. Next, check your spare tire and make sure it's in good condition with the correct tire pressure. Then, pack first what you'll need last. For example, if you plan on taking your golf clubs, pack them first. You won't need these while you're driving. Finish by packing anything you'll need easy access to.

Blow away wrinkles with hair care tools. You need to get the wrinkles out of your shirt or dress, but you don't have an iron handy. Time to plug in your hair dryer. First, sprinkle your garment with a little water. Then hold the dryer 1 to 2 inches away and keep it on low. Or, for small wrinkles, heat up your flat iron. Straighten out wrinkles like you would straighten your hair. Just make sure you clean your flat iron first with a damp cloth before you plug it in. And keep it on a low setting to prevent scorching your clothes.

MONEYSAVER

Pocket more money by buying a pass

If you're going to spend more than one day in a metropolitan area, purchase a multi-ride pass. The savings on bus and subway rides over several days is worth it, and you won't need to pay for a rental car, fuel, or parking.

For instance, a single-ride ticket costs around $3 in New York. But a seven-day pass runs about $30, good for unlimited subway and local bus rides until midnight each night. In Washington D.C., a seven-day regional bus pass goes for under $20. And the SmarTrip seven-day pass for short Metrorail trips runs around $35. You can also find single-day deals in some cities like Chicago, where the base fare is between $2 to $3 per ride, but a one-day unlimited pass is around $10. Just remember to ask about senior discounts first, and then do the math before buying a pass.

Don't pass up sightseeing perks. Buy multi-day passes to attractions. You'll save money and time by not waiting in long ticket lines. Say you want to explore Colonial Williamsburg. A single-day ticket runs around $42 and gets you into all of the Revolutionary City's sites. The ticket includes 35 exhibits, trade shops, museums, and complimentary shuttle bus service for one day. For a few dollars more, you can purchase a multi-day pass for the same attractions, including three days worth of shuttle service.

You can also check into buying a CityPASS in 11 cities or regions across North America including Atlanta, Boston, Chicago, Hollywood, Houston, New York City, Philadelphia, San Francisco, Seattle, Southern California, and Toronto. A pass bundles prepaid admission to each city's top attractions. For example, San Francisco's CityPASS includes unlimited transportation on all trolleys, buses, and historic cable cars for seven days, plus a bay cruise and admission to an art museum, an aquarium, and the California Academy of Sciences – all for just over $80. Purchase individual tickets and fares, and the cost would range from $130 to $160 for seniors over age 65. Visit *www.citypass.com* for details.

Never leave home without your buddy. Your GasBuddy, that is. This free smartphone app will list gas stations near you from the cheapest to the most expensive. Be prepared to enter the name of the city closest to you when you're ready to fill up. Then tap on the map view, and it will pinpoint exactly where to find each station. Anyone can use the app, but becoming a GasBuddy member comes with perks. Members update gas prices on the app, and earn points toward prizes like $250 prepaid gas cards. Membership is free. The app works on all smartphones including iPhones and Androids.

Know when to book a flight and when to wait. Bing's airline price predictor will tell you just that. The website analyzes millions of flights, and filters the information to give you the best deals. Plus, it will let you know if the fares are likely to rise or drop. Just enter your dates and destinations at *www.bing.com/travel*. Bing will display the best prices from aggregator sites, like Priceline, Expedia, and Travelocity. Then, if it looks like the fares will rise, Bing will recommend you buy the ticket right away. Conversely, if Bing predicts a drop in airfare, it will suggest you hold out. The risk of waiting, however, is entirely yours.

Take a bus for a buck. You want to travel from one city to another, but don't want to deal with airports. And the cost of filling up a rental car just isn't in your budget. Check into Boltbus and

MegaBus – both companies offer cheap bus fares to more than 100 cities across North America. BoltBus primarily serves the Northeast and West Coast. Each route sells at least one $1 seat. The trick to snatching up that seat is timing – the sooner you book, the greater your chances of grabbing a fare for a buck. Call 877-265-8287 or visit *www.boltbus.com* for more information. MegaBus serves cities across North America with free Wi-Fi and power outlets at each seat. The bus line also sells $1 fares. Booking way in advance will help you find the lowest ticket prices. Call 877-462-6342 or log on to *www.megabus.com.*

Stroll through security with ease. No need to worry about airport security if you have a medical condition or disability. The TSA now offers a card that can be downloaded and printed from its website. Use the card to jot down notes about your condition, disability, or medical device. You can show the card to a TSA officer, and trust him to discuss your condition discreetly. You won't escape being screened or patted down. But you will be able to protect your privacy by not having to explain your medical condition in front of other passengers.

Visit *www.tsa.gov* and click on "Travelers with Disabilities and Medical Conditions" in the "Learn More About" section for additional information. Then scroll down to find the link "TSA's Notification Card." Make sure you call TSA Cares' toll-free number at 855-787-2227 three days before your flight to discuss any questions or concerns.

Yard & garden

Quick tricks to beautify your outdoor space

3 unmistakable signs your lawn needs water. Don't wait until your lawn turns brown. Try these tricks to know when to water before it's too late.

- Look at your lawn through polarized sunglass lenses in direct sunlight. If it looks blue-gray instead of green, it's time to get busy with the garden hose.

- Walk through your lawn, then turn and look back. If there are footprints left from where you stepped, your grass needs a drink to give it more bounce.

- Push a 6-inch screwdriver into the ground. It should go in easily and all the way if the lawn has enough water.

The best time to water is very early in the morning. Water at night, and the risk of fungus and disease goes up. Water in the middle of the day, and a lot of the water will just evaporate. And it's better to water deeply and less often. Frequent, shallow watering can cause shallow roots, thatch accumulation, and compacted soil.

Most lawns need 1 to 2 inches of water a week, and it's good to give it a half inch to an inch twice to make the total. To measure, put an empty tuna can or similar container on the ground near the sprinkler before you turn it on. Let the sprinkler work for half an hour, then measure the water in the container. If it's a half inch, that should be enough. Try the screwdriver trick to check. If not, water a bit longer.

Once you've found the right amount of watering time, just do it twice a week. Your lawn will love you for it.

The secret to great grass. The first key to a lush lawn with less work and less money? Get your soil tested before fertilizing, sodding, or seeding. A basic soil test will tell you exactly how much fertilizer to apply for the type of grass you want to grow. There's no guessing and no wasted time or money.

Take a soil sample, then send or take it to your local cooperative extension office of the Department of Agriculture for analysis. Be sure to tell them that you'll be growing grass in the soil. You'll receive a detailed report in a few weeks with fertilizer recommendations and lawn care advice. There is a small fee for the service, normally less than $10. Find your local extension office online at *nifa.usda.gov/Extension/index.html.*

Warning signs for a malnourished lawn. You can spot a lawn that is low in nutrients even without a soil test. Just watch for these warning signs.

- Nitrogen. Sparse yellow to yellow-green grass with stunted growth. Weeds, particularly clover, are taking over the turf.

- Iron. Grass grows well but is yellow to yellow-green.

- Phosphorus. Dull, blue-green grass. The blades turn purple along the edges, then develop a reddish tinge.

Grass clippings will add nitrogen to your lawn as they decompose, so try leaving them on the lawn when you mow if lack of nitrogen is the problem. Also, there are fertilizers, both organic and conventional, specially made to provide whatever is missing in your lawn. If one of these problems comes up, ask for the right fertilizer at your local nursery or lawn care department of your favorite home improvement store. The experts will be able to give you specifics that are right for your area's soil.

3 ways to tame your garden hose. No need to buy something expensive — these free solutions will tame the tangle and keep your hose handy.

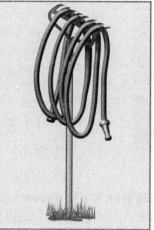

- Rake. Replaced your garden rake? Give the old one a clever update that's both useful and ornamental. Secure the handle firmly in the ground — no wobbling — then use the head of the rake for hanging a hose. Loop the hose loosely, and the spaces between the tines of the rake will keep it neatly in place.

- Wheel rim. Got an old car tire sitting around? Take off the metal rim, and attach it securely to your house or a fence. Your hose will curl up nicely around the rim and will unroll easily without tangling. Paint the rim to match your house, and it will blend right in.

- Bucket. Use a sturdy, metal bucket mounted securely to your house or shed, with the open end facing outward. Wrap your hose around it, and inside you can stash items such as gloves, sprayers, and nozzles. Even less work? Just coil your hose inside a plastic 5-gallon bucket and carry it where it's needed.

Put that holey hose back to work. Don't get rid of a leaky garden hose — transform it into a multipurpose soaker hose. Simply puncture the underside of the hose at regular intervals with a hot ice pick. Lay it, pinpricks down, in your garden bed between the plants. Attach one end to your new hose. Plug the other end with a plastic end cap. Cover your soaker hose with mulch and turn the tap on. Water will drip out of the small holes and thoroughly soak your flower or vegetable bed.

GREAT IDEA

Shield grass seed from pesky birds

Before you reseed a small patch of lawn, look in your basement or garage for an old window screen — or one that's not being used. Use it to protect your newly seeded area while the grass grows. Place the screen over the seeded patch, and weigh it down with a few stones to keep it secure. Birds won't be able to move it, and your seeds will be safe.

Cut back on mowing. Fed up with grass? Get lucky with clover. These hardy plants make thick, cushy ground covers just perfect for choking out weeds. Clovers are drought tolerant and never need fertilizing. Best of all, the low-growing varieties, such as white Dutch clover, rarely require mowing. Plus, the roots aerate compacted soil and add nitrogen back into the ground.

Or go low-maintenance with a no-mow herbal lawn. Many low-growing plants are fragrant, not to mention flowering. Try violets, creeping thyme, mazus (*Mazus reptans*), or pearlwort (*Sagina subulata*). For front yards where you rarely walk, consider yarrow, oregano, and phlox. If your lawn area is damp and doesn't get direct sunlight, you might want to go for a lush, green moss — sheet moss (*Hypnum sp.*) and fern moss (*Thuidium delicatulum*) are fast-growing and adapt well. Remember, moss likes water — the more it gets, the more it grows, but unlike grass, it needs only shallow watering. Your high-maintenance lawn care days could soon be over.

Take the strain out of carrying tools. Let your garden tools do the work for you — not the other way around. These clever ideas help make heavy tasks light.

- Instead of carrying around a weighty pump sprayer, put it on your golf bag cart and wheel it around your garden. The pull cart is designed for use on grass, and the sprayer should sit well on the base of the cart. Depending on the cart, you might need some duct tape or a bungee cord to help secure the sprayer.

- An old golf bag makes a terrific caddy for your long-handled garden tools, such as rakes and shovels. What's more, your gloves and hand tools fit neatly in the side pockets. You can put the golf bag on a golf bag cart for easy movement around your garden. After all, they're made for each other.

- Use a 5-gallon bucket to carry your small gardening tools. As a bonus, you can flip it over and sit on it as you weed, plant, or just take a breather. Add an S-hook to the bucket handle, and hook it on to your wheelbarrow, and you won't even have to carry the bucket.

- Attach a plastic window box to your wheelbarrow for a more permanent tool holder – just a couple of screws will do. Drill through the window box into the handles of the wheelbarrow, or use the drainage holes if they line up right. Pop in  the screws, and off you go. Keep small tools, your water bottle, even your cellphone, close by and easy to get to.

Be a better planter with a plan. You might be tempted just to go to the garden center and pick out what you like. But you'll make expensive mistakes if you mix and match plants that don't grow well together, or aren't suited for your soil. A little knowledge goes a long way. These sources can make your planning – and your planting – a lot easier.

- Guidebook. A simple guide for your geographical area will help you identify plants that will thrive. If your local garden center doesn't always have a knowledgeable salesperson available, take your guidebook with you. When you see something you like, check its requirements. And look at the pictures, too, because sometimes plants get mislabeled.

- Experts. If you aren't sure what flowers to plant, visiting garden shows will give you a lot of good ideas. You may be able to get advice about your specific needs and even buy plants you like on the spot. Garden tours can be even better. You'll get to meet people in your area who will be happy to share tips about their gardening successes.

- Neighbors. You don't have to take a tour to take a peek at the garden next door. A quick, reliable way to choose plants for your own garden is to see what's growing well in a neighbor's yard that gets similar light.

Free plants for your garden. There's no need to make a big investment in plants if you're just getting started in gardening. Here are some sources to consider when looking for something to grow. Be flexible, and see what's offered.

- Online. Check out the "free" section and the "farm and garden" sections of Craigslist. And go to *www.freecycle.org* — type in your general location and browse through the free offers for trees and plants.

- Landscaping crews. They often toss perfectly good plants when they change displays or redesign someone's yard. Ask nicely, and you may be able to adopt some.

- Garden club. Consider joining a local or online gardening club, which may host plant swaps among members. Or ask a neighbor about a trade.

- Membership. If you want trees, consider joining the National Arbor Day Foundation for just $10. You'll get 10 trees in return, along with access to advice and a support network for your tree-growing adventures.

- Nursery. If you're at a nursery buying and asking for advice, don't forget to ask if they have any plants they're throwing away. You may get some that need a little extra care, but when the price is right, a little added effort is worth it.

- Volunteers. Be on the lookout for volunteers – plants that come up unexpectedly – and make the most of these happy accidents.

GREAT IDEA

A worldwide web of gardening information

Learn how to grow anything, inside or out, with the help of these great gardening websites. Get ideas, find supplies, and connect with other gardening enthusiasts.

- Aggie Horticulture — Texas A&M AgriLife Extension Service, *aggie-horticulture.tamu.edu*

- Clemson University Cooperative Extension Service — Home and Garden Information Center, *www.clemson.edu/extension/hgic*

- GardenGuides — a growing resource for gardeners, *www.gardenguides.com*

- The Gardening Launch Pad's list of Master Gardeners' programs and extension services, *gardeninglaunchpad.com/extension.html*

- GardenWeb — iVillage Home and Garden Network, *www.gardenweb.com*

- The National Gardening Association, *www.garden.org*

- The Ohio State University PlantFacts database, *plantfacts.osu.edu*

- The United States National Arboretum, *www.usna.usda.gov*

- Watch Your Garden Grow — University of Illinois Extension guide to growing, storing, and preparing vegetables, *urbanext.illinois.edu/veggies*

Free fertilizer from an unlikely place. You won't believe what you can put in your garden soil that works just like organic fertilizer. Come springtime, you may have a good supply of ashes from your wood-burning stove or fireplace. Wood ashes are rich in nutrients plants love, and you can scatter them directly in your garden as fertilizer. For lawns, approximately 12 pounds will feed 1,000 square feet. For flower and vegetable gardens, use around 10 pounds for 500 square feet. A half pound will do the trick for individual shrubs or rose bushes.

Ashes increase the pH level of soil — a good reason to test your soil before you try this. Don't use ashes if your level is 7 or above. Scatter them carefully and keep away from acid-loving plants, such as blueberries and azaleas. Only use ashes from burnt wood, like hardwood trees, not pressure-treated, painted, or stained wood. And never use ashes from burned trash or cardboard.

Beware of danger lurking in your yard. Curious children and pets aren't aware of the dangers of pretty but poisonous plants, so you have to be. Keep little ones safe from these potentially fatal flowers, seeds, leaves, and berries. If a pet or a child shows signs of plant poisoning after being in your yard or garden, seek medical help immediately.

- Daphne. The berries of this ornamental shrub are highly poisonous. Eating just one can cause intense burning in the mouth and throat. Symptoms — headache, delirium, upset stomach, diarrhea, and convulsions.

- Digitalis — also known as Foxglove, Dead Man's Bells, Witches' Gloves. A beautiful but dangerous flower with poisonous leaves. Symptoms — nausea, vomiting, diarrhea, and abnormal heartbeat.

- Hydrangea. Flower buds are the main culprit, but the whole plant contains a poison that is similar to cyanide. Symptoms — shortness of breath, dizziness, and rapid pulse.

- Jasmine. Eating the berries can be fatal. Symptoms — nervousness and stomach upset.

- Larkspur or delphinium. The young plant and mature seeds are especially potent. Symptoms — burning mouth, nausea, and slow heartbeat.

- Lily-of-the-Valley. The leaves are especially dangerous, but the whole plant is poisonous, potentially lethal. Symptoms — confusion, headache, hallucinations, and cold, clammy skin with red blotches.

- Mistletoe. The berries are extremely poisonous. Symptoms — blurred vision, drowsiness, nausea, and diarrhea.

- Moonseed. The berries look like wild grapes, but don't be fooled. Symptom — convulsions.

- Narcissus. Its bulbs are the most toxic, but the whole plant is poisonous. Symptoms — nausea, convulsions, and paralysis.

- Nightshade. The whole plant is poisonous, particularly the unripened berries. Symptoms — dilated pupils, inability to speak, difficulty breathing, intense nervous and digestive upset, and convulsions.

- Oleander. One leaf can be fatal to a small child. Symptoms — vomiting, diarrhea, circulatory problems, and seizure.

- Rhododendron and azaleas. The whole plant is poisonous, and the effects can be from mild to lethal, depending on how much is consumed. Symptoms — drooling, teary eyes, vomiting, seizures, and coma.

- Wisteria. Its seeds and pods are poisonous. Symptoms — nausea, vomiting, and diarrhea.

- Yellow Jasmine or Jessamine, Carolina Jasmine. The nectar is poisonous even to honeybees. Symptoms — sweating, weakness, shallow breathing, convulsions, and paralysis.

- Yew. The berries and especially the foliage are toxic. Death is often sudden, without warning, but symptoms can include coldness, trembling, staggering, and collapse.

Pack a big harvest into a small space. Here's an attractive and efficient idea for growing a variety of herbs – recycle a hanging shoe caddy and have herbs handy when you want them. Pick a spot with good exposure – a wooden fence, potting shed wall, or even a door – then hang the caddy at a convenient height. It can be attached directly with nails or screws, or hung from hooks or a curtain rod for easy removal. Pour some water in the pockets to check the drainage. Poke small holes if necessary, then start planting.

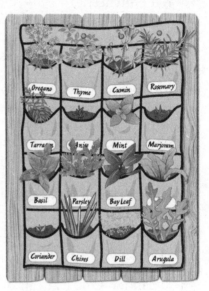

Choose the herbs you want, and the potting mix that suits each herb. Leave an inch or so between the top of the pocket and the soil, then add your seeds or plant. Finish your creation with the herbs' names on waterproof tape, pinned-on scraps of fabric, attached nursery labels, or any other attractive idea you can imagine.

Grow a salad bar in your yard. More vegetables mean more nutrients and a healthier life. The simplest, most cost-effective thing you can grow is salad. Start with a simple mixed salad – put lettuce, radish, and carrot seeds together in a container with sand to help it spread. Mix well and scatter them on a prepared bed and cover with a thin layer of dirt. As the veggies sprout, thin them for space, then let them mature. The mixture of plants helps keep both weeds and pests away.

Cool weather is especially kind to salad greens, so think about a fall planting of your favorite lettuce, as well as spinach, kale, Swiss chard, raddicchio, and arugula. A great trick for getting a constant supply of your green leaf of choice is to sow a lot of seeds in trays to get them going, but wait to transplant them in intervals of two weeks or so. Then instead of piles of lettuce all at once, you'll get a steady supply for your salad bowl. And you'll save loads compared to what you'd pay at the supermarket, especially if you like the more exotic leaf.

Another great bargain is growing your own tomatoes. Heirloom cherry tomatoes are an especially good value. They have a longer growing season and a larger overall crop. Plant basil with them for added flavor. And consider growing other flavor enhancers — dill, parsley, and scallion — to complete your bountiful harvest of good-for-you salad.

GREAT IDEA

Simple steps for safer transplanting

These two key steps will help you keep your perennials happy when moving them to a new location.

- Before — water plants the night before a move. It gives them a boost and helps keep stress away.
- After — keep plants shaded for a few days to let them recover. This is especially important for older perennials or in hot weather.

Get more bang from your bulbs with daffodils. Bulbs, especially daffodils, are a good investment in your garden. Buy a few and in time they'll fill your landscape. Daffodils are known as "the poets' flower." They are easy to grow, and they tolerate any kind of soil except boggy land. They multiply quickly, yet take years before they need to be divided. An added benefit — rodents find them unappealing and leave them alone. Then again, don't try overly hard to be thrifty. You might try to double your money by looking for daffodil bulbs with two "noses." It's true you'll get two flower stems, but these bulbs are more likely to go "blind" — stop producing flowers. Stick with a single-nose bulb for more flowers in the long term.

Encourage your plants to keep on blooming. When blossoms die, it gives the plant the idea its job of producing flowers is done. So it stops blooming and puts its energy into producing seeds instead. You can trick it into thinking its job isn't finished by dead-heading — or pinching off the dead blossoms before seeds form. If there are still buds on the stems, just remove the dead flower head. If there are no more buds, cut the stems back to the base.

If deadheading doesn't appeal to you, try planting flowers such as impatiens, begonias, ageratum, alyssum, and lobelia. As "automatic deadheaders," they do the work for you by dropping their dead blossoms without any help.

Tricks for choosing the right containers. Got houseplants or a container garden? For healthier, prettier plants, make sure you choose the best containers.

- Plastic is usually the least expensive choice. It's lightweight and provides good drainage. It cools quickly, keeping plants from overheating — but it's not very sturdy. Cold weather can make plastic brittle and break.

- Ceramic, or glazed clay pots, have good stability and retain moisture well. They come in a beautiful variety of colors and styles, which makes them more expensive. Something else to consider — heavy glaze can cause these pots to heat up and possibly damage roots.

- Terra cotta is also heavy and stable, with traditional good looks. It's porous, which is good for air circulation and absorbing mois-ture, but that also means your plants will need more frequent watering. Terra cotta can break easily, so it may not be the best choice if it's likely to get knocked over or moved around.

- Wood is versatile, natural, and helps warm the soil. It can be made into various combined features, such as planter/seaters and painted to coordinate with your decor. Unless it's rot-resistant cedar or redwood, it may need to be treated to prevent decay. Beware of chemicals that could be toxic to your plants.

- Metal containers are sturdy, and they look modern and trendy. Yet, they can really heat up in direct sunlight and damage your plants.

Clever containers help you pot your plants for pennies.

Don't spend all your fun money on fancy containers for your garden. There's a treasure-trove of potential pots all around – if you just know where to look. Here are a few ideas for turning normal household items and yard sale finds into charming planters.

For each project, prevent your potting soil from spilling out the bottom by lining the container with a piece of fine mesh screening, a bit of moss, or even a large coffee filter.

- Cinder blocks. These hollow building blocks are perfect for filling with plants. But don't stop with just one. Build a wall or tower by stacking them into any shape or design that fits your space. Leave as many blocks exposed as you like and fill with your favorite flowers. For tall structures, consider securing the blocks to each other with a concrete adhesive.

- Colanders. These are already designed for drainage, and the old-fashioned metal or enamel ones will add a nostalgic touch to your porch or patio. Place them on the ground, or add chains to the handles and you've got a hanging planter with loads of personality.

- Glass lampshades. Turn the shade upside down so the narrow opening is at the bottom. Add soil and your plants. What a bright idea.

Combine flower pots for charming, healthy plants. Terra cotta pots have a natural appeal most plastic containers lack. But they also dry out faster, and the soil temperature changes more than with plastic. A combination of the two, however, may be ideal. Plant in a slightly smaller plastic pot, and slip it inside a clay pot. Or maybe you have an attractive container you'd like to use as a planter but don't want to put soil in it directly. The solution is the same – a plastic pot that will fit inside. And if the planter is taller than your plastic pot, place an empty, upside-down flower pot below the filled one.

Quick cures for common houseplant problems. The same troubles show up in houseplants time and again. You don't need a degree in horticulture to put them right. Use these commonsense solutions to solve common complaints – and keep your house-plants healthy.

- Yellow leaves. Either too much or too little water or a nitrogen deficiency. Improve drainage by making sure the pot has good soil and enough drainage holes. Don't add gravel or sand. It's a myth that it helps. In fact, it makes the problem worse. Wait till the soil dries to water. Add fertilizer to boost nitrogen in the soil.

- Brown tips. Salt burn from too many minerals in the soil or from hard water. In the shower, flush the soil until the water runs clear.

- Stunted growth, small brittle leaves. Too little water. Water immediately, then again as soon as the topsoil dries out.

- No growth, dull leaves. Too much water. Improve the drainage, and wait for topsoil to dry before you add water again.

- Curling leaves. Too hot. Water and move to a shaded area.

- Tan or brown splotches. Sunburn or too cold. Move to a sheltered spot.

- White crust on soil. Salt buildup from too much fertilizer. Flush until water runs clear, and reduce fertilizer. For a lighter hand in applying fertilizer, try putting some in an old saltshaker and sprinkling lightly.

A smoothie for your houseplants. You can still put your food scraps to good use even if you live in an apartment or don't have a yard big enough for a compost heap. Stick your vegetable peels and fruit rinds in your blender, and purée them into a smooth liquid. Dilute with water and pour the mixture on your plants.

Recycled water gives your plants a boost. Time to stop letting water go down the drain without thinking about the cost. From now on, save water and use it to nourish your plants.

- Cooking. How often do you simply pour away the water used to cook vegetables or boil eggs? Instead, let it cool and give this nutrient-rich water renewed purpose by taking it out to your garden or giving it to your houseplants.

- Pet water. Pouring out your pets' bowls to give them clean water? Keep a container handy and pour the old water in there instead of down the drain.

- Shower or bath. Put a container in your sink or shower to catch excess water that would otherwise wash away. You may not get it all, but every little bit helps — and a little suds does plants no harm. The same is true after a bath. Any water you can reuse rather than sending down the drain is a saving on water costs and a benefit for the environment.

- Milk cartons. Before you recycle your empty milk cartons, fill them halfway with water and swish it around. The liquid makes a nutritious drink for alkaline-loving plants – African violets, particularly, love this homemade milkshake.

Enrich your soil for free. Why spend money on mulch when you can get it at no cost? Here are the best free mulches you'll find and a few you should avoid.

- Grass clippings. Be sure they're weed-free and free of herbicides, or weed killers. Then dry them and use as cover, about an inch thick. They'll suppress weed growth and add nutrients as they decompose.

- Autumn leaves. Rake the leaves into rows, about 6 inches deep. Set your lawn mower on the highest setting, and run over the rows repeatedly to thoroughly chop up the leaves. Use this fine mulch around acid-loving shrubs, flowers, or vegetables to add organic matter to the soil.

- Coffee grounds. In addition to your home brew, some cafes give away coffee grounds. Use just a thin layer, or they'll form a crust that will stop water from getting through. Also, too much will tie up nitrogen when they start to decompose. Be aware that coffee grounds can be acidic, which can lower the pH of your soil.

- Straw, hay, and wood chips are sometimes available for free, too. But be sure before you use them that they don't contain weed seeds. If so, they're a bargain you'd be better off without. If in doubt, avoid.

Successful mulching — the inside scoop. Mulch nurtures the soil, helps it retain moisture, and controls weeds. But be sure the time is right before you spread it. In springtime, give the sun some time to warm the ground before putting mulch around perennials. Too early, and they won't have the heat needed to get them going and growing strong. In winter, the best time to mulch is after the first hard frost. That ensures a stable temperature to help your plants thrive. And remember, if it doesn't get too cold where you live, many perennials are fine without mulch.

Using gravel as mulch can throw off too much heat in warmer climates. It reflects sunlight and can harm surrounding plants. Use darker, less-reflective material in hot, sunny areas. In dry or drought conditions, whatever the usual climate, wood chips can absorb what little rain falls. After the rainfall, the water evaporates from the chips without ever reaching the ground. Use dry grass or pine straw instead, to let the water seep through.

When it comes to mulch for lawns, it's usually best to let cut grass go back into the lawn during mowing. This provides constant feeding of new growth with the old. But there's an exception. If your lawn develops diseased areas, it's better to bag and remove cut grass rather than adding to the problem.

Holiday treat for your garden

Christmas is over, but you can still give your acid-loving plants a present. After you take down your Christmas tree, put it through a shredder. Then spread the mulch around your plants. It will provide cover and help to enrich the soil.

Keep soil moist with dryer lint. You need to empty the lint from your clothes dryer anyway, so put it to good use. Rather than throw it away, till it into the ground around your vegetables or flowers. It will help your soil retain moisture. It also makes a great addition to soil in hanging baskets, which are especially prone to drying out. Lint in the soil, or as a basket liner, will help keep hanging plants moist for longer while still allowing drainage. And if your lint is from a natural fiber, like cotton — no synthetics — it's also suitable for your compost pile.

Use the power of the sun to get rid of stubborn weeds.
Solarizing is an organic, chemical-free technique that harnesses the
heat of the sun to get your garden ready for planting. It not only
kills weeds, but also gets rid of pests and diseases. You'll need to
plan for your plot to be idle for 4 to 8 weeks, then follow these four
steps for success.

- Cultivate. After you've chosen your plot, till it thoroughly and
  remove debris. Take out any bits and pieces that could contain
  weed seeds.

- Level. Get your rake and break up any clumps left over from
  tilling. Smooth out the ground, making it as flat as possible.
  This will allow the plastic a tight fit later.

- Irrigate. Give the plot a good soaking — ideally down to about
  a foot deep. Be ready to place plastic on top as soon as possible after watering.

- Cover. Use clear plastic — thinner (1 mil) is better for heating,
  but if you're in a windy area, use slightly thicker (2 mils) so it
  doesn't get disturbed. Then weigh down the edges using soil
  or stones, and wait. How long? Usually, 4 to 6 weeks are
  enough if it's hot, but if it's cooler, windier, or cloudier where
  you are, leave the plastic on for 6 to 8 weeks.

Try to disturb the soil as little as possible after removing the plastic.
This will help avoid stirring up any weed seeds that could be lurking.
Your soil — weed-free and nutrient-rich — is ready for your plants.

Transform kitchen scraps into fertile soil. It's easy to create
wheelbarrows full of valuable compost. Here are five common problems and their simple solutions to get you started.

- Animals. Break up kitchen scraps into smaller pieces before
  adding them to the pile if critters are attracted to your compost.
  Mix the scraps with soil to disguise their smells. Always avoid
  meats, fats, and oils — even salad dressing on leftover greens.
  They're the most likely culprits to bring hungry animals running.

- Ants. These tiny insects are a sign that your compost is decomposing slowly, probably because it's too dry. Compost should be as moist as a damp sponge. Cover it if it's losing moisture, or take the cover off when it rains. In a dryer climate, water your compost pile. Mixing well with a pitchfork or other tool distributes the moisture and adds air. This turns up the heat of decomposition and makes it uncomfortable for ants, earwigs, and other bugs.

- Cold and slimy. Three things are usually to blame – too much moisture, not enough air, and too little nitrogen-rich material. To boost nitrogen, add coffee grounds or grass clippings and mix well.

- Odors. If your pile smells like ammonia, it needs carbon. Charcoal, paper napkins and towels, dryer lint, and leaves are rich in carbon. To remedy a trash odor, turn your compost with your pitchfork and break up the large pieces. You can avoid this in the future by chopping items into smaller pieces and mixing them into your pile.

- Too wet. Add brown matter to the mix. Good choices include straw, newspaper, dry grass, and leaves.

Place your compost pile in a well-drained, sunny area to encourage the heating process. Keep a side supply of dry grass, brown leaves, straw, and shredded newspaper or cardboard. Avoid hay because it often contains weed seeds. Add these materials in alternate layers for balance as you add kitchen waste. And remember – the better you chop up and mix all ingredients at the start, the sooner your compost will be ready for your garden.

Turn up the heat on seed-stealing squirrels. Squirrels love to eat, and they don't care where their next meal comes from. When gray squirrels were introduced into England and Ireland, they took food from native red squirrels and often drove them from their homes.

One way you can fight back is with hot pepper. You can buy suet and birdseed treated with cayenne pepper, or you can add your own hot pepper powder or spray to birdseed to keep squirrels from eating it. It coats the seeds, and leaves a nasty taste in the squirrel's mouth. Birds aren't bothered by the heat, but using too much can irritate their eyes. Chili flakes or seeds are also worth a try. Use gloves whenever you handle any kind of hot pepper, and avoid contact with your eyes, nose, and mouth.

If you don't like the idea of causing discomfort to squirrels, fill your feeder with seeds they're not fond of — such as safflower, nyjer thistle, or white proso millet seeds. Just one taste and your neighborhood squirrels may be looking for somewhere else to eat. And don't forget the usual weapons in the squirrel war — putting your feeder where a squirrel finds it hard to get to, protecting the feeder with baffles, or buying a style of feeder better at keeping them out. Squirrels are devious and determined, and multiple defenses may be your best bet.

Wage war on annoying mosquitoes. There are many ways to deter mosquitoes, but not many are chemical-free. Tell them to buzz off with these clever ideas that are safe for you and your family.

- Sandalwood incense sticks. The scent of sandalwood is an effective mosquito repellant. An Australian study found that this natural method was up to 73 percent as effective as Deet, a chemical insecticide that can affect your nervous system. What's more, sandalwood smells better and has none of the side effects. Place the incense sticks in the ground — start with one in front of you and one behind. Light them and you're ready to work in your garden. You can buy these sticks inexpensively online or at a local flea market.

- Battery-powered fan. A breeze of just 2 mph will stop a mosquito from getting where it wants to go. Let that portable fan on your desk do double duty in your garden. Place it on the ground and tilt it, or raise it up on an overturned bucket. You'll keep cool, and those pesky critters will be blown away.

- Sticky bug bat. Staple a plastic lid to a paint stir stick and smear it with petroleum jelly on one side. When mosquitoes – or other unwanted flying visitors – come calling, you'll be ready to stop them in midair. Or try an old ping pong paddle or a fly swatter covered with a plastic bag. Just make sure the sticky stuff is on the up side when you rest your bat on the ground.

Get rid of bugs and slugs with plastic bottles. Recycle your plastic drink bottles to make tidy traps for annoying pests. To make the basic trap, start by cutting off the top of the bottle about a third of the way down. It will look sort of like a funnel. Then turn the top upside down and put it back inside the bottle, neck first. Tape the edge if necessary.

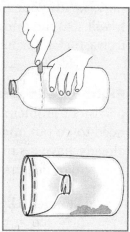

- Slugs. Put beer in the trap and lay it on its side in the garden. Slugs will slip inside for a drink, but they won't be able to get back out.

- Flies. Make the same basic trap, but poke a hole in the bottle cap and leave it on the bottle. Mix some sugar with water to make a sweet syrup and put it in the trap. Stand the trap upright to attract and catch flies.

- Mosquitoes. Do everything the same as the fly trap, but add a little bit of yeast to the sugar water. The yeast gives off carbon dioxide – a strong lure for mosquitoes.

If you have a row cover in your garden, there's an even simpler bottle trap. Put some sticky stuff – Tanglefoot or petroleum jelly – on a bottle full of water and place it upright under the row cover. The sun will warm the water during the day, then bugs will be attracted to it later as the air temperature drops. They fly to the warmth and stick to the bottle.

Simple tricks to protect your skin. Sometimes it's not convenient to wear gloves when you're weeding, planting, or pruning. But you may still want protection from dirt, lime, scratches, or poison ivy. Try a lightweight solution – slip your hand into a newspaper bag, or a bread bag from the supermarket. It will cover your arm but still provide good flexibility and touch. Put a rubber band around the top if it starts to slip off.

For more arm protection, cut off the feet of an old pair of socks to use as temporary sleeves on bare arms – combine with gloves if you want. If you'd rather work in bare hands but don't want to get dirt underneath your fingernails, draw your fingers over a bar of soap. It will seal the undersides of your nails, keep dirt out, and be ready to wash clean when you're done with your work.

Fight weeds with common household tools. Weeds are a persistent problem. There's no getting around it. But there's also no need to go out and spend money to solve the problem if you already have a simple toolbox. Use these common household and handyman helpers together with a little bit of elbow grease.

- Hammer. Dig the clawed end of a hammer into the soil, grab the weed at the base, and pull it out just like you would a nail.

- Pliers. Take a hint from your dentist. When persistent weeds won't come out by hand, get your pliers and go to work. You'll get a grip on the worst of weeds.

- Screwdriver. Use the flat-bladed kind. It's perfect for prying weeds out of cracks in driveways and between paving stones. It's also great for loosening tough weed roots before pulling them out by hand.

- Tweezers. Perfect for plucking tiny weeds and handy for getting hard-to-reach weeds out of tight spaces.

- Fork. The tines of an old but sturdy fork make great grippers for pulling out unwelcome garden guests.

- Apple corer. An old, serrated apple corer digs down deep and cuts the roots at the same time, and it's small enough to reach into tight spaces.

Plant bulbs and seeds without a backache. Instead of kneeling and crouching to create holes for bulbs and seeds, make it more like a walk in the park. A broken shovel with a D-handle makes a great new tool — a dibble. Sharpen the broken end to a point and use it to make holes as you walk the row you want to plant. Likewise, an old walking stick or cane with a metal tip can serve the same purpose. Or use the handle from an old rake or broom.

In addition to sharpening one end, use a yardstick to mark inch and foot measurements on it for a complete bulb hole tool. When you want to space your bulbs and seeds uniformly, you've got your measuring stick right there with you. And when you need to plant at a particular depth, measure the right length from the end of your stick, then get a rubber band and wrap it around at that mark — you'll reach the perfect level every time.

Help your tools last a lifetime. You can use household items you already have to make your garden tools work better and last longer. Try these simple tricks, and you'll spend less on replacements.

- Spades and shovels. Big or small, the treatment is simple. Use a wire brush to take rust off the blade. Sandpaper makes it even smoother, and running a file quickly along the edge will keep it sharp and easy to use. Rub in a little cooking oil to prevent rust and make digging easier. Keep a bucket of sand in your shed or garage, and stick your tools in it at the end of the day. It helps keep them dry, and you'll know just where to find them next day. For wooden handles, sand down any splinters and rub linseed oil on the whole handle to stop it from cracking and splitting as it ages — especially before you hang it up for the winter.

- Clippers. Put a little car wax on the hinge for a better cut. The paste that keeps your car shiny helps the clipper blades avoid a jam and glide more smoothly. You can also spray the blades with cooking oil – it keeps them lubricated and cutting freely. If some pine pitch or spruce sap sticks to the blades while trimming, put a little olive oil on a rag and rub. The blades will be smooth and clean again. Another wipe or two will take the sticky stuff off your hands, as well.

- Wheelbarrow. Make it roll with ease – keep the tire at the right pressure with your bicycle pump.

Easy store, easy pour. Here's a nifty way to make small, sturdy, plastic bags filled with seeds or fertilizer easier to handle. Before recycling a plastic bottle, cut off the top, including the collar and screw top. Pick a bottle with an opening that's the right size – the bigger the bag, the bigger the bottle. Unscrew the cap and feed the top of the plastic bag through it. Fold the edges of the bag over the bottle top and screw the cap back on. It's now airtight and secure. Want a handle, too? Use a plastic milk or juice bottle in the same way, but cut carefully to include the handle.

Simple, low-cost dry sink for your shed. There's no need to put expensive plumbing in your shed. Instead, make a dry sink. Use it for holding and rinsing flower cuttings, or controlling soil spill when you're potting. First, find something to use for the sink. It could be a big bucket, like those for drywall joint compound, or a plastic dish pan. It could even be an actual sink you find at a yard sale or thrift shop. If so, make sure you also have a bucket to put under the drain. Make an outline of your container on a wooden potting bench, then cut a hole that's just big enough for the container to slide into and rest snugly.

Make it even more useful with a portable water source for rinsing your hands. Get an empty laundry detergent bottle with a push-button dispenser, rinse it out thoroughly, and add water — instant convenience. You could also use a plastic beverage dispenser — the kind with a spigot, or an old water dispenser designed to sit on a shelf in your refrigerator.

Handy ways to keep your twine in line. Never misplace your roll of twine again. Try one of these clever ideas to keep it handy and tangle-free.

- Flowerpot. Put your roll of twine into a spare clay or plastic pot and run the end through a drainage hole. Place it upside-down, pull, and cut. Make it portable by adding a cover — tape a bit of cardboard over the top, and away you go.

- Baby wipes container. Whether it's a plastic box or flip-top cylinder, just remove the lid, add twine, and run it back through the opening in the lid before you replace it.

- Plastic pitcher. Reuse an old pitcher with a lid to keep your twine organized. If the lid has a flip-top, run the twine through the hole. Otherwise, pull it through the spout.

GREAT IDEA

New life for take-out chopsticks

Don't throw away those simple wooden chopsticks that come with your Chinese dinner. Keep them ready whenever you have a seedling that needs help. A chopstick poked into the soil makes a perfect stake to help support a small plant. A piece of string or a rubber band gently looped around the seedling helps keep it upright — or just let it lean on the chopstick as it grows.

3 ways to keep unruly stakes organized. The best time to organize your garden stakes is before you need them. Instead of leaving them in a messy pile, sort similar lengths and organize them in these handy containers.

- Plastic crates. Take two plastic crates that have lots of openings in the sides and base, and stack them upside-down on top of each other. Put stakes upright through the holes, and they won't go anywhere until you need them.

- Chimney pipes. Discarded chimney flues are sturdy and stand upright on the ground – perfect for keeping your stakes ready for use.

- PVC pipes. Use them as a sleeve for your stakes, and lean them in a corner out of the way.

7 sensational, easy-to-make plant markers. Plant markers not only help you identify your plants, they can be great-looking features for your garden. Best of all, they don't have to be expensive or hard to make.

- Broken flowerpots. Don't throw away broken clay pots – reuse the pieces by writing on the rim of the pot and sticking the broken edge into the ground. They look so good you might even break a few pots just for fun.

- Stones or bricks. Brush off smooth stones you find in your garden, or old bricks that are lying around. Paint a bit of fancy lettering on a smooth area, and make them uniquely your own.

- Small pot on a stick. Turn a mini terra-cotta flowerpot upside-down and write the plant name on it with a permanent marker. Place it on top of a stake.

- Seed packet. It's practical and clever to keep the plant's information close by. Put the seed packet on top of a stake, then cover it with a clear jar to keep moisture away.

- Nursery label. This is really useful if you have more than one variety of tomato. Cut a little slit at the top of a stake and slip the nursery label in – place them at eye level for easy identification.

- Wine bottle. Permanent colored marker on a wine bottle stuck upside-down in the ground makes a distinctive identifier.

- Golf club. Have old golf clubs you don't use? Instead of letting them gather dust in a basement or garage, put a label made from waterproof tape on the face of the club. Cut off the grip, and stick the shaft in the ground – they can double as plant stakes, too.

Scale back your work when watering a hanging plant.

It's not easy to see when your hanging plant needs water. Don't climb a ladder to check the soil – use an old fish scale for a simple and reliable visual check from the ground. Hang the scale on a hook, then hang the basket on the scale. Before you water, make a note of the starting weight shown on the scale – and then again after you water. Your plant will weigh more. When the weight goes back down, the plant is ready for more water.

In hot weather, when hanging baskets dry out faster, use a sneaky, slow-release solution. Put a few ice cubes on the soil and let them melt. It's easier than using a watering can. Also, the soil has more time to absorb the precious moisture, and you won't have excess water running out of the basket.

Index